D0894379

ANTONIO GALLENGA

*An Italian Writer in
Victorian England*

UNIVERSITY OF HULL PUBLICATIONS

Antonio Gallenga, 1860
From T. S. Sarti, *I rappresentanti del Piemonte e d'Italia nelle
tredici legislature del Regno*, Rome 1880

ANTONIO GALLENGA

An Italian Writer in Victorian England

———

TONI CERUTTI

Published for the UNIVERSITY OF HULL *by*

OXFORD UNIVERSITY PRESS

LONDON   NEW YORK   TORONTO

1974

Oxford University Press, Ely House, London W. 1

GLASGOW NEW YORK TORONTO MELBOURNE WELLINGTON
CAPE TOWN IBADAN NAIROBI DAR ES SALAAM LUSAKA ADDIS ABABA
DELHI BOMBAY CALCUTTA MADRAS KARACHI LAHORE DACCA
KUALA LUMPUR SINGAPORE HONG KONG TOKYO

ISBN 0 19 713419 X

© *University of Hull 1974*

C T1138
G 3
C H7

*Printed in Great Britain
at the University Press, Oxford
by Vivian Ridler
Printer to the University*

To my father

JAN 2 8 1975

PREFACE

WHAT brought home to British society of the nineteenth century the Italian reality of the Risorgimento in its political and artistic manifestations was the work of the Italian exiles who took refuge in England. The philanthropy and liberalism of the Victorian age proved very favourable to nationalist movements: political refugees were welcomed and accepted into English circles, and their sufferings found expression in some of the literary productions of the day. The lives and works of Italian exiles in England have already been an object of study, and a few monographs have appeared on the leading figures—Foscolo, Rossetti, Panizzi, and Mazzini. Very little, however, has been written on Antonio Gallenga, who was a critic, journalist, and politician, who first came to London as an exile in 1839, and eventually chose England as his permanent home—the place to which he could return from time to time from his wandering and restless life, and where he died in 1895. He devoted part of his life to Italian politics, teaching, and diplomacy, but his main activity was writing. His numerous publications reflect the evolutions and changes in thought which took place during the nineteenth century, and they also provide ample material on the making of modern Italy as seen through the eyes of a strong conservative who was at the same time a rebel. Moreover, after 1860, Gallenga's writings are one of the few cultural links between England and Italy, at a time when interest in the latter was rapidly decreasing.

It is the aim of this book to bring to light the relevant part of Gallenga's works and point out the role he played in the English and Italian world. Books and articles which deal with countries as far apart as Denmark and Cuba, Russia and Turkey, and which were written while he was a foreign correspondent of *The Times*, have been deliberately put aside, while his writings on America have been taken into account, representing, as they do, a vital part of Gallenga's Anglo-Saxon education. No full study of his life has so far been published. The only two works on him on which I have drawn are *Antonio Gallenga* by Aldo Garosci, which covers Gallenga's life up to 1858, and a series of articles by Franco Curato on the Frankfurt Parliament and Gallenga's diplomatic experiences.

I am particularly indebted to Professor E. R. Vincent and Professor Uberto Limentani for their assistance and valuable advice. I should also like to thank Professor C. P. Brand, Mr. W. J. Carlton, Mr. Peter Chandler, Mr. A. E. Howells, and Dr. D. E. Rhodes for their helpful suggestions. I am grateful to Professor Aldo Garosci for letting me consult Gallenga correspondence from *The Times* Archives, copy of which is in his possession; to the Mayer family and the Athenaeum Club for granting me access to their archives; and to Dr. M. Bersano Begey of the Biblioteca Reale of Turin. Last but not least, I should like to express all my gratitude to my friend Dr. Kathleen Speight for her knowledgeable guidance and encouragement.

CONTENTS

ILLUSTRATIONS

Plates 1-8 are reproduced from copies in possession of the Museo del Risorgimento, Turin, by courtesy of the Trustees

I

LUIGI MARIOTTI

ANTONIO GALLENGA was born in Parma on 10 November 1810, the eldest son of Celso Gallenga, a Piedmontese soldier in the Napoleonic army, who had settled there at the time of his marriage. His mother, Marianna Lombardini, died young leaving five children of tender age. As Antonio's father was a regular soldier he was often away from home, and his children were left in the care of their maternal uncle, Antonio Lombardini, a notary in the little town, who was responsible for their upbringing. Antonio Gallenga came therefore from a middle-class milieu, and his family did not hold progressive views. They were loyal subjects of Marie Louise, Napoleon's widow, who had become Duchess of Parma after the Congress of Vienna. Antonio grew up during the years when the memory of the Napoleonic wars still lingered in Europe, and when French culture still had a great influence in Italy. He had entered the University as a student of medicine, but his interests being mainly literary he soon transferred to classics. Having early evinced a keen interest in politics he found the University an ideal place in which to develop and complete his political education. Like many of his fellow-students he resented Marie Louise's easy-going but autocratic rule, and in several of his writings he has left us an interesting picture of life in the little Duchy in the days of the Austrian princess—seen, of course, through his own eyes. Marie Louise's government was undoubtedly tyrannical, but not harshly repressive. Gallenga, however, criticized it strongly as one of the worst forms of despotism. In his view it corrupted the social and moral structure of the Duchy through an apparent mildness, which nevertheless employed a strict censorship which prevented the establishment of any enlightened school of thought and stifled all liberal tendencies. Moreover, Marie Louise's profligacy and extravagance ruined Parma as much as her imperial husband's campaigns had devastated the city in earlier days.

It is not impossible that Maria Luisa was by taste and inclination addicted to all kinds of refinement, and naturally disposed to declare herself a patroness of art. . . .

She took the lying-in hospital under her patronage; built a bridge on the Taro, with twenty arches, three times the length of London Bridge, and a golden theatre—at least all covered over with a yellow material shining like gold. . . .

Her bridges, however, her theatres, her menageries and aviaries, her superb villas, and magnificent trains, her regiment of grenadiers, her profuse liberalities to mimes and charlatans—before long exhausted her revenue. Commerce and industry once more cramped within narrow boundaries, the taxes pressing undiscerningly[1] on the labouring classes, engendered general distress, and the state ran merrily into debt....

Parmesan manufactories were closed, as injurious to Austrian industry. Parmesan steamboats on the Po were stopped, as encroaching on Austrian commerce. Maria Luisa paid for board and lodging, when a guest at her parents' court. She paid her son's expenses, whom they held as a prisoner.[2]

For a while Marie Louise enjoyed a fair amount of popularity among her subjects, who considered her conduct the result of Austrian policy and called her *la povera tradita*. Her government apparently allowed some freedom: French papers circulated in the cafés and Jacobins sported the miniature of Napoleon on the lid of their snuff-boxes, but all this was a mere farce: repression was in effect active, and people who in the authorities' opinion held ideas somewhat dangerous for the establishment were removed from their posts. Occasionally some were sent to prison, and spies and police performed their task with great discretion in their attempt not to arouse popular feeling. Arrests were often made during the night, but, once jailed, prisoners were treated reasonably well, as Gallenga himself admitted:

Conspiracies had been found out at Parma in 1820, and the state prisons had been crowded with distinguished inmates. . . .

[1] Indiscriminately.
[2] 'Maria Luisa and Carlo Ludovico', in *New Month. Mag.*, Feb. 1848, vol. lxxxii, no. 326, pp. 240–1.

A few luckless Carbonari were sent to a little mock Spielberg, the fortress of Compiano, on the Apennines, but before the end of two years the day of clemency dawned, and they were all allowed to eat their Christmas pudding in the bosom of their families.[1]

In such an atmosphere, when Macedonio Melloni, an illustrious mathematician of the time, was appointed to the chair of physics at Parma University, Gallenga published his first work (printed by the famous printer Bodoni), a short pindaric ode in which he welcomed home the *figlio diletto* of Parma. The seventeen-year-old poet, who was at the time a student of classics, cannot claim any originality of invention for his poem, which was a mosaic of his favourite authors; but it reveals in his youthful enthusiasm the liberal spirit prevailing among the students, who were shortly afterwards the most active supporters of the 1831 revolt. Melloni's lectures did not always reflect the policy of the government, and when in 1830 they roused suspicion as being somewhat inspired by French ideas, he was asked to resign, and did so. This happened in late autumn when the students were already elated with the news coming from Paris after the July revolution, which had put an end to Charles X's reign and had given France a more liberal government under Louis Philippe of Orleans. The new monarch was welcomed both in France and abroad as the citizen king devoted to the cause of the Revolution. In Parma the dismissal of the young professor proved unpopular and Gallenga headed a students' protest against attending University lectures in physics until Melloni was recalled. On 2 January 1831 the new professor appointed by the government was confronted with an empty *Aula Magna* and could not deliver his lecture. There was no immediate reaction on the part of the authorities to this 'unofficial strike' by the students of Parma. But shortly afterwards Antonio and some of the other conspirators were put into jail in the nearby fortress of Compiano, where, however, they were treated with great respect, coming as they did from the best families in Parma. As Gallenga's father recorded in his diary, orders had been given for their good treatment.

They were kept in custody till the middle of February, when

[1] Ibid., p. 244.

the uprisings of Modena and Parma released them. Returning at once to Parma, they joined the revolt, which had already gained a too easy success. At the first sign of rebellion Marie Louise fled, and a provisional government was installed; for a few weeks Parma enjoyed an ephemeral freedom. When a month afterwards the Austrians came to restore the Duchess to her throne, however, little if any resistance was offered, and the only military action was the battle of Fiorenzuola which was, after all, little more than a skirmish fought with great enthusiasm but little experience by the young men of the town, Gallenga among them. After this, Parma surrendered to the Austrians without fighting.

The complete failure of the 1831 uprising in Central Italy and lack of military resistance were due to several causes. The whole movement had been badly organized, and fighting had been more for local reforms rather than for any national issue. Louis Philippe's policy also precipitated the situation. As Gallenga put it:

It was thought that the non-intervention might, by the means of sectional revolts, pave the way for the success of a general national effort; that the fear of a war with France would stay the sword of Austria in its scabbard. . . .

But the movement of 1831, like that of 1821, . . . was grounded on views of foreign diplomacy: all revolutionary measures were limited to prevent any provocation of hostilities, by a blind adhesion to the pact of non-intervention. . . . Still not a word was said about Italy, to give the insurrection the appearance of a national rising. All was paralysed, from its earliest start, by that inconceivable hallucination.[1]

Moreover, as often pointed out by historians of the Risorgimento, Parma was carried into the movement by the examples of Modena and the Papal States, where dissatisfaction with the local government was much stronger and had deeper roots. The provisional government in Parma was formed by moderate elements, who were cautious before taking any step to oppose the legal sovereign: Marie Louise was never dethroned, and eventually she returned as the lawful ruler of the Duchy. In *Castellamonte* —a romanticized autobiography of his years in Parma—

---

[1] *Italy, P. and P.*, vol. ii, pp. 12–13.

Gallenga has left a vivid picture of the violent contrast between the *arrière-garde*, which formed the provisional government relying on non-intervention, and aiming at some internal reforms, and the young intellectual generation ready to fight for the rescue of their country. People like Casa, Linati, and Jacopo Sanvitale spared Parma a heroic but useless slaughter, while many a patriot took the path of exile. Gallenga laid the blame for the rapid disintegration of the revolt on the leaders of the movement.

But not even the rapidity of their success, not even the unanimity of the people, could inspire the leaders with sufficient faith and determination. Indeed, the very facility of those first movements seemed to unfit them for the ensuing struggle. They seemed to flatter themselves that liberty could be maintained as easily as it had been obtained. They were willing to preserve in its purity that bloodless revolution in which they, very justly, prided themselves.

But it is fated that freedom can never be asserted on earth, without long and desperate strife; that it is never fully established until it is cemented with blood.[1]

Although Gallenga's view here is quite objective, it is doubtful whether in 1831 any other line of action could have achieved positive results.

The government's reaction against the rebels was not violent, and in the same year a general amnesty was granted to political criminals, but Gallenga was one of the few who were not pardoned. We learn from the police archives that he had gained for himself, on two separate occasions in particular, the reputation of being a violent, riotous young man. The first of these was after the battle of Fiorenzuola, when he informed the citizens of Parma from the balcony of the *Palazzo del Governo* of the end of non-intervention, urging the necessity of war against Austria. He concluded his speech by waving a dagger dramatically in front of a huge crowd. This threatening attitude was directly opposed to the views of the provisional government, for they wanted to keep the news of the defeat from the people in order to avoid any popular unrest. The second occasion was shortly afterwards, when he played a principal role in the abduction of the Bishop of

[1] Ibid., pp. 14–15.

Guastalla, a German and one of Marie Louise's favourites, who was held as a hostage for the lives of the citizens of Parma taken prisoners by the Austrians at Fiorenzuola. Gallenga was therefore regarded as a dangerous agitator and was never granted an amnesty. He was, no doubt, an impetuous and rash young man: all through his life one finds him suddenly leaving places, changing jobs and activities, finding new friends and making fresh enemies. Often he was forced into action by an inner restlessness, an inborn incapacity to settle anywhere, but it would be wrong to call him an anarchist. The thoughtlessness of some of his actions in his early days—such as the first of the two episodes just mentioned—can partly be imputed to his youth, but it was mostly due to the atmosphere in which he was brought up. Early romanticism, which in Italy coincided with the beginning of the Risorgimento, preached in essence the cult of the individual. Foscolo and Alfieri, however noble and patriotic their feelings, were basically, and above all, individuals, the writer, the hero, the artist, beings apart from the masses. This aristocratic view of art, morals, and politics implies an overestimation of the value and impact of the exploits of individuals. The fault of such a conception lies in the fact that feats of heroism and sacrifice acquire universal value only when they are the expression of a feeling shared by the majority and not merely by an élite.

Gallenga in his youth was a great believer in individualism and lacked almost completely any sort of social conscience. In this connection a little poem is significant, written in 1833 when he was planning to murder Charles Albert,[1] where the assassination is treated as a personal affair between the king and himself.

> Già troppo di te
> Natura fremè;
> Invano così
> Non tentasi il ciel;
> È giunto il tuo dì
> Tiranno crudel!
>
> Io teco cadrò,
> Non tremo, lo so;

[1] See Chapter V.

Ma il viver non fu
Che un lungo soffrir;
Precedimi tu
Ch'io voglio morir.[1]

Gallenga's experiences in the Old and the New World brought about a radical change in his ideas, but up to 1840 there are traces of his early romantic views. He remained an egocentric to the end, holding the highest opinion of himself, but while in his youthful days he had a firm belief in 'man' as opposed to 'people', in later years he replaced the individual by a society of men, a small select oligarchy chosen to be the leaders and to set an example to the world. This change in his views came about gradually, and, as just noted, was fostered by his experiences abroad, especially in the Anglo-Saxon world.

After an adventurous escape from Parma, Gallenga stayed with the family of one of his friends, the Mariottis, and later took their name and used it as a pseudonym. He then wandered across Northern Italy, and early in June sailed to France. Little is known about the first years of his exile, when he earned his living as a tutor in different families, first at Bastia in Corsica, later in Tangiers. Letters written while he was in France show his feelings of dissatisfaction and bitterness towards this new life. To Luigi Melegari in February 1833 he writes:

I am sick, very sick, and yet it isn't the uncertainty of my fate, nor my poverty that makes me unhappy. I weep over my country, I weep because I am compelled to stay in France, but above all I lament the futility of my existence and my inactivity. Almost three years have passed and I am still unable to take a step, to do something for my country.[2]

At this time he came into contact with Mazzinian circles and joined the recently founded Young Italy under the name of Procida. His joining the society was, so to speak, the logical

---

[1] *Oltremonte*, p. 71. 'Too long under your yoke / Nature quivered; / In vain and thus / Is heaven tempted; / Your day has come / Cruel tyrant; / With you I fall! / I don't tremble, I know; / Life was but / a long suffering; / Go before me / for I long to die.'

[2] Letter to L. Melegari, Toulon, 14 Feb. 1833, Museo del Risorgimento, no. 137: 32 (5), Rome.

conclusion of his being a patriot. Young Italy took the place of the Carbonari after the uprising of 1831. When in Parma Gallenga had met a few members of this secret society, but he had never joined it. While in prison at Compiano he and his comrades 'bowed with wonder and awe before the more recent carvings [*sic*][1] of the Carbonari of 1820, whose name we learned to pronounce with a secret reverence and gratitude, and whose successors we were proud,—nay happy—to behold ourselves.'[2] But their admiration was only for the men of 1820; they had no great faith in the energy and practical talents of the Carbonari in 1831, for a new approach to the national cause was already making headway among the younger generation.

Gallenga's connection with Young Italy had deep roots and lasted for several years. Moreover, his stay in France and his meeting with Mazzini in Geneva in the summer of 1833 put him into contact with different groups of exiles from various parts of the country. This widened his conception of Italy as a unity, but also made him aware of the strength of regional divisions, as can be seen in political writings of later years, when he defended the cause of federalism. At this time, he also developed a strong distaste for French culture and politics. France was a great disillusion to young Antonio, for the motherland of *Liberté, Égalité, Fraternité*, treated the Italian refugees as common criminals.

The paltry pension which Louis Philippe insidiously tendered to the Italian refugees in 1831, was turned into an instrument of oppression and corruption. Under the most frivolous pretext, and even without pretext, political guests were dealt with as prisoners; they were, like common malefactors, banished from Paris, Lyons, or Marseilles; from all large towns where they might have aspired to useful and honourable employment. Condemned to the dulness and idleness of provincial life . . ., ever in dread and suspicion of the spies that were purposely admitted to the same stipend[3] with them . . . , the Italian refugees in France were subjected to a mental anguish, by the side of which the bodily tortures of Spielberg were mere child's play.[4]

Even if political passion did colour with deeper hues Gallenga's

---

[1] Inscriptions written on the walls.
[2] *Castellamonte*, vol. i, p. 192.
[3] Pension.
[4] *Italy, P. and P.*, vol. ii, pp. 61–2.

picture of French hospitality, it is certain that he never felt wanted there. Mazzini had had the same experience, and in the summer of 1833 he had already moved to Switzerland. Gallenga's dislike of France as a society and a country lasted all his life. As late as 1883 he wrote:

In France the war of classes set in with almost cannibal ferocity, when the multitude rose in arms against the nobility, burnt and slew; and, to complete the work, abolished those *majorats*, or rights of primogeniture, without which the perpetuation—though not the accumulation—of lordly fortunes became impossible.

When the Reign of Terror came to an end . . . a few of the old feudal families struggled into new life, though with diminished lustre. But aristocracy without hereditary wealth was found to be a mockery; and France, deprived of a governing class, was unable to establish a Government. Though at times still formidable at war, and apparently prosperous in times of peace, that country was and is, under the best circumstances, *La France Acéphale*—a body without a head.[1]

At first, Gallenga's dislike of France was a question of personal disappointment, but later it developed into a serious appraisal of French democracy. He often pointed out how the principles preached by the revolutionaries of 1789 had failed in their practical application. After getting rid of monarchic absolutism, France went through a variety of political phases which, according to him, were 'a bourgeois Monarchy, a shame Republic, or a flash Empire'.

France cannot give other countries what she does not possess, and cannot appreciate and use to her own advantage. After sixty-seven years of struggle and bloodshed she is less than ever able to understand what freedom means. All her efforts, so far, have only led to the perfecting of centralization of the country, increasing the ascendancy of bureaucracy and the omnipotence of the police.[2]

He not only criticized the practical failure of the Revolution, but also condemned French political principles as being unsuited to the fostering of any sound basis in a nation. This attitude to

---

[1] *Democracy*, p. 19.
[2] 'L'Inghilterra e la pace', in *La Rivista Contemporanea*, Turin, Mar. 1856, vol. vi, p. 150.

France was quite personal and original at a time when democratic principles enjoyed such popularity among Italian patriots. It is, of course, true that after 1831 the trust which the Italians put in the French suffered a great blow, and Gallenga was not the only one who harshly criticized them. But the French conception of democracy served as the model first for Piedmont and later for the whole of Italy.

Gallenga's criticism extended to contemporary French literature as well. In his opinion the early thirties were

the best days of Victor Hugo and Balzac, Eugène Sue and Paul de Kock, George Sand, Jules Janin and Alexandre Dumas. . . . It is from these writers, to whom it would be impossible to deny the gift of the rarest fertility and versatility of genius, that the French caught their rampant Chauvinism; their dog-in-the-manger jealousy; their vaingloriousness, self-conceit and arrogance . . ., their want of faith in God and man.[1]

Anglo-Saxon literature of the day and Victorian moralism, with which he came into contact some years after leaving France, had great influence on this rather bigoted judgement. In some of its aspects, Gallenga's opinion of France can be compared to Alfieri's *misogallismo*.

In August 1833 Gallenga crossed the Piedmontese border with a forged passport, under the name of Luigi Mariotti, for although still banished from Parma, his pseudonym allowed him to travel safely elsewhere in the country. From that time till the year 1847 he made use of the name of Mariotti, all his books appearing under this name, and as such he is mentioned in private correspondence, articles, and in several records.

He stayed in Turin for a few weeks and at the end of September moved south. For some years he wandered across southern Italy and northern Africa—a restless, unhappy young man—eventually finding employment with the Neapolitan consul in Malta and Tangiers. In the latter place he spent about two years teaching children and taking part in social activities. As he recalls in his

[1] *Epis.*, vol. i, pp. 199–200.

memoirs, life in Africa was pleasant, but neither rewarding nor stimulating.

The Christian residents in Tangiers, as in other Mohammedan regencies, constituted at that time a sufficiently interesting polyglot community. Each consul-general and diplomatic agent was a little potentate, and all the subjects of the State he represented were his little court. He lived generally on intimate terms with his colleagues of other nationalities, and their visiting at each other's houses, and joining in picnic, garden, and other pleasure parties, and in riding, shooting, and boating excursions, gave rise to a state of society enlivened by all the charms of a pleasing variety and contrast.[1]

Whatever the circumstances that made him leave Tangiers, Gallenga felt that there was no future for him there. He also realized, rather sadly, that for the time being little if anything could be done for Italy, and lost all desire to go back to his country and take an active part in political life.

In August 1836 he embarked for New York, where he landed on 7 October, after an adventurous voyage across the Atlantic on board a small brig schooner, the *Independence*. His keen spirit of adventure and the hope of making a successful career had made him choose the United States. John Madison Leib, the U.S. minister in Tangiers, had encouraged him to go, with the idea of following an academic career there. 'It is of men like you that want is particularly felt in our trading community. We have plenty of storekeepers, land agents and politicians. Give us scholars and gentlemen, men of taste and refinement.'[2]

Leib had provided him with letters of introduction to some eminent Americans, among whom should be named Edward Everett, the Governor of Massachusetts, and Josiah Quincy, President of Harvard University. So Gallenga did not tarry in New York but moved to Boston, where he began his career as a teacher of Italian. His activity as an apologist in support of his country, which was the most valid contribution he made to the Risorgimento, dates from that time. When he first started lecturing and writing about his country he was prompted

---

[1] Ibid., pp. 4–5.   [2] Ibid., p. 18.

by practical considerations and personal ambitions, but later when his first books on Italy were published he became conscious of the possibility of their influencing public opinion.

When in October 1836 Gallenga presented himself to Edward Everett in Boston, he was hoping to get an appointment as teacher of Italian at Harvard University, but there was no vacancy at that time. The Chair of General Continental European Literature had been founded in 1816, when George Ticknor, the historian, was made Professor. He was succeeded in 1835 by Henry Wadsworth Longfellow, the poet. They both lectured on Italian literature, while Pietro Bachi, who was appointed *lector* in 1826, was in charge of language teaching. Bachi, whose real name was Batolo, was a Sicilian *émigré* who had left Sicily for personal reasons and settled in the United States, gaining a considerable reputation as a teacher, and publishing textbooks for students of Italian. He held this position till 1846. There was, therefore, no chance of Gallenga getting a post at the famous University. All the same, there was enough teaching of Italian available to provide him with work and a livelihood. After a rather hard beginning—he even had to borrow money from the local priest—Gallenga gained a certain reputation and was appointed teacher of modern languages at Harvard Young Ladies' Academy, a finishing school for girls.

In those days, the American academic and literary world was heavily dependent on Great Britain. The ties with England were still close: the United States retained much of the colonial spirit, and their culture had not yet fully developed as an independent contribution to the world of art. Moreover, the lack of an international copyright act facilitated the appearance of pirated editions of contemporary English works. No sooner had Carlyle's last book or Scott's most recent novel appeared, than they found their way to the American public, much to the financial disadvantage of the native authors. 'As to literary men —i.e. men living by literature—there were none in my days in America', wrote Gallenga about fifty years later, 'for Prescott, Ticknor, Bancroft, Sprague, and other historians, biographers, critics etc., were gentlemen cultivating letters as amateurs, loving

their work for its own sake, but relying either on a good patrimony or some other lucrative employment.'[1]

Any school of thought in the mother country, any new trend
of literature, was echoed in the ex-colonies and closely followed
there. The fashion for things Italian which had raged in England
had now reached the United States.

> Few modern languages, however, are more generally studied than
> the Italian. . . . The ladies of the Eastern cities of America are rivalling
> Europe in this, as in other branches of literary culture. One hundred
> young men are annually trained in the acquirement of it in Harvard
> College. All persons, who have any pretension to learning, have, more
> or less, had something to do with Italian.[2]

If the learning of Italian at the Young Ladies' Academy was
a frivolous entertainment, Ticknor and Longfellow were no
mean Italian scholars, nor was William Prescott, the historian,
who contributed several articles on the subject to the *North
American Review*. Italy was not, at this time, the only country
in which Americans of culture were interested: Longfellow's
articles and translations from Scandinavian sagas, Prescott's
essays on Molière and Cervantes, Ticknor's *History of Spanish
Literature* are a fair sample of their wide interest. Gallenga had,
therefore, landed in a culture-starved society which, having so far
not established its own tradition, was eager to welcome any
foreign contribution. The presence of several political exiles also
added to the popularity of Italian. When Gallenga landed in
Boston, Pellico's name and reputation were already well-known
and his sufferings at the Spielberg were a matter of sympathy and
sorrow, particularly when Federico Confalonieri, Pietro Maron-
cello, Felice Foresti, and other patriots found their way to the
United States after release from prison in Austria.

The situation was favourable indeed for a young Italian exile:
Gallenga not only soon got over his financial difficulties but found
himself welcomed into New England society. His occupation at

---

[1] Ibid., p. 361.
[2] 'Romantic Poetry in Italy', in *North Am. Review*, July 1838, vol. xlvii,
no. 100, p. 207.

Harvard Academy was not full-time, and he was able to spend most of his time reading and studying.

What a season that was too for reading, that of 1837! Besides the *De Omnibus Rebus et Quibusdam Aliis*, with which my American Encyclopaedia was making me familiar, had I not Walter Scott, whom we in Italy in our boyhood called 'the Ariosto of the North' . . .; had we not *Marmion* and *Ivanhoe*, and *The Bride of Lammermoor* . . ., *Maltravers*, and *Venetia*, and *Pickwick* . . . in their American reprints with the very bloom of novelty upon them? Had we not Carlyle's *French Revolution*, fresh from the publisher's hands, and Macaulay's essays in *The Edinburgh Review*, and his *Lays of Ancient Rome* and his *Montcontour* and *Ivry*?[1]

If we add to these a few other authors mentioned by Gallenga, such as Thackeray, we can see how soon he became acquainted with Victorian literature. His preferences among contemporary English writers are significant, since they are indicative of his own literary and moral tendencies.

Could any words of mine express the infinite good that all that reading did me? Could I ever do justice to the sound, bracing, purifying influence my introduction to the treasures of that living English literature exercised upon my moral character? What a healthy tone of feeling! What earnest thoughts and generous aspirations! What sober views of aims and duties of life were awakened! What new and, as I would fain flatter myself, better being was created within me![2]

When his English was proficient enough to attempt to write in the language, Gallenga decided that he wished it to be as much as possible like that of the authors he admired. There is no doubt that traces of their influence can be found in the moral tone of his writings and especially in his picturesque and often highly rhetorical style. But in those days other elements beside his reading of English writers contributed to his cultural formation. The Harvard Academy had no direct contact with the celebrated University, but being near to it, its associations with the academic world were close. Gallenga had, therefore, a chance of attending lectures given by the most famous American scholars, and he could freely mix in their circles. People such as Oliver Wendell

[1] *Epis.*, vol. i, pp. 196–7.   [2] Ibid., pp. 197–8.

Holmes, James Russell Lowell, Ralph Waldo Emerson, Margaret Fuller, to mention only some of the many quoted by him, were in some way connected with Harvard and fortunately for him he had easy access to them. When in 1838 he was asked to give a course of lectures on Italy in Boston his audience included Longfellow, Emerson, and Prescott. To address himself to such an audience Gallenga undertook a thorough and systematic re-arrangement of his knowledge of his country. In these lectures are to be found the seeds of *Italy, Past and Present*, which, partly based on his American notes, is his best achievement as a literary critic. The three years spent in the United States proved of inestimable importance, since they completed Gallenga's education and clarified his thoughts and ideas. The teaching he undertook in Boston revealed his true vocation and it was through a recon-sideration of his country in its historical and literary aspects that he became a historian and a critic.

Apart from lecturing Gallenga also published articles in the *North American Review*, the leading literary magazine of the day. They were in most cases reviews of contemporary Italian books. In them as well as in his lectures he tried to give a fresh and up-to-date portrayal of Italian life as seen by an Italian, full of the passion and enthusiasm and partiality which his position as an exile afforded him. His articles were later reprinted in England and eventually incorporated in some of his works.

While completing his education, Gallenga was contributing to the spreading of Italian studies overseas, and he soon became a member of Boston literary society, where he made some good friends. Among them were especially Longfellow, Prescott, and Everett. His acquaintance with Longfellow was of great impor-tance, as it was through him that he had his first book published. This book, which appeared anonymously in May 1838, bears the title of *Romanze*, and contains some fourteen ballads in 'good romantic style' written in the manner of Berchet and Grossi. A second enlarged edition under the title of *Oltremonte ed oltremare*, in homage perhaps to Longfellow's *Outre-mer*, appeared in 1844 in London. The value of the poems is merely autobiographical, since they provide some useful information about Gallenga's early life. As he himself admitted, he was no poet. His best lines are usually a poor imitation of some of the most famous Italian poems, such as Parini's 'Torna a fiorir la rosa', or Alfieri's celebrated sonnet 'Sublime specchio di veraci detti'. It is no wonder that Longfellow should promote the publication of these ballads for he was greatly attracted to the popular forms of poetry in several literatures. The legends of 'Evelina di Belgirate' or 'Inez de Castro', sung by an unhappy young Italian exile, could not fail to rouse his sympathy and he failed to detect the grotesque, almost gruesome flavour of some of Gallenga's worst lines:

> Guizza un lampo, l'aer cieco
> Fino all'alpi sveglia l'eco —
> Già riversa, già sommersa
> Va la vela dell'amor.
> Solo un grido — e d'Evelina
> Sol biancheggia ancor la vesta; —
> Non ben conscia, non ben desta,
> Muore in braccio al rapitor.[1]

Moreover, he was unaware of the lack of originality in some of Gallenga's lines. The Italian was not only grateful to the poet, but also felt strongly attracted to him.

Longfellow was then about thirty years old, beautiful as the god of day, with golden hair which he wore down to his shoulders, clear blue eyes, a fair, healthy complexion, and well-cut features. . . . I had some talk with him on subjects with which I thought I ought to have been tolerably conversant, and which gave me a high idea of his proficiency in those branches of literature which he had taught, first at Bowdoin College in his native Maine, and later at Harvard. . . . He spoke with genuine feeling of the beauty of our language; informed me that he was busy with a prose translation of Dante, which was published many years later. He asked me to recite some of the passages of the divine poem, which I knew by heart, regretting his inability to master the indefinable *nuances* of the Italian accent.[2]

---

[1] *Oltremonte*, p. 51, 'Evelina di Belgirate'. A lighting flashes, the blind air / Awakes the echo as far as the Alps. / Already overturned, already drenched / The sail of Love goes. / One sole cry—and Eveline's / white gown glimmers on the water; / Half awake, half asleep, / In her robber's arms she dies.

[2] *Epis.*, vol. i, pp. 170-2.

If the connection with Longfellow was useful to Gallenga on practical grounds (it was through the publication of *Romanze* that he acquired status and fame as a writer), his association with William Prescott and Edward Everett had greater influence on him. Prescott became his close friend, as can be seen in several of his letters, some of which were written after he had left America. He attended Gallenga's course in Boston regularly, and in 1842 reviewed *Italy, a General View of Its History and Literature*.

The work before us presents a view of Italian literature written in English. . . . Those who had the good fortune to attend the lectures of Signor Mariotti, some three years since, in Boston, will refresh their recollection of them in the more correct and complete form in which they appear in these volumes. . . .

However we may differ, too, from some of his conclusions, we must admit his liberal views, on all themes of moral and political interest, and the ardent, yet not intemperate patriotism which still binds the exile to the beautiful land of his birth.[1]

Gallenga was also well acquainted with Prescott's historical works. In 1840, during his short stay in Florence, he undertook the translation of *The History of Ferdinand and Isabella*, and while in the United States he probably read Prescott's articles on Italian literature.

Edward Everett, who always helped him in difficult times, was one of the first of Gallenga's pupils. He was a keen Italianist and already knew Italian well enough to read Dante. He was then forty-two and had in his younger years been Professor of Greek at Harvard. He had left this position to attend the University of Göttingen. When he returned to America, he was for a while minister and preacher in the Unitarian Church; eventually he turned to politics and was governor of Massachusetts when Gallenga first met him. According to testimonies of the time, such as Emerson's *Journals*, Everett was an eminent orator, as well as a man of wide political and cultural interests. Gallenga confessed that he learnt more from him about Dante than he ever taught him. In his admiration for him as a public speaker, he wrote that

[1] 'Mariotti's Italy' in *North Am. Review*, Apr. 1842, vol. liv, no. 115, pp. 340, 355.

in Harvard the event of the day was an address delivered by some of the greatest orators in the country, such as Edward Everett and Ralph Waldo Emerson.

Young Gallenga was greatly impressed by the oratorial gifts of a number of scholars, and American eloquence of the first half of the nineteenth-century left an undeniable mark on his English style. This is seen by comparing the opening of an address by Everett written in a fashion which F. O. Matthiessen calls 'the approved convention of the time'[1] with the Gallenga's beginning and close of his first lecture.

Gathered together in this temple not made with hands, to unroll the venerable record of our fathers' history, let our first thoughts ascend to Him, whose heavens are spread out, as a glorious canopy, above our heads. As our eyes look up to the everlasting hills which rise before us, let us remember that in that dark and eventful day we commemorate, the hand that lifted their eternal pillars to the clouds, was the sole stay and support of our afflicted sires. While we contemplate the lovely scene around us,—once covered with the gloomy forest and the tangled swamps, through which the victims of this day pursued their unsuspecting path to the field of slaughter—let us bow in gratitude to Him, beneath whose paternal care a little one has become a thousand, and a small one a strong nation.[2]

Down in a southern clime, amidst the silent waves of a tideless sea, there lies a weary land, whose life is only in the Past and the Future. . . .

The phoenix has been consumed upon her funereal pyre. Her last breath has vanished in the air with the smoke of her ashes; but the dawn breaks; the first rays of the sun are falling upon the desolate hearth; the ashes begin to heave, and from their bosom the new bird springs forth with luxuriant plumage, displaying her bold flight, with her eyes fixed on that sun from which she derived her origin.[3]

Both writers share the same magniloquence of speech and abound in images taken from religion.

Everett had been a divine, and so were most of the exponents of

---

[1] F. O. Matthiessen, *American Renaissance*, New York, 1941, p. 20 and *passim*.

[2] E. Everett, *Orations and Speeches on Various Occasions*, Boston, 1836, p. 587, 'Address delivered at Bloody Brook, in South Deerfield, Sept. 30, 1835, in commemoration of the fall of the Flower of Essex, at that spot, in King Philip's war, Sept. 18, 1675.'

[3] *Italy, P. and P.*, vol. i, pp. i, xliv.

American culture of the time. The links between religious and academic life had always been close in America, and Gallenga found himself in contact with the Reformed Churches and especially with the Unitarian movement, which in those days was extremely popular among educated classes. Like most Italians, he was born a Roman Catholic, but while at the University he shared the agnostic and materialistic views held by most of his comrades.

> Our medical students were, then, with scarcely an exception, materialists. Why not? . . . In their youthful presumption they thought they could account for every act of the mind as easily as they did for every function of animal economy. . . . It must not be thought, after all, that there is any very great harm in this sort of rash scepticism. It is honest, disinterested inquisitiveness. Every student in Italy must needs go through this fearful ordeal of doubt. It is the necessary consequence of too harsh enforcement of a blind, bigoted authority. . . . Our priests present us with a God as hideous as themselves.[1]

At the beginning of the nineteenth century, under the influence of French rationalism, the inspiration behind Italian culture had been secular. Shortly afterwards, however, with the advent of the romantic movement, and the appearance of *La morale cattolica* by Manzoni and the inspired writings of Mazzini, the Risorgimento acquired a religious flavour not always in conformity with Catholic doctrine. Gallenga does not differ from the general rule: his juvenile materialism was only a passing stage, and he soon returned to a faith in God and a belief in the influence of divine providence on human events. While in America, he attended churches of various denominations and this made him a Christian in a more universal sense. Any denomination to him was as good as another.

> Christianity relies for its preservation on its divine origin, on the simplicity of its primitive institutions, on its natural evidences, on the sanctity of its morals, on the gratitude of the world for its regenerating influence—its fate can never be involved in the ruin of any ecclesiastical system.[2]

---

[1] *Castellamonte*, vol. i, pp. 35–6.   [2] *Italy 1841*, vol. ii, p. 389.

Like most patriots, Gallenga was strongly anti-clerical and in the temporal power of the Papacy he saw one of the main causes of the moral and political degeneration of Italy, thus embracing Sismondi's theories.

In the first place, it is a point on which the best of Catholics, as well as the worst of infidels, perfectly agree; that whatever constitution the church may receive, after having undergone the modifications of which the necessity is so generally felt, no doubt can be entertained of the injustice and inexpediency of the temporal power of the popes.[1]

So he wrote in 1839, when reviewing Manzoni's *La morale cattolica*. He felt that reform in the religious field in Italy was most urgent, and advocated a return to a more primitive form of Christianity as well as to a greater freedom of thought in theological matters. Although he never joined any of the reformed Churches, there is a definite influence of Protestant thinking in some of his criticisms of the Catholic Church, such as his dislike of liturgy, of confession, and his opposition to the celibacy of the priesthood. His contact with the Protestant community also strengthened his belief in the Bible, not so much on theological grounds but because to him Christ was 'God's messenger'.

I am a Christian. I believe in God's messenger. And I believe in Manes, Confucius and Mohamet, and I believe in Homer, Dante and Shakespeare, in all of whom I recognize God's messengers . . ., whereever the development of man's mind manifests itself—there we must recognize God's revelation.[2]

All the same, he supported the need for an established Church for social reasons, in order to raise people's moral standards and educate them to a better ideal of life. While his attitude to the Church of Rome as a temporal power forms part of his political ideas regarding the Italian problem, Gallenga's attitude to religion as ethics is a proof of the didactic value of romantic thinking. The Risorgimento for him—and here he was following Mazzini's footsteps—meant moral renaissance as well as political independence. For him a complete regeneration had to start from religion, since faith is one of the basic feelings in man.

---

[1] 'Catholicism in Italy', in *The Christian Examiner*, Boston, Jan. 1839, vol. xxv, no. 90, p. 286.   [2] *Epis.*, vol. i, pp. 247–9.

For about two years Gallenga taught Italian and lectured in Boston and Cambridge, Mass., where he soon became a member of fashionable society, as he tells us in his memoirs, in which he has left an entertaining description of the life of the younger generation in those days. American men and women—women especially—were hospitable and Gallenga, then an eligible bachelor in his middle twenties, was often asked to dances and parties. However different the situation, his life there had something in common with his stay in Tangiers: he was accepted and welcomed into the local well-off society, but never felt part of it, because of his position and slender income. By the spring of 1838 he began to feel dissatisfied and decided to move elsewhere. There is no other logical explanation for his leaving Boston, apart from his psychological incapacity to adapt himself to New England society. With Everett's help he made two attempts to get himself attached to some other American institution of higher education, one in Philadelphia at the Girard College, and another at Nashville in Tennessee, where he arrived for an interview after an adventurous journey, colourfully depicted in his autobiography. Both attempts were a failure, since it was most unlikely that in the new and quickly growing, but still underdeveloped, parts of the country the teaching of a cultivated subject such as Italian could be of any practical use.

Eventually, he returned to New England where he spent the winter and most of the spring of 1839 teaching and writing, and by the end of April he had saved enough to pay for his trip back to Europe. Just before leaving Boston he made a last attempt to settle there by proposing marriage to Harriet Mills, the sister of a friend of his and the youngest daughter of a wealthy merchant. He had nothing to offer apart from his name and his love, and, needless to say, he was turned down. Bitterly disappointed he sailed for England on 1 May 1839.

II

LONDON 1839-1848

WHEN Gallenga landed in England, he little thought that this country would be his home for the rest of his life. In effect, he found the English milieu congenial and, in spite of long periods away, settled in Great Britain which became his adopted country. In 1847, at the time of his marriage, he asked for British citizenship and was granted it. His experiences in England divided more or less easily into two periods, the years before and after he joined the staff of *The Times*.

During the first period the movement for the unification of Italy acquired a national character and the first campaigns for independence were fought, and it was in these years that he carried out most of his political and literary work in support of the Italian cause, gradually gaining for himself a widespread reputation. Between 1839 and 1848, he spent most of his time writing about Italy, while during the first war of independence he began to play an active role in Italian politics. His first steps, however, were uncertain and faltering. He had come to London from the United States hoping to make a career as a teacher and a man of letters, but in the late thirties London already housed many Italian patriots who earned their livelihood by teaching Italian and competition was keen. Only a few among them had attained a degree of fame and prestige. Of these Antonio Panizzi, then Keeper of the Printed Books at the British Museum, and Gabriele Rossetti, Professor of Italian at King's College, London, had been the most successful. It was to the former that Gallenga went for help. He had been given a letter of introduction to him by a certain Mrs. Bonamy, an American and former pupil of Panizzi's. Panizzi's reception of Gallenga was not very encouraging, to say the least.

I had evidently chosen an awkward moment for my visit. He was out of temper, and my face, it appears, was not to his liking. He took the letter I was holding out to him—both of us standing—ran it over at a glance, and knitting his heavy brows, he crumpled it up, and said: 'There now! There is no end to these silly women! What right has Mrs. Bonamy to write to me at all? She says she was my pupil at Liverpool. How can I remember? Who will tell me her maiden name? And what can I do for you? Italian lessons? In London? Coals to New-castle! I never found any for myself. I lived here for two years at the rate of fourteen pence a day—fourteen pence, I tell you; it is a starving trade in London.'[1]

As Gallenga was soon to find out, Panizzi, like other well-known exiles, had been pestered by the frequent intrusion of his com-patriots, who took refuge in England. Some of them were politi-cal refugees, but others mere rascals who were trying to take advantage of the situation. Moreover, the teaching of Italian in London was, no doubt, a starving trade, and it is quite under-standable that Panizzi advised him to move elsewhere, as he him-self had done in previous years. But Gallenga was determined to stay and so he wrote shortly afterwards:

Dear Mr. Panizzi,
    More following my friends' advice than my own inclination, I put an advertisement in The Times in the hope of finding some private pupils.
    I should like to leave with Rolandi and Messrs. Taylor and Walton, the University booksellers, the name of people to whom anyone interested in my offer could apply for reference. . . . I think that, as former professor at the University, you are the most suitable person to be consulted on such a matter.[2]

Eventually he found work as a tutor and also succeeded in having articles published in English magazines, as is seen in another letter of 1839, in which, while applying for a ticket of admission to the British Museum Library, he somewhat pompously informed Panizzi of his literary progress.

    I wished at the same time to inform you that I have entered into contact with the Metropolitan Magazine for the insertion of a series of

---

[1] Epis., vol. ii, pp. 21–2.
[2] B.M., unpublished, undated letter Mariotti to Panizzi, in Panizzi Papers, Add. 36727 fol. 260.

papers on Italy, on which I intend to lay the basis of a work of some importance. I also sent an article to *Fraser's Magazine*, which has been accepted, and another to *Bentley's Miscellany* for which I am waiting an answer. Nevertheless my circumstances are far from being bright and I still recommend myself to your memory.[1]

While in this precarious financial situation, Gallenga was offered the opportunity of returning to Italy. Early in July 1839 he had met Mazzini again, who was then living in London and who welcomed him back and introduced him to his Anglo-Italian friends. Among them, Antonio met Enrico Mayer, the Leghorn banker and educator, who had for some years been travelling in Europe studying the problem of public education. He asked Gallenga to translate some of his articles on education into English. In Tuscany, where he lived, Mayer worked with the Abbot Lambruschini, editor of *La Guida dell'Educatore*, and with the Vieusseux circle. Politically he was a moderate and a believer in peaceful reforms, and had so far enjoyed complete political immunity. Though Mayer dissented from Mazzini's views, the two men were still friends in the early forties. It was not surprising to find at Mazzini's house people of entirely different political creeds, because in those days the national movement still presented a united front, in spite of the fact that the trend to separate and split into several parties was spreading fast. The break between Mayer and Mazzini had occurred by January 1841, as can be seen in a long letter Mazzini wrote to him, which ends—rather sadly—as follows: 'Follow your path, whatever happens, I am determined to follow mine.'[2]

Young Gallenga was very attracted to Mayer's ideas, and when the latter offered him the chance of returning to Italy, he gratefully accepted it. Mayer guaranteed him political immunity in Tuscany and helped him to find employment with an English family, then living in Florence, the Crawfords. By the middle of April 1840 he was back in Italy, his friendship with Mayer and the protection of an English family giving him comparative

---

[1] B.M., unpublished, undated letter Mariotti to Panizzi, in *Panizzi Papers*, Add. 36727 fol. 259.

[2] *S.E.N.*, vol. 20, p. 40, Mazzini to Mayer, London, 18 Jan. 1841.

security. He was known to the police under the assumed name of Luigi Mariotti, and the *laissez-faire* policy of that time meant that the authorities were indifferent as to his real identity. The Crawfords were in sympathy with the theories of Young Italy: in later years their younger daughter Georgina, then a girl of twelve, married Aurelio Saffi, the Italian patriot and friend of Mazzini, and they were among the very few who remained faithful to Mazzini and his cause till the end. In the early forties they welcomed to their house in Florence liberals and patriots, many of whom came from the local upper classes, and Gallenga mixed freely with them. However, he soon felt out of place, quarrelled with his employer, and by the end of July was back in London. In later years, when commenting on his leaving Florence, he presented a negative portrayal of Tuscan society of the day.

Anything more charming than the conversation of these well-bred persons could not well be imagined. There were no other ladies present than those of the family; yet, strange to say, it struck me as if there were something feminine in the tone of the voices, the softness of the accent—to which my ears had of late become unaccustomed— something in the caressing manner and winning affectionate address, to which the *tutoiement* of the Southern idioms admirably lends itself. All that was so old as to have become almost new to me. . . . Dare I confess that with all its charms that easy life soon became wearisome to me? Those nine years' wanderings had completely unfitted me for that monotonous quiet. I felt thoroughly *dépaysé*. . . . There were many among those Florentine idlers whom I liked, not many for whom I could feel much respect. The tone of their mind struck me as frivolous; their patriotism, which was general and sincere, seemed merely an affair of fashion; their love of literature and art only a luxury.[1]

Gallenga's condemnation of Florentine nobility is unusual and unjust. There were, true enough, idle aristocrats like those he mentions, but there were also people like Capponi, Vieusseux, and Mayer—all of whom he met—who were actively engaged in promoting the social progress of their country as well as the growth of national feeling, and who, under the grand-ducal government, could act quite freely. As Hancock put it,

[1] *Epis.*, vol. ii, pp. 66–8.

it may at first be rather disappointing to discover that in Tuscany there was nothing which had the least resemblance to tyranny; that the people were contented and happy; that the Grand-Duke was a mild, studious person who attempted with pathetic perseverance to keep the love which his subjects had once given to him, and who was repaid at last with scorn, hatred, and bitter accusations which were untrue. . . . In Tuscany there were none of the usual obvious causes which produce revolutions.[1]

The growth of the revolutionary spirit was due to factors other than that of violent oppression. It was largely a natural inheritance of the enlightened spirit of the eighteenth century, which made the most advanced sections of society react against the paternalism of the government, which, in effect, tolerated liberal institutions, but did not support them. This note of peaceful antagonism between the *Buon Governo* and the Liberals gave the Tuscan Risorgimento right from its early days a quality of moderation which had so far been lacking in other Italian states, and which made its appearance elsewhere during the forties only when some of the other governments relaxed, to some degree, their despotic rule. Gallenga himself, when writing on education in 1841, praised the work of Tuscan intellectuals, while he openly condemned the grand-ducal government as paternalistic. So, though there is little evidence for it, it is to personal reasons that one must impute Gallenga's failure to settle in Florence. He had, so to speak, entered it through the back door, and his position as a political exile, even under a false name, prevented him from coming into prominence. His ambitions were frustrated and his dislike of working in a dependent position precipitated the situation. Giving somewhat trivial reasons, he left the Crawfords and went to live by himself, although Mayer had warned him that the loss of English protection would be most unfortunate. Shortly afterwards, he was warned by friends that the police were growing suspicious and he was advised to leave.

His sudden departure was a great disappointment to Gino

[1] W. K. Hancock, *Ricasoli and the Risorgimento in Tuscany*, London, 1926, p. viii.

Capponi. Capponi, who in 1840 was almost completely blind, had been in need of a reader for English books, and had employed Gallenga. With his help he read *The History of Ferdinand and Isabella*, sent to him by the author, William Prescott—he too almost blind—with whom he had kept up a friendly correspondence for some years. He was so taken with the work of the American historian that he asked Gallenga to translate it into Italian. On hearing this, Prescott wrote to his former friend Mariotti:

It gives me great satisfaction that you should undertake the translation of my work in the beautiful Tuscan. It would grieve me to have the work to fall into incompetent hands . . ., but with you I should feel very safe—and I have no doubt the work will gain, instead of losing, in its foreign costume.[1]

He was, naturally, as disappointed as Capponi had been at Gallenga's sudden departure and his failure to produce the translation, which was eventually finished by Antonio Tempestini. Antonio never gave Prescott any definite reason for his leaving Florence, apart from some vague remarks, as appears from their correspondence.

I have left my country somewhat reconciled to my lot of exile, and considerably cured of homesickness. We hear so much from our French, English and German visitors about the justice and fitness of the fate of our country that we are almost forced to think that all is for the best and that dependence and divisions, Pope, priests and convents are a blessing for us!

So be it. I have no power, though I would gladly give my life for it to change its destinies. But I do not like to see my country as it is, and it grieves me much less to lose the blessing of its air and climate and die of useless regret and repining abroad.[2]

In the same letter, in part contradicting what is said above about the state of the country, he informed Prescott that 'there is a novel ardour for historical studies', and although 'perhaps all this is not gold', nevertheless, the fact that so many books were being

---

[1] W. H. Prescott, *Correspondence*, Boston, 1925, p. 143, Prescott to Mariotti, 28 July 1840.

[2] Ibid., pp. 159–60, Mariotti to Prescott, 18 Sept. 1840.

printed and sold was already a sign of life and activity. All this seems to be further evidence that Gallenga's reasons for returning to England were of a personal kind: in fact, he could not fail to see that active liberal forces were at work in his country and were gradually gaining ground, but, though admiring the people who were behind them, he lacked the patience and the constancy of a moderate reformer.

Back in England, Gallenga welcomed any news of peaceful reforms, such as the establishing of a national copyright, the relaxing of the censorship of the press, the yearly meetings of Italian scientists, and pointed out to the English public that those were clear signs of the emancipation and the renaissance of Italy. People like Capponi and Vieusseux had fostered an inner regeneration of the country based on peaceful revolution the purpose of which was to *Italianize Italy*.

The Italians had been so long estranged from each other; the name of their country had been so long buried in oblivion; their local interests had been so artfully directed into different and opposite channels, that their patriotic ideas—I speak of the unenlightened classes—had still something vague and undetermined: the natural boundaries of the country seemed to shift from one district to another, so as to induce the traveller to conclude that, geographically as well as politically, there is no Italy.

To efface from the minds of the people these last remnants of illiberal provincialisms, rather engendered by ignorance than ill-will; to foster the redeeming idea of Italian nationality, the intelligent classes in Italy were actively employed.[1]

Gallenga's stay in Florence, however short, proved valuable, not only because he gained first-hand knowledge of conditions inside the country, but also because it greatly influenced the development of his political thinking. This can be clearly seen in an article on popular education which appeared in the *Foreign Quarterly Review* in 1841.

Right from the beginning of the Risorgimento, public education had been one of the main concerns of Italian liberals and

[1] *Italy, P. and P.*, vol. ii, pp. 381-2.

patriots. By 1841 a few experiments had been launched and
a number of schools had been opened, most of them supported
by private funds, such as the Tuscan *asili* or nursery schools,
and the Mazzinian school in London. About popular education
Gallenga writes:

> Popular education in England, in America, in almost every other
> civilized country, may or should have no other object than to promote
> the greatest happiness of the lowest classes by improving their intel-
> lectual and moral condition. But in an enslaved, divided, distracted
> country like Italy, education is not considered as an end, but as a means.
> The work of regeneration must lead to a deed of emancipation. Popular
> instruction must be among the most active elements of nationality.
> The Italian people must be raised to the dignity of rational beings,
> that they may be fairly entitled to claim their rights as an independent
> race of freemen. Education, we have said, must be the beginning of
> a fundamental revolution.[1]

But if the aim of popular education was the same in the various
Italian states, the interpretation of the word 'education' differed
so greatly that he felt the need to define it.

> The main object of education should be to fit man for life. It ought
> to instil into the youth's mind that there is a society already in existence,
> in which he is to fill a place, in which he will have duties to perform,
> hardships and storms to endure. It ought to teach a man to know him-
> self, to resign and reconcile him to his lot; to recognize and adore the
> hand of Providence, even in those social arrangements which may
> strike him as unjust and arbitrary.[2]

These words, which were inspired by the doctrine of *La Guida
dell'Educatore*, clearly show how far Gallenga had travelled from
the day when he brandished a dagger in front of an astonished
crowd in Parma. They were, of course, written at a time when
'moral force' and 'passive resistance' seemed likely to win the
battle for emancipation. But even later, when he had to admit
that complete independence from foreign rule could not be
gained without actual fighting, the idea that man must fit into

---

[1] 'Education in Italy', *Foreign Quarterly Review*, July 1841, vol. xxvii, no. 54,
p. 321.
[2] Ibid., pp. 298-9.

a pre-existing society remained firm in his mind. He now began to consider national emancipation as a development towards liberalism and away from absolutism, rather than as the fruit of a violent revolution. Although the national idea had spread quickly all over the country since the beginning of the century, it was still confined to a minority which included most of the middle-class bourgeoisie. As Gallenga pointed out—and quite rightly so—the working classes, especially those living in the country, were not yet in sympathy with it. They were acquainted with very little beyond the boundaries of their villages and towns. Hence the need to educate them. When commenting on the introduction of compulsory education in the Lombardo-Venetian provinces by the Austrian government, he gave it his full support.

There is no doubt that the Austrian government, when proceeding to the organization of primary instruction, only acted in compliance with the urgent demands of the most enlightened part of the nation, and that the funds for the erection and maintenance of schools have been and are chiefly furnished by private donations and voluntary contributions. . . . All this may go far to prove that the natural good sense and intelligence of the Italian people needed no great compulsion to enter into the views of their legislators. Still but few of the lowest classes can be made to understand and value the blessings of education, and the rest must be guided to their own good by the argument of force. . . . It is only with this object that the centralizing omnipotence of a despotic government may more readily prevail against the natural sluggishness or stubbornness of a degraded population, that the Italian patriots have resigned education into the hands of their rulers. . . . [There is] every reason to expect that the diffusion of useful knowledge would soon lead them [the Italians], at least, to as much rational latitude and freedom of inquiry as is now enjoyed, under the same absolute rule, by the subjects of the Prussian monarchy.[1]

He was, of course, aware of the danger of state intervention and so were most Italian liberals, but some years later, when incorporating these notes in *Italy, Past and Present*, he did not condemn state-controlled schools; on the contrary, while he advocated education for everyone in an ideally free country,

[1] 'Education in Italy', *For. Quart. Rev.*, vol. xxvii, no. 54, pp. 320–1.

Gallenga put forward as a solution the idea of an educational system run by the combined efforts of the government and private individuals. The state would be in a position to guarantee regular functioning and to enforce compulsory attendance, while private intervention would counterbalance the political implications of a state system. One can see in these pages on education the first steps towards an enlightened conservatism, which characterized Gallenga's political convictions in later years. It was from the upper classes that the future leaders of the new Italy must come, and in their hands lay the possibility of bringing about the physical and moral welfare of the lower classes. A liberal government would work for the people, but would not need to be formed or elected by the proletariat.

His moving towards conservatism was a slow process and up to 1848 his attitude towards the national movement was a mixture of approval and criticism of the activities of patriots and governments. His opinion of Charles Albert and Mazzini, for instance, underwent several changes in a short period of time, from extreme hatred to great admiration and vice versa. His uncertainties and changes of opinion reflected the uncertainties and changes which took place in Italy. They gave his writings a peculiarly moderate tone which gained him the approval and the support of many English people, especially those who considered Mazzini's views extreme.

When he returned to London in July 1840, Gallenga found that some of the articles he had left in the hands of his publishers before going to Florence, had been published and had been well received. He continued writing for several magazines and was soon being asked for more articles than he could produce.

The editor of the *Foreign Quarterly* is pestering me for more articles and more news from Italy, but from where can I draw the material to satisfy his demand?[1]

So he wrote to Mayer from London, complaining about his lack of news from Italy. He did, however, manage to publish a large number of essays: before 1843 he was a regular contributor to

---

[1] Mayer Archives, unpublished letter, Mariotti to Mayer, 10 Apr. 1841.

the *New Monthly Magazine* and he wrote frequently for the *Foreign Quarterly Review* and the *British and Foreign Review*. In April 1841 his first book on Italy appeared under the title *Italy, General Views of Its History and Literature in Reference to Its Present State*, later changed into *Italy, Past and Present*. It was favourably reviewed and attracted the attention of men of letters, such as Edward Bulwer-Lytton and Benjamin Disraeli, then at the height of their literary fame. They were so impressed with his work that, with Dickens and Carlyle, they gave him testimonials when, in 1847, the chair of Italian having become vacant at King's College, London, Gallenga applied for it, but was unsuccessful. Of *Italy* Bulwer-Lytton wrote:

> The book is admirable, useful, instructive. I am delighted to find an Italian coming forward with so much noble enthusiasm to vindicate his country and obtain for it its proper interest in the eyes of Europe.[1]

Disraeli was not less generous in his praise.

> I recognise the rare characteristic of genius—a large conception of the topic, and picturesque diction founded on profound thought, and the passionate sensibility which becomes the subject—a subject beautiful as its climate and inexhaustible as its soil.[1]

The book also opened to him the door of London literary circles.

> In a few days after its publication, that book had won for me an altogether new social position. Lady Morgan, Lady Blessington, and other ladies who had recently written on Italy or on a subject connected with that country, were loud in my praises. . . . Lady Molesworth, Mrs. Milner-Gibson, and other leaders of fashion among a certain class in Belgravia, took me by the hand, and rare were during that season the afternoons or evenings, in which I was allowed to attend to my occupations, or to enjoy the quiet of my lodgings.[2]

Encouraged by the social and literary success of his *Italy*, Gallenga tried to obtain a post in an English University. Since his days in Boston one of his greatest ambitions had been to follow an academic career. While in Harvard, the presence of Pietro Bachi

---

[1] Quoted in: L. Mariotti, *The Blackgown Papers*, London, 1846, p. i.
[2] *Epis.*, vol. ii, p. 102.

had spoiled his chances of becoming a *lector* in Italian. When he first moved to London there was no vacancy available at the University, in addition to the fact that he had produced hardly any work of literary value and was completely unknown as a scholar. Even given the chance it was most unlikely that Gallenga would have succeeded in securing an appointment. His teaching, therefore, was confined to private lessons, most of it to young ladies who, according to the fashion, were expected to know Italian as well as music and embroidery. But now Gallenga's hopes were revived, and in 1841, with the support of Edward Everett and Samuel Rush Meyrick, he applied for a professorship at the Taylor Institution of Modern Languages at Oxford, then in the making. Everett, who most fortunately for Gallenga had been appointed U.S. minister to the court of St. James, proved the same generous friend to the Italian in Great Britain that he had been in the United States. He helped him to find private lessons and assisted him with his application to the Taylor Institution. Samuel Rush Meyrick, a lawyer and former Oxford student, was a well-known antiquary and collector of arms: in 1826 he had been in charge of the organization of the armoury at the Tower of London, and later of the collection at Windsor Castle. He was an author of books on heraldry and had consulted Gallenga, to whom he had been introduced by a mutual friend, on historical points concerning Italian coats of arms. Though he helped Gallenga he thought that he stood little chance of success, mainly because as an Italian, he was born a Catholic. So Meyrick, as outspoken as Gallenga himself, wrote to him, commenting on Oxford bigotry:

Oxford, as I before told you, is full of bigotry, prejudice and illiberality, and the Dean of Ch[rist] Ch[urch] is considered the most ill-bred man in his manner of any in existence. You have done wisely to leave copies of your book with him and with the Vice-Chancellor, for the liberality of sentiment it contains with respect to religion, will make them either doubt your being a Catholic, or conclude that you are by no means a rigid one.[1]

The establishment of the Taylor Institution proceeded very

[1] A.B.M., unpublished letter, Meyrick to Mariotti, 16 Dec. 1841.

slowly and we can find Meyrick's statement about Oxford dislike of Roman Catholics confirmed in an unpublished letter written by Everett to Gallenga, two years later when his application had not yet been officially examined.

> On occasion of a late visit to Oxford, I conversed with Dr.Wynter[1] on the subject of your application. Dr.Wynter spoke very kindly, or rather favourably on the subject of your qualifications. He appeared to be acquainted with your book, he respected your candour on the subject of your religious convictions, but said he thought it would be deemed expedient not to appoint any person of the Roman Catholic Church. From what I have heard of the progress of the Taylor College, I was led to think that it would not go into operation very soon.[2]

Everett was correct about the delay in the formation of the Taylor Institution, the building of which was completed only in 1847, when the first Professor of Modern Languages was appointed. As to Gallenga's candour with regard to religion, he was, as previously demonstrated, inclined towards some generic form of Christianity not necessarily identifiable with a specific Church, and most of his violent opposition to the Church of Rome sprang from anti-clericalism more than from actual condemnation of its doctrine. It was, therefore, not surprising that the Oxford dons should consider him still a Roman Catholic. By 1856, when Aurelio Saffi was appointed lecturer in Italian, objections to a Catholic had obviously lost ground.

While Gallenga was trying unsuccessfully to enter Oxford University, Dr. John Inglis, third Bishop of Nova Scotia, offered him the Chair of Modern Languages at King's College, Windsor, in Canada. Although there was little scope for the teaching of languages there, and the Bishop had probably wanted a foreign professor for reasons of prestige, Gallenga immediately jumped at the opportunity of securing for himself an academic position and accepted his offer. Just as he had left for Florence, rashly, almost at a moment's notice, so now he left London for the New World. In January 1842 he sailed on board the *Britannia*, one of the first

---

[1] Philip Wynter, D.D., then President of St. John's, who in 1840 was Vice-Chancellor.

[2] A.B.M., Everett to Mariotti, 31 July, 1843.

Cunard liners which on the same voyage was taking Dickens on
his first visit to the United States. Gallenga, who felt for the novelist the same warm admiration he had for Carlyle, was eager to
know him, and before leaving had asked a mutual friend for a
letter of introduction to the writer. Dickens himself was willing
to make his acquaintance, but unluckily the two men never had
a chance to meet. Three days after leaving Liverpool, when the
Italian sent him his card together with his friend's letter, the
novelist had already taken to his berth. The sea was so rough that
neither Dickens nor his wife moved from their cabin.

A head wind! Imagine a human face upon the vessel's prow, with
fifteen thousand Samsons in one bent upon driving her back, and
hitting her exactly between the eyes whenever she attempts to advance
an inch. Imagine the ship herself, with every pulse and artery of her
huge body swollen and bursting under this maltreatment, sworn to go
on or die. Imagine the wind howling, the sea roaring, the rain beating:
all in furious array against her. Picture the sky both dark and wild,
and the clouds, in fearful sympathy with the waves, making another
ocean in the air. Add to all this the clattering on deck and down below;
the tread of hurried feet; the loud hoarse shouts of seamen; the gurg-
ling in and out of water through the scuppers; with every now and
then the striking of a heavy sea upon the planks above, with the deep,
dead, heavy sound of thunder heard within a vault; and there is the
head wind of that January morning.[1]

Gallenga chose that very awkward day to try and get in touch
with him: Dickens was unable to move from his cabin but was
troubled by the thought of the Italian boldly pacing up and down
the saloon, maybe expecting him to turn up any moment.

I imagined him one of those cast-iron images—I will not call
them men—who ask, with red faces and lusty voices, what sea-sickness
means, and whether it really is as bad as it is represented to be. This
was very torturing indeed; and I don't think I ever felt such perfect
gratification and gratitude of heart as I did when I heard from the
ship's doctor that he had been obliged to put a large mustard poultice
on this very gentleman's stomach. I date my recovery from the
receipt of that intelligence.[2]

[1] C. Dickens, *American Notes*, Greenwich, Conn., 1961, p. 28.
[2] Ibid., p. 30.

After a troublesome crossing lasting sixteen days, Gallenga reached his destination and landed at Halifax, Nova Scotia, while Dickens and his wife continued their journey to America. When he was back in London, he wrote to the novelist and this time Dickens welcomed him to his home, jokingly saying that he had not forgotten their 'merry meeting at sea'.[1] From Halifax Gallenga moved to Windsor where he soon settled, but equally soon grew tired of it. Here again he found himself in as amiable a milieu as he had found in Tangiers and Boston, but with little intellectual stimulus. He was in charge of the teaching of Italian, French, and Spanish, but the students were few and their major interest was theology. He spent part of his academic year in Halifax, where he was asked to lecture to fashionable society but most of the time was spent in 'ignoble idleness'. He remained fifteen months in Nova Scotia, after which having enough money for his trip back to Europe and having found a successor for the College, he returned somewhat depressed to England. It was quite naïve of Gallenga to have hoped for an academic life of high scholarly standards in the colonies, especially when, only some years before, he had complained about the cultural provincialism of New England, which, though lacking a European tradition, was an active centre of studies. But his grim financial situation had made him take a step which he soon regretted. The success of his *Italy* was only nominal, and it brought him little pecuniary reward. As he put it, 'the book languished throughout the year', and his publisher, Mr. Otley, of Saunders and Otley, told him that it was a dead loss, 'dead as a coffin nail'.

However, when in April 1843 Gallenga returned to London, he began to make ends meet, for there was still a great demand for the teaching of Italian in spite of the fact that those were no longer the days 'of Byron and Shelley, of Roscoe, Leigh Hunt, Rogers and Landor, and those other stars of the Regency, which had caused all their educated countrymen to rave about Italy.'[2] Most of the teaching was to him dull and uninspiring—the sort

[1] On Dickens and Gallenga see W. J. Carlton, 'Dickens Studies Italian', in *The Dickensian*, May, 1965, vol. lxi.

[2] *Epis.*, vol. ii, p. 92.

of teaching reserved for a finishing school for girls—but it was
not so for his students. He taught Italian to Dickens, with whom
he had entered into friendship, and who on the eve of leaving for
Italy wrote to John Forster: 'A blessing on Mr. Mariotti my
Italian master.'[1] There is little indication in *Pictures from Italy* that
Dickens took any special interest in contemporary Italian politics,
apart from the close of the book, where perhaps one can trace
some evidence of a sympathy with Italian nationalism.

> Let us part from Italy, with all its miseries and wrongs, affectionately,
> in our admiration of the beauties, natural and artificial, of which it is
> full to overflowing, and in our tenderness towards a people, naturally
> well-disposed, and patient and sweet-tempered. Years of neglect,
> oppression and misrule, have been at work, to change their nature and
> reduce their spirit . . ., but the good that was in them ever, is in them
> yet, and a noble people may be, one day, raised up from these ashes.
> Let's entertain that hope.[2]

Greater warmth of feeling towards the Italian cause can be found
in some of his letters, and in one to Henry Chorley in 1860, the
name of Gallenga appears together with those of Mazzini and
Manin, as being the Italians who had made him aware of their
country's problems.[3]

Gallenga was, by now, becoming better known as a lecturer
as well as a writer. In 1845 he twice addressed the British and
Foreign Society in London, reading two papers of a light character,
The Age We Live In and *Bull and Nongtongpaw or National
Characteristics*, in both of which he satirized the insularity of the
English. In the following year he was asked to lecture on Dante
in Manchester. Although there is little evidence about his lecturing
abilities, he must have been quite successful, since some years
later they thought of asking him again. But if having pupils like
Dickens and the occasional lecturing were rare events to be
enjoyed, there was much social life to compensate for the drud-
gery of his teaching. With the help of Mazzini, at first, and

[1] J. Forster, *The Life of Charles Dickens*, London, 1928, p. 305, Dickens to
Forster, 1 Nov. 1843.
[2] C. Dickens, *Pictures from Italy*, London, 1907, pp. 509–10.
[3] Idem, *Letters*, London, 1882, vol. iii, pp. 190–3.

then with the success of some of his publications, Gallenga came into close contact with the section of English society which showed sympathy for Italy. Their interest, not sterile or superficial, was often a way of expressing themselves either artistically or socially. They not only backed the Italian cause among English public opinion, but were also free and generous in their help to Italian patriots who had taken refuge in Britain. In his memoirs Gallenga has left us a fascinating gallery of literary portraits of eminent Victorians, who befriended him and helped him in his career. Most important of these was Sarah Austin, the writer and translator, whom he had met as early as 1839.

Mrs. Austin was the kindest of women, kind especially to the Italians, one of whom, Fortunato Prandi, had been her intimate friend, and whom she had aided in the translation and publication of the *Memoirs of Andryane*, a State prisoner at Spielberg. She gave me letters for many influential men, all of whom were lavish of their promises of assistance in any kind of employment which I might suggest as suitable to my taste and abilities.[1]

Mrs. Austin introduced him to another writer, Ann Jameson, the author of a *Diary of an Ennuyée*, who already knew Italy, and who was to return there a few years later as a friend of the Brownings. At her home, where he was often a guest, he met Robert Browning, still quite unknown as a poet, and who had just returned from his first visit to Italy, where he had toured the Venetian provinces.

[Browning was] a young man with a bright countenance, long hair down to his shoulders, and dark eyes, with the light of intelligence and the fire of enthusiasm flashing from them. . . . Browning was then full of Italy, a country wherefrom he had just returned, and where, as he told me, he had been rummaging about the farrago of the rhymesmiths of the *Cinquecento* among 'whose rubbish he found gems of great price'.[2]

During the same period Gallenga made the acquaintance of Lady Noel Byron, the widow of the poet, who devoted herself to charitable works and was sponsoring public education. She

[1] *Epis.*, vol. ii, pp. 42–3.   [2] Ibid., p. 45.

worked closely with James Kay-Shuttleworth, the English educator, who was the first secretary of the committee founded by the Privy Council to administer government aid for public education in England. Mayer had introduced Gallenga to Lady Byron, who asked him to translate some of her writings on schools of charity for *La Guida dell'Educatore*. Recollecting his visits to her, Gallenga left an interesting picture of the widow of the poet. She used to entertain him at length on the subject of education as if anxious to impress him that her zeal for the cause and progress of humanity engrossed all her energies to the exclusion of any other thought.

Lady Byron was then forty-seven years of age. She had been fifteen years a widow, and had seen the last of her husband twenty-three years before the date of my visit. She barely looked forty; though she dressed simply and almost poorly, with her hair in smooth bands under a cap, and a plain dark merino dress up to her chin, almost a nun-like habiliment. Her complexion seemed to me rather dark for an Englishwoman—marble-like, quite colourless; but her features were faultless and the expression was sedate, serene, with hardly a trace of a grief long since buried.[1]

One day, when the weather was fine, they talked about the Italian climate and Gallenga brought up the subject of the Italian situation.

I said I little cared to see Italy again in her present prostrate condition, and quite inadvertently let slip the line:

'Victor or vanquished, thou slave of friend or foe'

then soon recollecting whose words those were, I was struck dumb and looked foolish; but the lady never winced, never made a sign as if she had ever heard the line; as if *Childe Harold* had never been anything to her, or she to *Childe Harold* and its author.[2]

Like her husband, Lady Byron was a good friend to Italy. Her name appears in the list of people who sponsored Mazzini's school at Hatton Garden, and she was often seen there. Together with her name and that of Ann Jameson one finds, among the supporters of the school, those of the Carlyles and Arethusa

[1] Ibid., pp. 28–9.   [2] Ibid., pp. 29–30.

Milner-Gibson, all of whom befriended Gallenga. The Carlyles, who kept open house in London, often asked him to their home, and young Gallenga was fascinated, as many were, by the writer's striking personality. He had always professed the greatest admiration for the Scottish historian and thinker, and meeting him was a rewarding experience.

In the evening I found the grisly philosopher seated in a low arm-chair near the fire, with his feet up the chimney-piece, Yankee fashion, with half-closed eyes, and a meerschaum between his teeth, holding forth in his drawling Scotch sing-song, and so much in the phraseology with which I had become familiar in his writings—especially in his *French Revolution*, which I knew almost by heart—that I often turned to him wondering whether he was merely talking, or reading, or reciting.[1]

He was also a regular visitor at the home of Arethusa Milner-Gibson, the wife of Thomas Milner-Gibson, the politician, and who presided over one of London's most fashionable salons. To her he dedicated a new edition of his poems, *Oltremonte ed oltre-mare*. Together with Lady Morgan, the Irish novelist, she introduced Gallenga to society. Their friendship came abruptly to an end, however, when, after the first war of Italian independence, Gallenga abandoned and publicly attacked Mazzini. His friendship with Lady Morgan, on the other hand, lasted till her death in 1859. To her he dedicated another of his books, *The Blackgown Papers*, published in 1846. This is a collection of short stories, which had previously appeared in magazines, and presents all the worst features of the gothic and sentimental novels, only now and again showing some documentary interest, as in the tale *Morello, or the Progress of the Organ Boy*, which illustrates the wretched conditions of Italian boys imported by professional beggars who exploited them—a social evil which Mazzini tried to fight with the founding of his school in London.

In 1847 Gallenga married. His wife was Juliet Schunck, the daughter of a wealthy German-Jewish family. He had met the Schuncks in Manchester: they belonged to the intellectual élite of the town, and gave him hospitality when he was there in 1846

[1] *Epis,,* vol. ii, pp. 105-6.

to lecture on Dante. Juliet was sixteen years his junior and a rich young lady provided with a large dowry plus a yearly income. When they married he resumed his real name as can be seen from one of Mazzini's letters to an Italian friend, Lamberti.

Mariotti, alias Gallenga, for he is now using his own name, has married a young, gentle English girl who already has five hundred pounds a year and will have one thousand one day. *Bravi tutti!*[1]

Mazzini's allusion applies to many Italian exiles who solved their economic problems by marrying wealthy English ladies: Gallenga was no exception, and Mazzini's light remark seems to insinuate some doubts as to the sincerity of his love for Juliet. Gallenga was jealous of his private life, and so little is known about it that one can only guess at their relationship. In the writings where his first wife is mentioned, he speaks of her with great tenderness and respect, but these sources are not reliable, for they are, so to speak, official papers, either written for the public, or to some distant acquaintances. Like Harriet Mills in Boston, Juliet was remarkably rich, and after her premature death Antonio married again. She died in 1855 of scarlet fever, and her husband remarried in 1858: three years are perhaps a long enough time to mourn a beloved wife, but only a year after her death, he was courting Ada, the very young daughter of one of the most in-fluential political men in Turin, Luigi Farini, who, it should be noted, was his contemporary, for he was born in 1812. Gallenga even proposed to her, but was not accepted. Apart from this, there are no real grounds for supposing that his feelings for Juliet were only mercenary. As in his public life, Gallenga suc-ceeded in reconciling idealistic and practical considerations: as love for his country never prevented him from pursuing his own career, so his love for a woman always went hand in hand with his desire for money and social connections.

His marriage put a definite end to all financial worries and, in spite of his disappointment at not being appointed to the chair at King's College, he could now face the future with greater tranquillity. Between 1847 and 1848 he published an enlarged

[1] *S.E.N.*, vol. 32, p. 115, Mazzini to G. Lamberti, 21 Apr. 1847.

edition of *Italy, Past and Present*, reassessing the Italian situation in the light of more recent events. His position was further consolidated when the Chair of Italian at University College, London, became vacant. This time his influential friends and his reputation as a man of letters did not fail to secure it for him. At the time when he was appointed professor Gallenga had travelled a long way from the day in June 1839 when he had landed at Portsmouth with hardly any money in his pocket and a few letters of introduction from American friends. He had established himself as a professional writer and a critic. His writings covered a wide range of subjects from poetry to fiction, but his reputation rested entirely on his political and literary works. All of these, in one way or another, were related to the Italian scene. His propaganda work for the national cause coincided with the genuine interest for the Italian situation which was alive among some of the leading English figures of the day. The writings of Gallenga, together with those of other exiles, helped to keep this interest alive and bring it to a wider public, thus influencing English public opinion, which for several years was extremely favourable to Italy. The Italy which Gallenga presented to the English was a living reality. He wrote about and for his country, to prove that the time of Italian revival had come, that 'the fate of Italy was mature'. His articles were largely informative and, since they were primarily written for current magazines, they often reveal journalistic features, such as long digressions on current topics, the introduction of trifling episodes and allusions which may have appealed to the reader of the day, but which seriously impede the sequence of thought. Even when editing his papers for a book, he could not resist the temptation to pack into a single volume as much of his output as he could, regardless of the fact that some of it was quite irrelevant to the theme of the work. Once one accepts the fragmentary character of Gallenga's writings, however, a close examination of his political and literary production can be rewarding.

III

ITALY, PAST AND PRESENT

Italy, Past and Present contains most of Gallenga's literary and
critical articles, linked together and expanded so as to give a
panorama of Italian history and literature from its origins to his
own days. Gallenga's ideas reflect so much of the spirit of his
time that it is rather difficult to trace their original sources.
His education was fundamentally Anglo-Italian. In Italy he was
brought up in the years when the quarrel between classicism and
romanticism still lingered on; in America he knew Prescott and
Ticknor personally; in London he was in close contact with
Mazzini, through whom he met Carlyle. Romanticism came to
him through the writings of the *Conciliatore* and the works of
Berchet, Mazzini and Manzoni, Sismondi and Ginguené, as well
as those of Carlyle and Scott. This can be seen in the introduction
to *Italy*, where he asserts that there exist indissoluble links between
history and literature and one cannot fully consider and assess a
work of art without taking into account the historical conditions
of the time in which it was produced. Art must spring from life,
and the life of a country is its history. This is the chief principle
'radiant with the light of truth' put forward by the new romantic
school. Moreover, the man of letters has two missions to fulfil: he
must portray an age in its moral and social aspects, and 'divine
the spirit of the times and go before it'. The classical school, which
interpreted art as something apart from life, had failed in its
task. It must be noted here that by classicism Gallenga meant
that school which imitated the ancients, and not the original output of classical authors. He agreed with Schlegel, when he asserted
that classical culture is romantic as long as it is a product of its
time.

The acceptance of romantic theories implied a complete change
in the field of literary criticism. If the literature of a country was

to be judged according to its relations to the time and place from which it sprang, a history of it could only be written in the light of national history. For Gallenga this must not be a mere recollection of facts and events, but an examination of their causes and effects in relation to social progress. History and literature, therefore, form a sort of ideal unity the progress of which marks the phases of human evolution.

The history of nations is naturally divided into so many distinct epochs; the same or analogous revolutions take place in regular periods, and their history is never so well studied as during those intervals of silence and torpor during which the exhausted nation supplies its empty veins with new blood, and hardly develops strength for new action; as the geologist, who would explore the crater of a volcano, must wait for an hour in which the mountain lies still and cold, as if spent by the last eruption, and preparing in silence and darkness the glowing materials for the new one.[1]

So that while on one hand, the idea of development in the succession of human events was put forward, this development was conditioned by the alternating of recurring cycles, some of which represented decadence and, on the surface, regression. These inevitable moments of silence and torpor were ideally suited for studies and research

for there is, even in the most distant and disparate events, an admirable chain of causes and effects, some links of which it is not always impossible even for human shortsightedness to trace.[2]

Regression and decadence were never entirely so, and within the framework of cyclical recurrences mankind moved towards its goal. As Croce put it, the idea of development marked the achievement of the new times.[3] For Gallenga this idea depended on divine intervention, as he clearly expounded in the final paragraph of his introduction to *Italy*.

There is, at last, a PRESENT for Italy. The stroke of the last hour of the PAST ushers us in the first hour of the FUTURE. Days follow but resemble not each other. There is no delay or intermission in the

---

[1] *Italy, P. and P.,* vol. i, p. xxxi.   [2] Ibid., vol. i, p. xxxi.
[3] B. Croce, *Storia della storiografia italiana nel secolo XIX⁰*, Bari, 1921, p. 56.

fulfilment of Heaven's will. . . . God has, at last, mercy on long-enduring
Italy! Her princes may yet desert her. Her Pope, even if infallible, is not
immortal. But God is eternal and is with her. Happy, if she learns to
trust in Him and herself alone! Her sorrow has been weighed her: fate
is mature.[1]

Gallenga not only placed absolute trust in a transcendent principle,
he also believed that it was possible for man to trace the causes
that lie at the root of human existence by some rational process
based on his own interpretation of a chain of human events.
Such study helps us to understand not only our present condition,
but also our future. The connection between past and future so
greatly stressed by Gallenga was not at all logically demonstrated
in his writings for his theory was not based on any sort of historical
materialism. Like Mazzini, and Carlyle, Quinet, and Michelet, he
approaches the problem in an almost mystical way. Men, books,
and events are seen in a messianic light, fulfilling or not fulfilling
the mission inherent in them. Such an approach gives his writings
a tremendous dramatic value: every man and every fact is so
vividly depicted in an elevated style and enriched by biblical
expressions that some of his pages offer interesting and entertaining reading quite apart from their critical content. When it
comes to actual criticism, such preconceived theories on art and
its mission do not always prove positive. The historical interpretation of literature, which was one of the greatest achievements
of romanticism, undoubtedly facilitates the correct understanding of a work of art. Any detail concerning the time and life of an
author may help in interpreting his writings, but does not add
anything to the intrinsic value of the work itself. It is even more
dangerous—and this appears to be the main limitation of Gallenga's criticism—to judge literature in accordance with its moral
commitments, especially when by morality one means Victorian
puritanism and patriotism. However noble in their intentions,
they greatly narrow the field of artistic creation. Gallenga's
criticism is often anchored to moral and practical issues as is
evident in this passage on *I Promessi Sposi*.

What patriotic object . . . could the novelist propose to himself when

[1] *Italy, P. and P.*, vol. i, pp. xliii–xliv.

he made a monk and cardinal his favourite heroes: when in an enlightened though oppressed country, in the the age of Galileo and Sarpi, he found no greatness, no virtue, but under the cowl or the mitre? Why did he choose his subject out of a period of oppression and woe?[1]

Equally dangerous is the application of some of his ideas to the historical process, which becomes at times a mere chronicle of individual vices and virtues, as can be seen in the description of the fall of Florence in 1530 when besieged and taken by the troops of Charles V.

A sullen determination, such as despair alone is apt to engender, has seized the rulers of the beleaguered city; they resolve never to yield to any extremity, and to bury themselves with their families amidst the ruins of their country. Malatesta Baglioni, one of the mercenary leaders whom the Republic held in its pay, understood nothing of that heroic resolution, and entered into secret negotiations with the besiegers, to avert the fate of those deluded enthusiasts, and save them in spite of themselves. He opened the gates to the enemy, and turned his artillery against the town.[2]

On the other hand, Gallenga's belief in human development and progress, while at times forcing the issue in relation to history and literature, lies at the very basis of some of his acute observations on different events: his pages on the Reformation and the Counter-Reformation in Italy show this well, especially where he says that what prevented the spreading of the new Churches in Italy was the lack of adequate political institutions and not a profound attachment to the doctrine of the Church of Rome.

The doctrines of Luther and Calvin, encouraging a spirit of free inquiry, could not fail to be warmly received in a country naturally inclined towards them, by the recent memories of its liberal institutions, by its superior refinement and culture. ... [But] when the opposite factions were brought into violent collision, and it became a necessity for every state as well as for individuals to come to an open profession of faith, the Italians were no longer masters of themselves. The whole country lay prostrated at the feet of the armies of Spain, of that power which gave so ample proofs of relentless, sanguinary bigotry,

---

[1] *Italy, P. and P.*, vol. ii, p, 113.   [2] Ibid., vol. i, pp. 247–8.

Whatever opinions might have prevailed in Italy friendly to the Protestant faith, they would inevitably have been drowned in blood.[1]

Although Gallenga stated that he was not writing the history of Italy and of her literature, but merely giving a general view of the country, his book contains enough information to outline its historical and literary evolution. Moreover, in spite of the limitations and dangers of his ideas, he was far more of a critic than Mazzini or Carlyle, and the implications of patriotic and moral issues involved in his theories on art are more than once forgotten when the critic takes over. For instance, he greatly admired Ariosto, in spite of the fact that the author of *Orlando Furioso* was not a politically committed poet, in an age which saw the spreading of foreign power in Italy and the loss of independence, and even admitted that Ariosto was fulfilling his mission as a poet,

so far as the office of poetry can be merely to afford an easy and—with the exception of a few cantos—innocent delight; so far as it can have no other aim than to give rise to a rapid succession of infinitely varied and always pleasing emotions, without pointing to any determined object, without proving or illustrating any important truth.[2]

This evaluation of Ariosto's poetry conflicts with what has just been mentioned as regards Manzoni's art. Gallenga was in fact blatantly contradicting himself: the idea was already at the back of his mind that the appreciation of a work of art cannot be limited by preconceived theories without depriving literature of some of its greatest creations. Schlegel had felt this contradiction too, and De Sanctis made the same point when he wrote that the error of the historical school lay not in its belief in historical values, but in its historical conception of the beautiful.[3] This inner contradiction which at first seems to undermine Gallenga's writings is what gives value to his application of the historical method to literature.

In dividing the history of his country into ages, he was echoing

[1] Ibid., vol. i, pp. 278–9. See also A. Garosci, *Antonio Gallenga*, Turin, 1964, p. 191 and *passim*.

[2] *Italy, P. and P.*, vol. i, pp. 309–10.

[3] F. De Sanctis, *Teoria e storia della letteratura*, Bari, 1926, vol. ii, p. 75.

Vico's theories, which had only recently become known. He partly accepted them, but also put forward his own interpretation of *corsi* and *ricorsi*. In fact, he soon became aware of the dangers of too strict a division and his alternating ages of torpor and activity transcend the actual limits of time, so that they can coexist one beside the other. For instance, the second age of Italian history, that is to say of the time of the Communes, which for him, as for most romantics, was

a blessed age, when the heart of the writer was glowing, and the hand trembling with the agitation of public life, when the scholar was at once a citizen, a warrior, a magistrate;[1]

covered the whole of the fourteenth century, but it also continued through the following centuries 'wherever a faint breath of liberty was found to foster it'. So he goes beyond the artificiality of a chronological classification, and makes his age coincide with a given phenomenon rather than a given period of time. This system can be of value in following some trends of thought and literary taste and assessing them. It also helps to support Gallenga's idea of human development, mitigating a too naïve faith in a linear evolution of mankind.

His ages of Italian history are: the age of darkness, from its origins till the middle of the thirteenth century; the age of Dante, including the thirteenth and fourteenth centuries; the age of the *Signorie* or of domestic tyranny, covering the fifteenth and sixteenth centuries; the age of foreign dominion, beginning with the descent of Charles VIII, and ending with the reign of Leopold of Tuscany (1765–90) when the age of national reawakening begins. It is interesting to notice that while in the 1841 edition the Napoleonic era was included in the last age, in the 1848 edition it was transferred to the previous one. The change is significant for in less than ten years the question which closed his book, *Shall Italy ever see better days?* had been answered in the affirmative, and the emancipation of the country was now seen as an internal issue, depending on factors other than the French intervention in Italy.

In *Italy*, *Past and Present*, history is more widely illustrated than

---

[1] *Italy, P. and P.*, vol. i, p. xxxvii.

literature. We approach different ages from an historical angle—
by historical is here meant, above all, political. Gallenga had
some justification for doing so, for he was trying to correlate
history and literature, which he succeeded in doing in spite of the
fact that the information is often episodic and too detailed, and
that, notwithstanding his criticism of eighteenth-century erudition, he did not fully escape its influence.

The first age opens with the fall of the Western Roman Empire.
The history of Italy is here seen in a European light: the invasion
of the Longobards is compared to the invasion of the Saxons
in Britain, the Normans are followed in their conquest from the
North Sea down to Sicily. In so doing Gallenga made ample
references to the works of Sismondi, Ginguené, and Hallam. It
is because of these non-Italian sources and because it was written
for an English-speaking public that the book has an international
flavour. Moreover, he aimed particularly at bringing Italy into
focus as one of the European countries—however lacking in
independence—and not as a mere colony of the Austrian Empire.
All elements which showed the continuity of a national tradition throughout the centuries—regardless of whether artistic,
racial, political, or linguistic—were given particular stress. The
greatness of Italian civilization is asserted right from the start.

Italy in the Middle Ages was like Mount Ararat in the deluge; the
last reached by the flood, and the first left. The remains of the Roman
social world were either never utterly dispersed in that country, or far
later than any where else; and, if we are to date the close of the Middle
Ages from the extinction of feudalism, that revolution was effected
in Italy no less than three centuries before the time of Charles VIII of
France, the epoch assumed by historians as the close of the period. The
history of Europe in the Middle Ages must necessarily be referred to
Italy, as the history of the ancient world has always been referred to
Rome. The great ascendancy of the papal power, and the influence of
Italian genius on the literature and the fine arts of all countries, made
Italy essentially the centre of light, the sovereign of thought, the
metropolis of civilization.[1]

This is, of course, true of the centuries after the year 1000. Before

[1] Ibid., vol. i, p. 4.

then Italian influence was not so great as Gallenga would have us believe. In effect, Rome itself did not escape the imputation of decadence and corruption, while the northern tribes which invaded the country were highly praised, for they brought with them new blood and more austere customs and traditions. The fusion of the Latin and the German worlds was chiefly due to the spreading of Christianity and the preaching of the Gospel. The early Christian Church, quite rightly considered an element of progress, too soon turned into an instrument of corruption and depravation, while the tribute paid by Gallenga to the virtues of the northern invaders is typical of romanticism in its revaluation of the Middle Ages and anti-classical campaign. A positive aspect of the contamination of the two cultures was the advent of chivalry.

That mixture of enthusiasm and extravagance that made the cause of the weak fair and sacred in the eyes of the brave—that noble school of loyalty and truth, of devotion and gallantry, of humanity and liberality—that sacred flame that tended to purify love from its earthly alloy, and raised an altar to woman—chivalry was the right arm of Christianity in its sacred mission of peace and justice. . . . Chivalry was the alliance of force with right.[1]

The crusades were the result of such a spirit.

The crusades brought a temporary peace to Europe. . . . That blind necessity of bleeding, which the human families obey nearly every quarter of a century, was, in this occurrence at least, effected with the least consciousness of fratricide. The crusades were a folly indeed, but the Christians only recovered from it to plunge into the equally fatal but less pious follies of the wars of the Roses, of the Armagnacs and Burgundians, of the Huguenots and the League, of Cromwell and Napoleon.[2]

From what has so far been quoted, it is clear that at times Gallenga approaches history from a literary point of view. His illustrations of chivalry seem to be rooted in some of Berchet's ballads or Scott's novels, and his descriptions of the pious follies of the crusades seem to draw their origin from the reading of Tasso more than from the study of historical texts. And yet he showed

---

[1] *Italy, P. and P.*, vol. i, pp. 47–8. [2] Ibid., vol. i, pp. 48–9.

a vivid sense of historical perspective when he pointed out that, though apparently inspired by religion, the crusades were a non-religious phenomenon, for they fostered great social changes, and stood for that spirit of initiative and adventure which led man to great new discoveries.

The crusades were the forerunners of the liberties of Europe. Rights and privileges were sold, charters granted at auction, to raise money for those venturous pilgrimages; slaves were manumitted; duties of vassalage, old debts, and tributes, legally abolished, or wilfully forgotten or settled by death. The magna charta of England and the parliaments of France date from that epoch of general convulsion. . . .

The crusades led the way to India and America.

They roused a spirit of enterprise and curiosity that was never to rest while there should be space to run, and elements to subdue. It revealed the existence of boundless regions and inexhaustible treasures. . . . The luxuries of the East were spread before the enraptured adventurers of Europe; the soil itself of the West teemed with the development of eastern seeds, and unknown harvests smiled on the Lombard and Neapolitan plains.[1]

The struggle of the Communes against the German Emperor was another sign of the rising spirit of freedom and independence: the twelfth and thirteenth centuries, were, therefore, a time of social and political progress in the country. The literature of the period, however, lacked any genuine inspiration. Early Italian poets were briefly dismissed: Gallenga was aware of their linguistic and stylistic importance in relation to the development of the language, and did not deny the formal perfection of some of their compositions, but considered them the bards of an artificial and dead world. There was, according to him, a deep discrepancy between the life of the country and its literature, for Italian had established itself later than any other Romance languages, and its first literary productions were under a strong foreign influence, mainly that of Provençal poetry—to which he added Arabic poetry, thus accepting Sismondi's view of the importance of the Arabs on Western culture.[2]

---

[1] Ibid., vol. i, pp. 49–51.
[2] J. C. L. Sismondi, *De la littérature du midi de l'Europe*, Paris, 1813.

A free nation, engaged in wide speculations of commerce and industry, in endless experiments of municipal democratic institutions, labouring under the feverish excitement of active life, and enlightened by the rapid diffusion of useful knowledge in her numerous schools, could only look upon the frivolous dreams of chivalrous poetry in the light of an idle pastime. . . . The court and castle had had their own literature; it was now time that there should be a literature for the people.[1]

The answer to this quest was to be found in the works of Dante. When introducing the Florentine poet, Gallenga dealt at first with his life and gave full space to the part Dante played in the history of his town. In describing him, our author allowed his imagination to run riot.

Wherever [Dante] passed, from one to the other of the Italian universities, to Bologna, to Padua, he found the love of study, and the culture of taste in the fine arts, blended with the ardour of liberty, and with the martial spirit of the age;—for letters and arts want excitement; they can sail with all winds, but not without wind; great minds expand in proportion to their own exertions; they exult in the heart-stirring commotions of the great drama of life, in the conflict of factions, in the tumult of wars. . . .

Wherever he passed, the poet traversed the wide plains of Lombardy, smiling with plentiful crops, the reward of a laborious husbandry, aided by a spirit of enterprise that rescued marshes and swamps from the bed of rivers, opened canals, and raised dikes, edging and fencing that garden of the vale of the Po, whose fertility forms, even in our own days, the envy of foreigners.[2]

Gallenga considered Dante's political theories as essentially concerned with the welfare of Italy, and not so much as advocating the establishment of a universal monarchy. He looked upon Dante's conception of the Holy Roman Empire as a forerunner of nineteenth-century nationalism and for him the whole of *The Divine Comedy* is pervaded by patriotic feelings: the episodes of Sordello, Cacciaguida, and the like 'have hallowed the poet's memory in the heart of his countrymen'. This interpretation of Dante's political thinking was a common feature in Dantean

---

[1] *Italy, P. and P.*, vol. i, pp. 83–4.   [2] Ibid., vol. i, pp. 92–3.

studies of the first half of the nineteenth century. It was based on Foscolo's critical papers, from which Mazzini had drawn inspiration for his article *Dell'amor patrio di Dante*, written in 1827. When some years later Mazzini edited Foscolo's commentary on *The Divine Comedy*, he stressed again the national qualities of the poem, without considering that Dante always felt he was an exile, once he had been banned from Florence. Gallenga, who was fully conversant with the writings of both writers, followed in their footsteps, and abandoned Sismondi who had so far been his guide.

His attention, however, soon turned to Dante's poetry. After briefly dismissing his minor treatises, Gallenga ventures into a long exposition of *The Divine Comedy* which is not devoid of critical interest. The renewed popularity that Dante enjoyed both in Italy and abroad during the Romantic period largely rested on the conviction that he wrote for the people, and in a language which could be understood by the people. His use of the Italian tongue, which had appeared to classical scholars as lacking in refinement and obscure, seemed to be a superb example of Romantic poetic diction *ante litteram*. His was a language derived from every-day speech and arranged in metric form taken from popular religious verse. Moreover, ultramundane visions were a favourite theme with Christian writers and readers of the Middle Ages. Gallenga greatly praised the popular tone of the poem, but in doing so he sounded, quite unintentionally, a comic note.

No poet ever struck upon a subject to which every fibre in the heart of his contemporaries more readily responded than Dante, when he undertook to write his Universal Gazetteer of the kingdom of death—his hand-book for travellers to Heaven and Hell.[1]

His interpretation of the *Inferno* fluctuates between admiration for Dante's tragic muse and contempt for the medieval conception of the place of damnation. In spite of its dramatic moments the *Inferno* is 'a monkish hell in good earnest, with all its howling and gnashing of teeth'. The presence of the devils and the horror of the various forms of punishment created an atmosphere which

[1] Ibid., vol. i, p. 121.

was gruesome and humorous at the same time. Gallenga captured the grotesque—almost comic—side of the first *Cantica* so evident in Dante's creation of some of his devils. By the side 'of the proud and almost sublime Pluto of Tasso, and Satan of Milton' Dante's demons are certainly inferior characters, who, nevertheless, well convey his conception of evil. Gallenga did not completely underrate the poetic value of the *Inferno*, and summed up his rather contradictory views by saying:

[although] Mr. Leigh Hunt, and other modern critics, may justly object to so very hot and ungentlemanly a place of punishment . . ., it is impossible to mistake the tragic tone that pervades the poet's mind, all along its dolorous progress; among the vainest sports of his unruly fancy, no less than in its gloomiest inspiration, the oddity or wildness of conception is always set forth with terrible earnestness of diction. The powers of utterance are always in keeping with the depth and vastness of thought. There is a life-like palpableness in every object brought before us, which can be accounted for by nothing short of the actual evidence of the senses. . . . An eloquence impressive, efficient in the same measure as it disdains all attempts at effect—a fancy that casts and moulds not—creates, and never stoops to mere description—an inventiveness that fears no weariness, knows no exhaustion; startling, revolting, wringing our heart, rending it fibre from fibre—a phantasmagory of loathsome, dire suffering, never stopping at any climax of horror, of agony, but always seeking 'beyond the deepest hell a deeper still' till it revels on [*sic*] the misery of beings.[1]

If his notes on the *Inferno* succeeded in reconciling his admiration for Dante with his Victorian sense of decency and propriety, his observations on the *Purgatorio* and *Paradiso* are far more valid, coming at a time when the interest of many critics was centered on the first section of the *Commedia*. Dante's imagery seemed to him the best feature of the poem, and he placed *Purgatory* and *Paradise* above *Hell*, because of the spiritualized and rarified elegance of Dante's poetic diction. Although Gallenga did not attempt a detailed analysis of the poet's language, he succeeded in rendering the atmosphere which pervades the two *Cantiche*. He captured the tenderness of feeling which characterizes the

[1] *Italy, P. and P.*, vol. i, pp. 124-5.

Mazzini teaching in his school, London 1841 Engraving by Mantegazza

The battle of Santa Lucia, 1848

Purgatorio and which was reflected in the delicacy of its tone and inspiration.

[Purgatory is] a conception full of love and charity, in so far as it seemed to arrest the dead on the threshold of eternity; and by making his final welfare partly dependent on the pious exertions of those who were left behind, established a lasting interchange of tender feelings. . . . With little more than two words, the poet makes us aware that we have come into happier latitude. Every shade we meet breathes love and forgiveness. The strange visitor is only charged with tidings of joy to the living, and messages of good-will. The heart lightens and brightens at every new stratum of the atmosphere in that rising region. . . . The friends of the poet's youth one by one arrest his march and engage him in tender converse. The very laws of immutable fate seem for a few instants suspended to allow full scope for the interchange of affectionate sentiments. The overawing consciousness of the place he is in for a moment forsakes the mortal visitor so miraculously admitted into the world of spirits. He throws his arms round the neck of the beloved shade, and it is only by the smile irradiating its countenance that he is reminded of the intangibility of its ethereal substance. The episodes of the purgatory are mostly of this sad and tender description. The historical personages introduced seem to have lost their own identity, and to have merged into a blessed calmness.[1]

The same warm style, full of praise is used for the *Paradiso*, for he felt, more by intuition than by a conscious effort, that theology and philosophy could become matter for poetry—that poetry depends not on what is written about, but on how it is written about.

Dante's Heaven is indeed heavenly. Angels' smiles beam through his verses. . . . As in the region of eternal doom the souls of the reprobate were oftentimes deformed by their turpitudes so as to become indiscernible to all knowledge; so are now the chosen ones beautified beyond recognition, . . . joy shows itself in Heaven by increase of light, and every smile is a flash.

There is something wild, vague, overpowering in the strange phantasmagory of all these myriads of lights. They revolve around us as we read, like the undefinable splendours that, some of us may recollect, haunted our cradles in childhood, when a whole canopy, as if of

[1] Ibid., vol. i, pp. 125–7.

C

coloured dots of vivid flame, glittered above our heads in the apparently boundless vastness of space, and rolled slowly and steadily about, till it seemed to set beneath us, and we hung upon it, at the height of many thousand fathoms, as if ready to plunge, cradle and all, into the luminous abyss, when we started up half in wonder, half in dismay, and roused the whole household with our infantine screams.[1]

Gallenga's pages on Dante naturally found a place in Toynbee's *Dante in English Literature from Chaucer to Cary*, but his notes on Petrarch went unnoticed, for they did not rise beyond the negative judgement passed on him by Italian romantic critics. After illustrating his life and character at length, Gallenga briefly sums up the qualities of his poetry in a few scanty lines in praise of his style, which hardly do justice to the artist. He then concludes by saying that the cult of his contemporaries for the poet of Laura would be greater had Petrarch borne to his tomb the palm of martyrdom rather than his crown of laurel.

Boccaccio has a better fate than Petrarch, both as a man and a writer. As a man because he was proud and independent and not the servile minion of princes. As a writer, because he gave us in his *Decameron* 'the virtues and vices of the human family, the whole world in a stage'. The best page Gallenga wrote on him is the one dealing with the environment in which the action of the *Decameron* is placed. Although most of what he said may appear obvious to the modern reader, it is well worth quoting, because this is one of the first pieces of criticism in which the dramatic contrast between the tragic description of the plague in Florence and the merry life of the ten narrators was clearly and vividly rendered.

From Thucydides to Botta, Manzoni and Bulwer, there has been no lack of descriptions of pestilence.

Both romancers and historiographers seemed always well aware of the great results that would be derived to their narrative, from the exhibition of a whole race struck by that most direful of scourges. Yet Boccaccio's stands unrivalled for truth and evidence; and the happy idea of choosing, by way of contrast, so gloomy an *overture* to effusions of so gay a nature, has been too often, we think, and too lightly

[1] *Italy, P. and P.*, vol. i, pp. 130–1.

set down as an extravagant aberration from the rules of taste. The sufferings so keenly described in the proem are intended to throw light upon the more brilliant pictures of the enchanting country in the neighbourhood of Florence. The ten gay recluses, who, desirous of withdrawing themselves from the public calamity, have repaired to the genial shades of their country-seats, there endeavouring to abstract themselves from their terrors, in the enjoyment of every luxury, and in the pleasurable entertainments of a sympathetic society, seem constantly to be haunted by the phantoms of the scourge they have left behind; and among their flowery walks, their songs, their carols and feasts, the warbling of the birds, the murmur of the springs, those gallant story-tellers, and not less the fancy of their readers, seem constantly distracted by the groans of the dying, and the funeral knell of the desolate city.[1]

Like Foscolo in *Le Grazie*,[2] Gallenga mentioned the *shocking* directness with which Boccaccio portrayed human society, but absolved the Florentine from any imputation of obscenity, since his tales had an eminently moral aim, 'as they boldly unmasked all kind of hypocrisy, and stripped vice of its alluring disguises'. The elegance and complexity of his style, however, did not appeal to Gallenga, who agreed with most of his contemporaries in their negative judgement of it: for him too, 'the wonderful precision and energy of Dante was diluted and vitiated in the round periods of Boccaccio'.

The second age closes with a chapter dedicated to Machiavelli which is mainly biographical. Gallenga accepted the view upheld by his contemporaries that the Florentine historian was a forerunner of Italian nationalism, but like Balbo and other romantics he considered him dead to all enthusiasm. What comes to the surface here is the atmosphere in which *Il Principe* was conceived and written: lack of national unity, everlasting strife between the neighbouring cities, foreign intervention, all these are vividly depicted. Against this background of turmoil and impending decadence of the country, the moral character of Machiavelli stands out as an example of virtue and patriotism. His great moment came when, on his death-bed, the historian was

---

[1] Ibid., vol. i, p. 204.
[2] U. Foscolo, *Opere edite e postume*, vol. ix, p. 275, vv. 755–64, Florence, 1883.

surrounded by the most eminent citizens of Florence who, at last, appreciated his uprightness and virtues.

From a bed of sickness, the dying statesman and citizen, too great to give way to any feeling of personal resentment, raised his voice for his country, and his last words were of applause and encouragement to its restorers.[1]

We have now reached the age of Italian principalities, and we are given a full account of the turning of the republican Communes into dictatorial *Signorie* governed by a prince or a tyrant, and its effects on public life and art. Gallenga had little sympathy for Renaissance life and most of his judgements are biased and arbitrary. Humanism appeared to him to be mere erudition: Platonism and the philosophical disputes of the fifteenth century seemed to him to be little more than a display of childish vanity on the part of the scholars. If he was right in saying that for about a century the renewed interest of the men of letters in classical culture contributed very little to literature in Italian, he was wrong in condemning humanism and Platonism as arid and devoid of interest, for the early philological and philosophical disputes of the Renaissance contained the germs of that inquisitive mind which led to new discoveries and scientific progress in the sixteenth and seventeenth centuries which he so highly praised. Moreover, the sources of inspiration of Ariosto and Tasso, both of whom Gallenga greatly admired, were to be found in the revival of classical studies. In short, he failed to see how humanism developed into Renaissance, and of the former experience he underlined only the negative aspects, such as the literal imitation of Petrarch and the ancients, and the dullness of some literary and philological controversies.

He warmly welcomed the return to the use of the vulgar tongue in the second half of the fifteenth century, which, superficially, he attributed to political reasons. After over a century of independence and economic welfare the standard of living in Italy had risen and people could afford the refinement of culture. It would have been, says Gallenga, to act against the spirit of the time to

[1] *Italy, P. and P.*, vol. i, p. 246.

reject schools, academies, and art. Equally naïve and superficial are his opinions of the first major poets who wrote in Italian again, Lorenzo and Poliziano, whose poems together with Pulci's *Morgante* are mentioned as a proof of the *popular* tone of the new literature.

The love poems of Lorenzo do not soar above the common level of mediocrity; his carnival songs and rural stanzas, though more spontaneous and original, make us painfully aware how deplorably the Italian language had degenerated from the ease, elegance and purity of Petrarch.

Poliziano's verses, written, as they were, at an earlier date, were more exquisitely finished as to style. That is, however, all that can be said in their favour.[1]

Even more severe was his judgement of *Morgante*, expressed in the florid, colourful, and pompous language we are now learning to expect from him and which for a foreigner shows an outstanding richness of vocabulary.

It is a vile, vulgar performance, which had its origin among the orgies of a dissolute court, disgusting for his strange mixture of mock bigotry and scoffing irreligion, an unrelieved exhibition of ignoble, bacchanial sensualism.[2]

No better fate was in store for the other poets of the period with the exception of Ariosto and Tasso. Before them, only Boiardo, the author of *Orlando Innamorato*, received fair treatment. Gallenga recognized the faults of the Count of Scandiano, but fell in love with the chivalrous theme of his poem.

The appreciation of Boiardo's fantastic world, while the mythical world of Poliziano's poems was dismissed and rejected, is significant not only of Gallenga's literary taste but of the taste of his own day. The romantic epics, although undeniably the product of the Renaissance mind, took their inspiration from medieval legends; so did many of the romantic writers of the early nineteenth century. The chivalrous poems were as far from the medieval spirit as the ballads of the nineteenth century, but they sprang from the same source. The mythical world of Poliziano escaped Gallenga, just as the world of Foscolo in *Le Grazie*,

[1] Ibid., vol. i, p. 292.   [2] Ibid., vol. i, p. 293.

because they were both rooted in classical mythology. Ariosto followed in Boiardo's footsteps, but far more than the latter he possessed 'that sovereign mind presiding over the whole, that unity which has power to subject the immensity to its laws'. In reading what Gallenga wrote on *Orlando Furioso*, one cannot help noticing how his individuality shines through his English style and at times overshadows the individuality of the author he is writing about.

We delight in the contemplation of its vastness, we like to run after its boldest flight, to abandon ourselves to its playful humour, in the same manner as one of the knights of those fables, in his hour of perplexity, lets the reins loose on the neck of his charger, to be led by the instinct of the sagacious animal.

So much for the work of the imagination. But when, after making a sport of himself and his readers, the poet ventures on a sudden appeal to our sympathies; when he paints man abandoned to himself, grappling with superhuman difficulties, with no tutelar genius but his steady will, no enchanted shield but his undaunted virtues—the world of fiction suddenly disappears from our eyes, and there we stand, as if suddenly converted to the belief of those fables which had been woven in a spirit of jest and raillery.[1]

Briefly, Gallenga is pointing out two elements in the poem which later attracted the attention of the critics: the richness of imagination and invention—that is to say the unrealistic element of the poem—and the portrayal of individual virtues, which make destiny a part of man, and not an external force. Here these two elements are united, thus reconciling the poetry of Ariosto with the romantic view of moral commitment in art. This interpretation, however, could not be carried very far, and Ariosto remains for Gallenga, above all, the poet of imagination and not of the heart.

If his observations on Ariosto are penetrating, what he had to say about Tasso reflected his admiration for the unfortunate poet, but did not add anything new to the appreciation of *Gerusalemme*. In the first half of the last century, the legend of Tasso was at its height. Gallenga was no exception to current fashion, and

[1] *Italy, P. and P.*, vol. i, p. 307.

Tasso was judged and assessed on biographical elements. His greatness lay in his works as well as in his sufferings. It was only when describing the development of the theatre in Italy that Gallenga showed a critical interest in some of Tasso's writings. For instance, in his judgement on *Aminta*, he is well before his time, and Tasso's influence on and important position with regard to the rise and fortune of pastoral drama were clearly stated. Opinions on this play have so greatly changed throughout the centuries that the warm admiration which Gallenga felt for it cannot fail to attract the attention of the reader.

It would not be easy to define to what particular merit *Aminta* owed its success on the stage, and continues to form the delight of gentle readers in our days. It is certainly not owing to its dramatic interest, for it has little or no action; and that little—from want of mechanic ingenuity in the construction of ancient theatres—is made up by narrations, and almost provokingly kept out of sight of the spectators. But its peculiar charm arises from a series of tender thoughts and feelings, delicate, ingenuous, pure; it is due to an elegant and poetical, but always passionate and true language; to a softness, a languor, an irresistible voluptuousness of style.[1]

Gallenga's negative judgement of Poliziano and Lorenzo returns with regard to the Petrarchists and the lyrical poets following Tasso. If he is right in treating most of them as minor authors, the reasons for his condemnation of their art go beyond the field of literature. He quotes Vittoria Colonna and Michelangelo as the main exponents of Petrarchism. While his opinion of the latter has found supporters—and in spite of their roughness some of his sonnets are no doubt great poetry—Gallenga's evaluation of the formal and cold lines of the Marchioness of Pescara is based essentially on moral grounds. As would be expected, the lyrical effusions of platonic love were beyond his interest, but patriotic poetry was much nearer to his heart, and, in consequence, found in him a better interpreter. What to him appeared to be the greatest evil of the literature of the day, or rather the major fault of the men of letters of the Renaissance, was their abstraction from everyday life and problems, their servility towards

[1] Ibid., vol. i, p. 340.

princes and foreign sovereigns—in short their lack of civic virtue.
This attitude was not only reflected in their epic and lyric productions, but also echoed in their patriotic poems.

To this proneness of the generality of the men of letters of the
sixteenth century to unbidden acts of servitude, they added, by way of
contrast, an enthusiastic but retrospective fondness for the name of
their country; not indeed of the trodden and plundered land that lay
bleeding at their feet, but that of the classic hero's dust which reminded
them, at every step, of ages of greatness and victory which could never
return.[1]

Gallenga found this nostalgic yearning for the greatness of the
past in Leopardi's patriotic poems too, and he saw that nationalism in both Leopardi and the *cinquecentisti* was the expression of
a refined cultivated taste of a few men of letters, and did not
reflect a popular movement. Moreover, it did not imply a faith
in the present or the future of the country, and therefore it was
detached from contemporary reality and took refuge in the
portrayal of past glories. In Gallenga's eyes the writer of the
Renaissance was no longer the prophet of his country, like Dante,
or the painter of habits and customs, like Boccaccio, but—with
very few exceptions—he was alone in his ivory tower, the bard
of a dreamy mythological world, preoccupied with his material
welfare, the servant of princes. The real contributions of the Italian
Renaissance to human progress were to be found, according to
him, in the field of science, architecture, and painting, as well as
in the sphere of historical and philosophical studies. The names
that Gallenga associated with historical studies are those of Machiavelli, Guicciardini, Segni, Varchi, and Sarpi. He admitted
that, with the exception of Machiavelli, perhaps, they were all
partisans and therefore highly biased in their judgement, but
added that all of them excelled 'in that self-possession which,
divesting the related events of all exaggeration or palliative,
presents them bare but striking evidences, against the monsters
whom they consign to the unerring desecration of posterity.'
Together with the historians, philosophers, such as Telesio, Bruno
and Campanella, show the positive aspect of the Renaissance,

[1] *Italy, P. and P.*, vol. i, p. 350.

since in their works as well as in their lives, one can see the coming of intellectual emancipation from the bigotry of religion and of Aristotelianism. Such emancipation, however, was to yield its fruits outside Italy, in countries where the Reformation succeeded in establishing a new form of worship, and free thought. So historians, scientists, and philosophers preserved that spirit of freedom which had been an Italian patrimony for centuries in an age of political and moral decadence.

One has to make many reservations about Gallenga's interpretation of Renaissance literature and thought. The relation between literature and history is often forced and carried too far when he tries to establish a direct link between the two. Where he does succeed in establishing it is in his way of portraying so many events. While Castiglione and his book are dismissed in a line or two, and *Il Principe* is not mentioned at all, the world of Italian patrons and their artists, and the exploits of Italian tyrants are fully explored and represented. See, for example, his pages on Leo X and on Benvenuto Cellini, whom he called the 'Gil Blas of the sixteenth century'. It is in portrayals of this kind that Gallenga is most successful. His *Italy* is a good introduction to some works of literature, because it recreates the atmosphere in which many books were conceived and written. This does not only apply to his presentation of the Renaissance but of almost all periods of Italian history, as we have already seen in the case of the crusades.

The fourth age is an age of foreign domination and national decadence. The Italian princes, who had been fierce, proud tyrants in earlier days, were now 'deprived of all intrinsic importance' and, while politics and literature reached a very low standard, the scientist remained the lonely representative of the creative genius of the past, in spite of the fact that Spanish rule and the Church's fight against the Reformation conspired together to destroy that spirit of free inquiry which was an essential feature of philosophy and science. The inquisition which had already begun its persecutions in previous centuries, and which counted some of the most eminent thinkers—such as Bruno— as its victims, continued. Galileo too suffered at their hands, but the recantation of his theories appeared to Gallenga a moral

victory and not a defeat, and he gave an almost Brechtian interpretation of his character.

Galileo would not give his enemies the satisfaction of burning him
alive. He knew that, whilst he lived, there was no rest for them. . . .
He abjured—he abandoned his theories; but when he felt assured that
they were utterly, incontrovertibly, eternally demonstrated; when he
was certain that they had become the inheritance of the latest posterity.[1]

The prose works of Galileo were not considered by Gallenga as
part of Italian literature. This explains why, once he dismissed
the scientific prose of the seventeenth century, the decadence in
the field of letters appeared to him to be almost complete. A few
poets only escaped his severe judgement, for instance Marini and
Filicaia. Of the former he thought that a few stanzas from his
Adone could still 'be numbered among the best specimens of
Italian versification'. He also praised Filicaia, who, in his opinion,
was the only poet who wrote under the 'immediate impulse of
genuine feelings', and whose patriotic poems 'would live eternally
in the heart of the Italians'. A very different view of his poetry was
given by De Sanctis who quite rightly said that Filicaia looked
backwards to the greatness of the past, of which there were no
traces in contemporary Italy, and his patriotic poems are cold and
stately compositions devoid of any emotion, thus applying to
him what Gallenga said of the *cinquecentisti* and Leopardi.[2]

Gallenga, who had confined the *Seicento* to a few pages, gave
ample space to the *Settecento*, which was a period of social and
artistic reawakening for the whole country. He opens his review
of eighteenth-century literature with an examination of the works
of Metastasio and the poets of Arcadia, for whom he felt a lukewarm admiration. In spite of the narrow range of their inspiration, they made an attempt to keep in check the exuberance and
the intemperance of diction of the *secentisti* and this he was prepared to praise and respect. It was, however, with writers other
than Metastasio and his followers that, like most Italians of the
1840s Gallenga found spiritual affinities. First of all, with the

[1] *Italy, P. and P.*, vol. i, p. 410; p. 412.
[2] F. De Sanctis, *Storia della letteratura italiana*, Milan, 1917, vol. ii, pp. 166–7.

historians, since it was in their writings that the national element
was kept alive in an age of political servitude, or, to use Gallenga's
words, 'in an age of political dearth'. Hence the warm praises
awarded to Muratori, Giannone, Tiraboschi, and Maffei. In
their monumental works of erudition the political and literary
past of the country was preserved for posterity.

This prevalent spirit of erudite inquiry which taught the Italians to
dwell too fondly on the past, if it was beneficial to elevate the national
character, inasmuch as it gave that people full knowledge of themselves,
it had also the effect of engendering those false aristocratic notions by
which the Italians have been, and are still, inclined to bring forward the
exertions and achievements of their forefathers, as if entitled by them
to a life of dissipation and indolence.[1]

This is only a mild criticism of erudition, if compared with what
Gallenga had said in his introduction to *Italy*. There he attacked
the absence of the idea of development in history, that is the
illuministic approach to history as compared with the romantic.
By 1840 such an approach was obsolete and meaningless. But if
considered against the cultural background of the eighteenth
century it had an important role to play and he fully appreciated
this. The more he progressed in the analysis of the *Settecento*, the
more he felt that it was a period of reawakening in almost all
branches of learning. In the field of literature it was drama which
produced two of the greatest artists: Goldoni and Alfieri. He
greatly praised the theatrical gifts of Goldoni and considered the
Venetian a born comedian, thus refuting Sismondi's negative
judgement which had been accepted by foreign critics and which
had been the cause of an underrating of his comedies abroad.
Gallenga, however, did not fail to see the flatness of some of
Goldoni's heroes, who were conceived as types rather than round
characters, as often happens in a comedy of manners.

[Goldoni's] heroes too often remind us of the green-room. Their
faded lineaments are apparent through the meretricious varnish of
their theatrical paint. Neither was the poet's own character such as to
raise him to the conception of a *beau-idéal* of moral worth. The sport

[1] *Italy P. and P.*, vol. i, pp. 423–4.

of fortune during his lifetime, he had acquired all the apathy and reck-lessness of a confirmed fatalist. 'All the world's a stage', was his device. As he gave little or no room to feeling in his bosom, so did he equally exclude it from his plays. He seemed to be born to laugh at the follies and miseries of mankind, and this he understood to be the sole and exclusive office of comedy.

Of this task he admirably acquitted himself. His fertile, inexhaustible, original humour; the rapidity and spontaneousness of his dialogue; the variety and eccentricity of his characters; his truly comic vein, stand unrivalled in Italy.[1]

Alfieri was for Gallenga the greater of the two playwrights, for he drove Metastasio and his effeminate heroes from the stage and restored dignity to tragedy and drama.

Alfieri was in Italy the last of classics; and happy was it for that school, that it could, at its close, shed so dazzling a light as to shroud its downfall in his glory. . . . He substituted dramatic for melodic poetry; manly passions for enervate affections; ideas for sounds. . . . We must look upon Alfieri not as the predecessor or contemporary of Goethe and Schiller, but as the successor of Racine and Metastasio. It is only with the prosy *tirades* of the former, and the honeyed *recitativi* of the latter, that the iron framework of the fierce *Astigiano* can be fairly compared.[2]

Gallenga's judgement of Alfieri comes at an interesting stage in the evaluation of the dramatist by the romantics. Many of them had been against him and his rehabilitation in the pages of Mazzini and Gioberti was mainly based on biographical elements. Gal-lenga did, up to a point, deal with Alfieri's life and supported in part the legend of his pride and love of freedom, but soon turned to his works and his heroes and, for once at least, the artist was to him more interesting than the man.

Alfieri forgot, or, perhaps, wilfully neglected the precept of Horace, *ut pictura poesis*. . . . His tragedies are only a group of four or five statues; his characters are figures of marble, incorruptible, everlasting. . . . He describes no scene. Those statues stand by themselves, isolated on their pedestals, on a vacant ideal stage, without background, with-

---

[1] *Italy, P. and P.*, vol. i, p. 444.   [2] Ibid., vol. i, pp. 448, 451.

out contrast of landscape or scenery; all wrapped in their heroic mantles; all moving, breathing statues perhaps, still nothing but statues.

Wherever be the scene, whoever the hero, it is always the poet that speaks. It is always his noble, indomitable soul reproduced under various shapes; it is always one and the same object pursued under different points of view, but to which every other view is subservient. The struggle between the oppressor and the oppressed; the genii of good and evil have waged an eternal war in his scenes.[1]

Gallenga's pages on Alfieri are his best as a critic, and in reading them it is only to be regretted that instability of temperament, superficiality, and restlessness prevented him from pursuing his studies further.

In spite of his sympathetic attitude towards the literature of the period, Gallenga's pages on the eighteenth century contain some serious omissions. Parini is mentioned only briefly in the first version while in the final edition of *Italy* a long footnote was added, containing an extract from *La Notte* and its English translation, as if Gallenga had felt that Parini deserved to be better known, and yet he made no attempt to give the poet a proper place in the history of Italian literature.

We are now nearing facts and events which were within Gallenga's living memory and evaluation becomes more difficult. This is felt in his presentation of the three major pre-romantic poets Monti, Foscolo, and Pindemonte. The first two are placed on the same level, with the result that Foscolo is highly underrated, while Pindemonte is given a short paragraph—what he would deserve in a survey of this kind. He remains for Gallenga the master of gentle and delicate feelings, the high priest of melancholy, who was not in unison with the unsettled period he lived in. Monti is praised for the beauty and skill of his style, which is compared to 'a rich, pompous dress', covering, however, 'only barrenness and shallowness, only ashes and smoke'. As for Foscolo, Gallenga admired the man in him, but not the artist.

Foscolo, like Alfieri, rather a great soul than a powerful mind,

[1] Ibid., vol. i, pp. 452–3.

mastering men and events, mastered by his passions, in a perpetual struggle with himself, reining his imagination, and paralysing his forces, only showed that he was a genius without fulfilling the true mission of a genius. . . . Satisfied with having won the favours of fame by a short courtship of four hundred lines, with having poured out his soul in the pages of his Venetian hero, the author of *I Sepolcri* and *Iacopo Ortis* sank in disappointment and inaction to die in distress and bitterness of heart. Sometimes, in his inordinate love of erudition, he would make a show of his classical lore, with almost puerile vanity: sometimes he would toil with a deplorable perseverance at the mechanic construction of a few lines, which afterwards, in utter exhaustion, he left unachieved.[1]

So much Gallenga had to say of *Le Grazie*, which he perhaps never read and never understood. Foscolo's name returns in the following volume on contemporary Italy: in effect, he seems to belong to two different moments, namely, the period of foreign dominion and the period of national reawakening. But there Foscolo returns only as the author of *Iacopo Ortis*—a novel which he greatly admired because of its patriotic theme—and the Italian who first endured the pains and sufferings of exile.

Apart from these poets, other names of *letterati* of the second half of the eighteenth century appear—most of them philosophers and historians. Gallenga's opinions on the thinkers of the Enlightenment are superficial and generalized. Once again what he succeeded in capturing was the atmosphere in which they wrote. To Gallenga, the advent of enlightened absolutism in Italy was promoted by a basic nationalistic feeling—nationalistic here indicates love of the Italians for their individual states, and it is not to be identified with love for Italy as one country. The popular basis of despotic government made it easier for the new rulers to assert their power. With the introduction of new reforms they aimed at gaining the love and confidence of their subjects. It was at such a time that Vico, Beccaria, and Muratori produced their works and sowed the seeds of what Gallenga called 'moral regeneration of the country', not only helping the princes in their reforms, but also forcing them to continue in the path of co-

[1] *Italy, P. and P.*, vol. i, pp. 473–4.

operation with their subjects. For some years despotism and progressive thinking went hand in hand. The French revolution and the subsequent invasion of Italy accelerated a process of regeneration and modernization of the country which was already in progress. According to Gallenga, the speeding up of such a progress was not entirely advantageous for the Italians, for had it been allowed to proceed 'unhurried and unimpeded, the transition from thought to action would have been slower, perhaps, but more deliberate and unanimous'. Socially the coming of the French appeared to have achieved little. Politically it had a great influence in changing the quality of Italian nationalism, reintroducing the name and concept of Italy as one nation, in spite of the fact that the Italy created by Napoleon lasted a short time and was mainly a French institution.

Gallenga's attitude towards Napoleon is twofold: on the one hand he greatly admired him, as he had all the qualities of the great man and the hero; on the other — he held him responsible for many of the evils which befell Italy, for his intervention turned a peaceful revolution into a violent uprising. Botta's attitude towards Napoleon and the French seemed to Gallenga to sum up the good and evil of French intervention. What the historian Carlo Botta pointed out to his compatriots was the impossibility of relying on foreign intervention for the emancipation of the country. In this he was in opposition to the majority of the new liberals who looked upon the French as liberators, and considered French thinking an ideal model to follow. Gallenga was fully on his side, where the French were concerned. But Botta often displayed a pessimistic attitude to history, for the unhappy events which he witnessed during his life—such as the fall of the Venetian republic—made him despair of the future of his country, and this did not appeal to the patriot Gallenga.

But shall there be no refuge against evil, except suicide or indifference? Shall virtue find no supporters, because its former champions perished in fight? Shall Italy never be independent, because the patriots of 1814 were discordant and unfortunate?

No! God commands us to follow the impulse of conscience; to toil and struggle, unmindful of the results of our efforts. The ultimate success rests entirely in his hands; and he knows how to turn our very reverses to the accomplishment of his unerring judgements.[1]

Italy's past ends with these words. Whatever one may think of Gallenga's evaluation and judgements, the book has so far presented a unity of conception and development which is lost in the following volume, *The Present*. Even for a more painstaking scholar than Gallenga it would have been difficult to assess contemporary men and events in a proper perspective, without committing gross errors of judgement. In the case of our author he was himself so involved and committed in the political situation, that any sort of impartiality was impossible. The final paragraph of the first volume is significant; from now onwards the note of propaganda in favour of Italy, joined to a harsh criticism of political views opposed to his own, becomes prevalent and the book acquires a journalistic tone. Its interest lies in the amount of information it supplies on contemporary Italian life, and not in its general picture of the period.

The volume on contemporary Italy begins with the downfall of Napoleon and the Congress of Vienna. The years which passed between 1814 and 1847, the time when Gallenga was writing, saw many changes in the country: the establishment of the secret societies and their subsequent decadence, the coming of Young Italy, the first uprisings, and the relaxation of despotic rule in the forties. The advent of romanticism in Italy coincided with this period of political turmoil. Although it did not originate in the country, and it developed there comparatively late, romanticism completely changed the quality of Italian culture, for it made Italian writers look for inspiration from their own times as well as from national sources. The ties between literature and politics became very deep: to be a romantic meant to be a patriot, for it implied the acceptance of the existence of an Italian national tradition, regardless of political divisions and boundaries which split the country into several states. In this atmosphere a new genre flourished: the historical novel. Like romanticism it was not a native production, but it came from abroad. The first

---

[1] *Italy, P. and P.*, vol. i, p. 479.

translations of Scott's novels into Italian so greatly enflamed the public that soon Italian writers started their own production of novels which drew inspiration from Italian history. In spite of his great admiration for Walter Scott, Gallenga had some reservations about the artistic and moral value of such works; like Mazzini, Tommaseo, and Manzoni, and many others, he took this stand on the side of history in the dispute on the relationship between history and imagination, that is truth and fiction. The issue was a moral one. Like Manzoni, Gallenga proclaimed the superiority of history over fiction: the historical novel to him was a point of transition between the works of erudition, where history remained a scholarly but sterile production, and the works of the new historians, where it became the source of dramatic and poetic writing. Such history, according to him, had already been written by Sismondi and Carlyle.

Let only the poet undertake to write history. Let a man of profound and vigorous genius, penetrated with a religious feeling of veneration for truth, assume the high and *new* office of an imaginative historian. Sismondi and Michaud on the Continent, Carlyle in England, have shown, to some extent, how history can be arrayed in almost as attractive a dress as poetry. Nothing is more calculated to rouse the fancy and warm the heart than this great biographer of the human species—this registrar of the errors and follies of the perpetual contradictions of man.[1]

Gallenga's views on history and the historical novel represent a moment of the long dispute which involved so many Italian writers. When he wrote about it the argument was drawing to a close. His reasons for rejecting it can be better understood if one looks at its poor quality. No outstanding work was then produced, if one excepts *I Promessi Sposi*. Even there, the fusion between the historical and fictional element was not always successfully achieved. In effect, the whole argument brought against the historical novel by some romantics is rooted in moralism rather than based on literary criticism, and yet the rejection of so many works is critically valid. Their falseness and insincerity depended on the absence of an artistic, not an historical, truth. The weakness

[1] Ibid., vol. ii, p. 122.

was in the writer and not in the genre. It is enough to remember Gallenga's admiration for Alfieri's dramas to see how weak is his argument against the travesty of historical evidence. Gallenga then launches into a detailed examination of the novelists of the day. Not much of what he wrote about them is worth remembering, with the exception of what he said of Massimo D'Azeglio's very famous *Ettore Fieramosca* inspired by the *disfida di Barletta*, a combat which took place in 1503 between thirteen picked knights of France and Italy, and which was won by the Italians. This episode seemed to Gallenga a happy choice for a subject, because it complied with his ideas on the use of history in the novel. He thought that the story of an historical novel must

not belong to too ancient a period of history, for a larger share will be left to imagination than is consistent with sober probability; neither must the date be too recent, lest stubborn facts should pin down fancy, and allow no free scope for invention.[1]

The challenge of Barletta had all the qualities required, for although strictly historical it was distant enough in time to allow free scope to the artist. Moreover, what greatly endeared the book to him was its patriotic theme. After the failure of the first uprisings, when Italians appeared to the whole of Europe unable to fight for their own independence,

was it not by divine intervention that the novelist reminded his countrymen that, in another epoch, the misfortunes of Italy had been ascribed to want of military firmness on the part of her children; and that, on that occurrence at least, the bitter taunt was forced down the throat of those who uttered it, by a fair combat, in the face of the sun.[2]

Here, of course, is the patriot speaking and not the critic. Gallenga then laments the lack of Italian fictional works dealing with contemporary events, and blames it on political censorship. The fear of persecutions made many writers take refuge in the past, and in this way some of their works escaped the censor, in spite of their open patriotic inspiration. Gallenga was aware that the success of these books lay in their relationship to the contemporary situation. Similar reasons were at the basis of the popularity of romantic drama. Like the novel, the theatre took inspiration from national history. However, love of one's country was not enough to breathe new life into a genre which, after Alfieri, and apart from Manzoni's tragedies, had not produced any outstanding work. The dramatists of the day still wandered between classicism and romanticism. In spite of their choice of subjects, they remained faithful to the model of the ancients. This contamination bore no fruit. Of all playwrights, Gallenga mentioned two names only, Pellico and Niccolini, as worth saving from silence. He saw in young Pellico a great dramatic talent destroyed by the sufferings of the Spielberg, but he had little admiration for *Le mie prigioni*, Pellico's well-known memoirs.

The *Prisons* of Pellico is not the work of a bigot,—not of a man who has forsaken his cause, or wishes for a reconciliation with his unrelenting foe. It is the long, painful effort of a man who has traced his sufferings to his Maker, blessed him for the trial he was pleased to inflict, adored his will in his instruments. Sublime virtues! But the long solitude of his sorrows had made him alone: he had withdrawn himself from the cause he had served; he had stifled all the natural indignation of a patriot. He had pardoned not only his own wrongs, but those of his country. . . . If all his countrymen should embrace his maxims, it would be over for ever with Italy.[1]

Not many critics would agree nowadays. Even more difficult to accept is his view of Niccolini, an almost completely forgotten playwright, whom he considered rather a poet than a dramatist, but whom he greatly admired. He found the lyrical outbursts of his characters poetically valid, even if dramatically negative. Notwithstanding his exaggerated praise of the dramas of Pellico and of Niccolini, he was not unaware that contingent circumstances and the vogue of the moment gave them an undeserved reputation. It was only in the field of lyric poetry that Italian literature had something to offer which was everlasting. Gallenga opened his review of romantic poetry with the name of Leopardi, whom he barely understood and knew only in part, and whom, like Alfieri, he considered one of the last of the classics.

[1] Ibid., vol. ii, pp. 178–9.

Lyrical poetry in Italy, numbered still, till very lately, a very ardent cultivator, amongst the most rigid followers of classicism, in the person of Giacomo Leopardi. His patriotic soul knew no other utterance that the old-fashioned *Canzone Petrarchesca*. Five or six effusions in that style, the work of his whole life, illustrated by a vast mass of philology and erudition, have been read with almost superstitious veneration by Italian youth, for the last twenty years. They are cold and stately, highly finished performances, with a great deal of common-place mantled by flowing grandiloquence . . . they are specimens of what might be called monumental literature.[1]

There is a tribute to Leopardi's fame, and a fair assessment of his patriotic poems, but not a word is said about the *Canti*—whether through sheer ignorance of the poems or a complete misunderstanding of them we do not know. It is interesting to remember that Leopardi had met with little favour across the Channel, for until the year 1850 when the Gladstone article on him appeared, he was hardly known in England at all, and Gallenga's words on him added to the general underrating of the poet.[2] Giovanni Berchet, an exile who had lived in England and had just returned to Italy, met with a better fate than Leopardi. Gallenga considered him definitely superior to the poet of Recanati.

His *Romanze*, the most immediate expression of Italian nationality, during the first dolorous experiments of its violent awakening, were, without contradiction, the most romantic production of Romanticism. . . . None of the modern poets had better conceived the pining depression, the ardent impatience, under which the Italians were labouring; none to express the inveterate rancour long cherished in Italy, and especially in Lombardy, against the Austrian name. The spirit of the exiled bard roamed amidst the favourite haunts of his childhood. He descended into the privacy of afflicted mansions, he interrogated the tears of bereaved sisters and wives, and revealed their secret anguish to the sympathies of Europe.[3]

For Giusti, too, Gallenga had correct words of praise

Giusti's humour is of the quietest. . . . It is raillery in a quick but subdued

---

[1] *Italy, P. and P.*, vol. ii, pp. 210–1.
[2] See W. Gladstone, 'Leopardi', *Quarterly Review*, Mar. 1850, vol. lxxxvi, no. 172.   [3] *Italy, P. and P.*, vol. ii, p. 212.

tone, a gentlemanly sneer, more, to say the truth, after the manner of French *persiflage*, than in the sanguinary tone of Italian pasquinade. The style is distinguished by nerve and laconism; by an adroit spontaneousness which is, however, the result of careful study.[1]

If in the case of the theatre he misjudged Pellico and Niccolini, Gallenga proved a better critic of Berchet and Giusti, assessing them above the crowd of popular poets now almost forgotten but then extremely famous such as Carrer and Mercantini, who only followed the fashion of the day; he did not, however, see the limitations of their inspiration and style.

So far no mention has been made of the greatest writer of the time: Alessandro Manzoni. Gallenga's chapter on him, in fact, comes before his analysis of any other romantic writer. But he is placed at the end of this review because it is easier to understand some of Gallenga's reservations about Manzoni's art if one bears in mind what he had to say on civic and political commitment in the novel.

Manzoni pointed to heaven; the only true country, the only home of mankind. The earth was for him a den of wild beasts; a wild field for the demons of evil to run riot in. A religious fatalist, he acknowledged in the tyrant the instrument of inscrutable Providence. . . . His sacred hymns, his tragedies, his Ode on Napoleon, almost every chapter of his novel, are eminently Catholic.[2]

More critically valid are his observations on his lyric poetry, for he realized the newness of Manzoni's poetical language and was one of the first to praise it for its simplicity, not devoid of literary allusions.

The effect they *Inni Sacri* [have upon] the reader is analogous to the magic sensation wrought upon us by a stately peal of deep organ in a vast Gothic minster. It acts on the nerves even more than the mind. The charm resides in the loftiness of measure and rhyme, in the happy application of the familiar, yet ever-amazing scriptural language, in the warmth of true love that glows throughout every line.[3]

Gallenga offered his readers a translation of the *Pentecoste* from

[1] Ibid., vol. ii, p. 215.   [3] Ibid., vol. ii, p. 106.
[2] Ibid., vol. ii, pp. 71, 73.

the *Inni Sacri*, and of a few passages from the two tragedies, together with one of *Il cinque maggio*. *Il cinque maggio* and *I Promessi Sposi* were already well known in Great Britain, and translations of both were already available to the public. Not so the two tragedies, which by their own very nature were destined to meet with little success on the stage. If our author was right in stating that the value of the two dramas lies in their lyric rather than their dramatic content, his criticism of Manzoni's novel was heavily biased by moral and political reservations, as we have already pointed out. He also found some major faults in the literary aspects of the book. For him, one of the most relevant was a basic want of unity of action and interest. What Gallenga meant was the lack of fusion of the historical and the fictional element, as well as the episodic character of the novel.

> Manzoni's characters are all equally inactive. . . . They do little good and less harm. It is only the pestilence—good, accommodating pestilence—that settles all scores. Men are only puppets, dressed up, tricked out with great care, each of them perfect in his own way, but most preposterously jumbled together. . . . All inconvenient persons are disposed of, in a summary way, by the contagious disease; and, released from their worst terrors by the death of their enemy, freed from rash vows by priestly authority, purged from political interdicts by the interference of powerful friends, the betrothed are at last united.[1]

Gallenga's judgement is too sweeping if applied to the whole of the novel, but it remains basically true for some sections of it. Moreover, Manzoni's realism of speech and portrayal of character —which had been praised by Gallenga in the tragedies and the poems, and which remains one of the best features of the novel and the one which gives it unity—was by him condemned as being 'commonplace' and uninteresting. Gallenga was so much under the influence of the fashion of the day where novel-writing was concerned that he failed to see the greatness of Manzoni's achievement in creating language suited to his characters.

> His dialogues are mere common-place. Comic sometimes, for comedy may be compatible with prose, but none of his personages

[1] *Italy, P. and P.*, vol. ii, pp. 89–90.

are ever allowed to spout poetic sentiments any more than they are made to speak in rhythmical language. . . . But the poetry which we look for in vain from the hero's lips breathes from the poet's own soul. Their thoughts are often noble or gentle, though they can find no words to give them utterance. The poet delights in giving them a helping hand now and then. Witness the farewell of Lucia to her country. . . . Overcome by emotions, she hides her face as if composing herself to sleep, and weeps undisturbed. It is well she holds her tongue; were she to give free vent to her gloomy meditations, her plain language might shock us . . . but it is the poet that speaks, and Lucy will not feel inclined to quarrel with her eloquent interpreter.[1]

Not so moving and touching was Renzo's *goodnight* to his fatherland, but then, as Gallenga put it, 'the poor clown speaks for himself'. His condemnation of Manzoni's style is not at all convincing. Another nineteenth-century writer, Luigi Settembrini, who shared most of Gallenga's opinions and prejudices as regards *I Promessi Sposi*, valued Manzoni's language quite differently when he wrote that his is the first book in Italian literature which can be read and understood by all kinds of people, since

it is written as we speak, as any honest and ordinary man would speak without affected turns of phrase, conventional and bookish words and expressions. For Manzoni writing means thinking and feeling . . . [and] the words always come to him from the heart.[2]

After having spent so long analysing the relationship between history and fiction, Gallenga could not fail to direct his attention to the writing of history. 'The Italians are writing their history', said he, praising the great amount of scholarship which went into this field of research, but lamenting that no history of the whole country had yet been written. Moreover, none of the works then published appeared to him to have created that poetic history he so much admired in Carlyle and Sismondi. Historical studies were, therefore, a branch of learning completely separated from literature, and their vitality was yet another sign of the forces which were at work in Italy and of its turning into a nation. However difficult it proved at times for the *letterati* and the historians to have

[1] Ibid., vol. ii, pp. 91–2.
[2] L. Settembrini, *Lezioni di letteratura italiana*, Florence, 1964, vol. ii, p. 1077.

their books published, their work was fertile and useful, hastening as it did the formation of a national conscience. The political evolution of the three decades between 1814 and 1848 could be fully understood only if, together with the violent uprisings which took place from time to time, one took a close look at the peaceful revolution which was taking place within the Italian states, and which had started again after the long break caused by the Napoleonic wars. The relaxing of despotic rule after 1840 was, according to Gallenga, mostly due to moral pressure exercised by the philosophers, thinkers, and writers. The situation on the eve of the first war of independence was similar to the one which preceded the French revolution and the coming of Napoleon. At the end of 1847, Gallenga was hoping for a peaceful coexistence of the Italian states, which would slowly prepare for the unification of the country and eventually form a united front against Austria. The promoters of such a peaceful revolution found their exponents in D'Azeglio, Balbo, and Gioberti, whose political theories were now enjoying a popularity almost equal to the one enjoyed earlier by Mazzini. Gallenga was, for a short time, under the illusion that they could succeed where Young Italy had failed. This short-lived illusion was dispelled by the events of 1848, which once again plunged Italy into war.

IV

POLITICAL JOURNALIST

ALTHOUGH most of his time was devoted to literary work and teaching, Gallenga never ceased to be interested in Italian politics. After his return from Florence in 1840 he decided not to go back to his country again until there was a real chance of fighting for the national cause. It was only in 1847 that things seemed to have changed inside the Peninsula, with the exception of the Austrian dominions. As he wrote at the beginning of the year:

These are no longer the times when the most frequented shop in Naples was closed, merely because it had the word *Caffè d'Italia* written over the door. All is now 'national', all 'Italian'. . . . Hardly one of the exiles, excepting perhaps Mr Mazzini, but has either been re-called or suffered to repatriate on the slightest hint of his desire.[1]

In the summer he thought of returning to Italy, as can be seen from the letter he wrote to Gino Capponi, his former friend and employer, who was now a member of the Tuscan government.

The grave and happy events which are changing the fate of Italy have often tempted me to abandon everything, come back and take part in public life.

Some days ago the impending hostilities between Austria and Rome had almost decided me to return, but more recent news spoke of peace and therefore I have stayed here.

However, I saw the name of your Excellency in the list of the Cabinet in Tuscany. . . . While I am glad that the power is gradually coming into the hands of our men, I think I can openly beg you to tell me whether you deem that I could be of any help to our country, because of my long exile and living among free people. Should you consider that my services could be of any advantage to the

---

[1] 'Present State and Prospects of Italy', *New Month. Mag.*, Feb. 1847, vol. lxxix, no. 314, pp. 255–6.

government which you belong to, I would only be too pleased to offer my services.[1]

Gallenga's offer was declined, as he did not leave for Italy till the following year. He was, however, eager to do something on behalf of his country and contributed some articles to the English press depicting current events in Italy. During his long exile his political belief had undergone a gradual, but steady change. He had left Parma as a young enthusiastic Mazzinian. On the eve of the first war of independence, he backed the moderate liberal party.

Like D'Azeglio and other liberals, Gallenga considered war necessary for the final redemption of the country, but it had to be war against foreign powers, that is Austria, and not against the Italian princes. 'The Italians', he wrote, 'have conquered their princes', who were 'a worthless material'. In this new atmosphere there was a good chance that 'the germ of a national federation which had virtually existed for many years in the hearts of the people' would develop into an actual Italian league.

On hearing of the revolt in Milan in March 1848, which started the first campaign for national independence, Gallenga left for Italy with a group of exiles. He travelled via Paris—where he parted company with Mazzini—Mont Cenis, Turin, Milan, and eventually reached the Piedmontese army at Asola, near Mantua. He was eager to fight, and was hoping to be accepted by the Novara Cavalry Regiment, but his application was refused because of his age—he was now nearly forty—as well as because of his lack of military experience. Bitterly disappointed, he enlisted with a small band of volunteers, the Griffini Column, and remained with them for some weeks. The column was among the best organized of the volunteer troops, but was not free from the faults common to an irregular army. Gallenga, who had long cherished romantic dreams of military glories, was disillusioned by the behaviour of young enthusiasts unaccustomed to any form of discipline. Several years later he wrote:

I felt strangely out of place among my comrades of the Griffini

[1] Gallenga to Gino Capponi, 7 Sept. 1847, Biblioteca Nazionale Centrale, Florence.

Column, a motley crew, a few of whom were very young students from the University of Pavia, but the greatest number the mere riffraff of Milan, all of whom had shown themselves heroes at the barricades on the 'five great days'.[1]

He fought side by side with them at Santa Lucia, a battle of no great military importance which took place at the beginning of May, and which was the only considerable military action in which Gallenga took part. Shortly afterwards, he left the column to join another band which had come from Parma under his younger brother's command. As Antonio recorded in his memoirs, the younger Gallenga explained to him the actual difficulties of warfare and added that if the war went on 'it would have to be fought by soldiers and not by adventurers'. In his opinion the volunteers were a mere 'rabble' of little use on the battlefield. He also advised Antonio, whom he considered unfit for the hardships of camp life, to leave the army, and added that the pen and not the sword should be his weapon. If, however, he was so keen to serve as a soldier, he advised him to return to Milan or Turin and get attached to some Piedmontese or Lombard corps.

Following his brother's suggestion, Gallenga left for Milan, where he hoped to have his service of 1831 recognized, but in actual fact he did not enrol and never returned to the front. His short military experience was not fruitless, as appears from some of his criticisms of the first war of Italian independence. He was portraying himself and his fellow soldiers when he wrote:

The volunteers could have been turned into soldiers. Some of them, like the Griffini Column, and the volunteers from Parma and Piacenza remained on the battlefield till the very last, and fought bravely. But those few were wrongly employed and this was a serious mistake. Since they had not been trained as front-line troops, it was judged best to employ them as *bersaglieri*. Respectable citizens . . . some of whom were corpulent, gouty and wearing glasses, were ordered to run through the fields and jump over shrubs, competing with the Piedmontese *bersaglieri* who are the most lithe and indefatigable troops in the whole army.[2]

[1] *Epis.*, vol. ii, p. 175.
[2] 'Agli Italiani di Piemonte e Lombardia', *Il Risorgimento*, Turin, 18 Aug. 1848.

On his way to Milan, Gallenga stopped at Parma. He had not seen his native town for some eighteen years, but people remembered him, for his adventurous escape and long exile had made his name popular. His coming from the battlefield added to his reputation. He was still regarded as an extremist and a Mazzinian because of his activities in 1831. As soon as he arrived in Parma he made public his differences with the leader of Young Italy in an open letter to one of the local moderates, Piroli, which was printed and circulated in the town. In it he admitted that Mazzini and himself were close friends, drawn together by a brotherly affection.

> I often differed from him where politics were concerned. . . . Now that both of us are back in Italy, we are still good friends but do not expect either of us to sacrifice our ideas for friendship's sake. . . . The parties which are active in Italy are in essence two: that of the *Unione* and that of the *Unità*.[1]

Gallenga was in favour of the *Unione*, which proposed the establishment of an Italian league as a first step towards unification. He also advocated the abolition of the smaller Italian states—such as the Duchies—in order to strengthen the position of Charles Albert in the north. On 8 May he publicly addressed a huge crowd, which had gathered in the main square, and urged the citizens of Parma to vote for the annexation to Piedmont. His speech made a great impression and he was selected to be one of a deputation to go and discuss the problem with the Provisional Government. Gallenga's initiative had a decisive influence in hastening the annexation of Parma, as can be seen in the report which appeared a week later in *Il Risorgimento* and which highly praised it.

> LONG LIVE GALLENGA! I think that the only just and rightful actions performed in Parma were the gunshots of the 20 in the morning, and this Gallenghian exploit.[2]

Back in Milan, Gallenga continued his political activity. He was

[1] Letter to G. Piroli, May 1848, Raccolta Bertarelli, Museo del Risorgimento, Milan.

[2] L. Scarabelli, 'Correspondence from Parma', *Il Risorgimento*, 17 May 1848.

engaged in writing for *La Lombardia*, when he was suddenly called back to England, where he had left his family: his baby daughter, Gallenga's first child, had died, and his wife was very ill.

He left Italy at the beginning of July. When Juliet's condition improved enough to allow him to return, the Italian war was lost. Gallenga took up quarters in Turin where most of the vanquished army had sought refuge.

A more disheartening and perplexing situation of affairs than what we met in Italy at this juncture, it would be impossible to imagine. With the King, and the remnants of his beaten army, swarms of homeless and in many cases, penniless fugitives from all parts of Italy had crowded in upon exhausted Piedmont. Among them were the bitterest enemies both of the King and of his people. The municipal jealousy which had shown itself between Lombards and Subalpines on the first success of the campaign was not likely to be soothed by the smart of its final reverse. . . . Treachery on one side, supineness and cowardice on the other, were the charges with which the contending parties met each other in their envenomed controversy.[1]

Gallenga thought it essential to pacify the Italians. In the hope of putting an end to political controversies, in August he sent a first article to *Il Risorgimento*, under the title of 'Words of a Peacemaker to the Italians of Piedmont and Lombardy', which won him the full approval of Cavour—who ran the paper *de facto*, if not personally—and thus his political career in Piedmont began.

Apart from the Parma episode, the role played by Gallenga in the first period of the 1848–9 campaign was limited. His military experience was short and not at all important, but enough to give him an idea of the disorganized state of the Italian forces, and, after the Salasco armistice (9 August 1848), he took an active part as a journalist and a politician in contemporary Italian affairs.

The first thing to do now was to settle political differences among the Italian parties. It was essential to achieve unity, if there was to be any success against Austria. In a series of articles which appeared between August and September, Antonio

[1] *Epis.*, vol. ii, pp. 200–1.

Gallenga tried to prove that the national cause had never been betrayed. The reason for the defeat lay in some strategic mistakes which undermined the easy successes of March. *Una fatale illusione sulla facilità dell'impresa* made the Italians unaware of the effective strength of the Austrian Empire. Local governments began to discuss internal political issues long before the common enemy had been expelled from the Italian soil. The absence of a central command essential for the organization of the troops coming from all over the country, and the slowness and indecision of Charles Albert's policy added to the final disaster.

Had Charles Albert advanced bravely between Mantua and Verona, and had he left Nugent's troops behind, they would have been immediately driven back across the Tagliamento. But the Lombard provinces and Milan itself would have fallen a prey to the emboldened garrisons. Charles Albert wanted to cover everything and protect everyone. His error of judgement was due to good intentions, but it was nevertheless fatal.[1]

Moreover, the Piedmontese troops found themselves confronted with the inherent diffidence and mistrust of the lower rural classes, who lacked a political conscience and who mistakenly regarded the war of independence as another of the many pillaging campaigns they had witnessed throughout the years. In the Po valley the peasants' cowardice was complete: 'those poor fields had too often been the theatre of atrocious and devastating campaigns at the times of the French: now they believed that their only means of salvation was to hide everything and flee.' After the signing of the armistice the situation was very critical. As Gallenga pointed out, the Italians were in a sad predicament.

We are back where we started, at the beginning of a war which can be very obstinate on both sides. It is vain to foster any illusion by exaggerating the importance of diplomatic mediation. . . . What conditions is, in fact, Austria prepared to accept now that she can boast of an unexpected military success?[2]

Gallenga had little faith in Anglo-French mediation, which was

---

[1] 'Agli Italiani di Piemonte e Lombardia', *Il Risorgimento*, 19 Aug. 1848.
[2] Ibid., 9 Sept. 1848.

at work trying to compose the dispute between Austria and Piedmont. His instinctive mistrust of French politicians and his knowledge of English foreign policy made him sceptical of the outcome of such negotiations. He knew that Great Britain and France alike had no real interest in Italy as a country: the chief aim of English politics was the preservation of the balance of power in Europe. As for France, it might have been profitable for some Parisian politicians if Austria had lost some of her power. Italians must, therefore, rely on their own forces, which could provide some form of defence against the invader and would, if carefully organized and united. It was time to lay political questions and personal vanities aside, for these were times which demanded 'one sole mind, one sole heart'. For Gallenga a temporary dictatorship would have been the ideal solution, but he thought it impossible because Italian people were too individualistic to let themselves be governed by one man. Though Gallenga's opinion on this is questionable, it is undeniable that none of the leading figures of the moment enjoyed adequate political prestige and popularity to become the moral and political leader of Italy. In the months which followed the defeat federalism appeared to be one of the best means of achieving some form of unity, and Gallenga continued to give it his full support. With Perez and Ferrara, he promoted the establishment of a *Società Nazionale per la Confederazione Italiana*, which was officially founded in Turin on 6 September. The formation of the Society was one of the several attempts made in 1848 to bring about an Italian league. Although some of the people who lent it their support firmly believed in federalism, many—not excluding Gallenga—considered it as a first step towards a centralized government. In the programme of the Society a kingdom of Northern Italy— including Piedmont, the Duchies, and Lombardo-Venetia— under the rule of the dynasty of Savoy was put forward as the leading state of the Confederation. It is no wonder, therefore, that most Italian princes regarded it with suspicion. The main obstacle with which it was confronted was the mutual distrust of the Italian sovereigns. For a short while, however, its popularity was such that Cavour, Lambruschini, Melegari, and many prominent figures of the moderate party, gave it their support. Enrico Mayer declined the invitation to take part in the Congress, which was held in October, because of his foreign nationality (he was a German subject), but he declared himself in favour of it. Vincenzo Gioberti—then at the height of his political career— was elected president, while Gallenga became one of the secretaries. He probably wrote the *Proclama al Popolo Britannico*, published in *Il Risorgimento* and signed by Gioberti, president, and Gallenga, secretary. He knew what great influence public opinion could have over the British Cabinet, and so tried to draw the attention of the English press to the Society.

We come before you, ye umpires between Austria and Italy. We claim Italy as our own birthright. . . . We have, at last, acquired a will of our own. Every day, since that fatal 1814, has found us one step in advance. Every day stifled a conspiracy, quelled an insurrection.[1]

He was doing his best to promote federalism, making full use of his rhetorical gifts in writing for the newspapers, when he was appointed chargé d'affaires for Sardinia at the German National Assembly. In 1848 following the Paris revolution which took place in February, most German states had rebelled against their princes. The easy revolutionary successes in various states were accompanied by plans for establishing some sort of political unity and a national assembly was summoned in Frankfurt, and it was there that Gallenga was sent on a diplomatic mission.

Like all similar attempts, the *Società Nazionale per la Confederazione Italiana* failed in its task. The breaking of the armistice and the defeat of Novara soon put an end to its existence. At the time when Gallenga was in Frankfurt, political intrigue was already undermining it. The Society had been founded by moderate elements, but, as Abercromby wrote to Palmerston, it soon turned into one of the ultra-liberal political circles.

A few sittings of this Association under the direction and influence of the Abbé Gioberti were sufficient to change the whole character of the Society. . . . Should it wrest from the hands of the Government the direction of the League, and be strong enough by the exercise of public

[1] 'Proclama al Popolo Britannico', *Il Risorgimento*, 23 Sept. 1848.

3   *The Peace of Paris, March 1856*
By J. Longe

4 The death of
Jacopo Ruffini
in jail,
Genoa 1833
Engraving by
Mantegazza

opinion to impose the terms which in the opinions of the members of that Society may be considered the best, I fear that . . . we may expect to see a greater development given throughout Italy to purely democratic principles.[1]

The National German Assembly had opened in May with the aim of bringing about a federation of German states. The development of the German situation seemed likely to affect the war in Italy, and the interest shown in nationalism by German liberals made the Italians believe that they could find an ally in the Central Power. Almost all Italian governments—both old and new —sent representatives to Frankfurt in order to follow the situation more closely. Piedmont had appointed one in June in the person of Evasio Radice. When he left Frankfurt because of disagreement with the existing Piedmontese Cabinet, Gioberti was asked to head the Italian mission. Owing to Gioberti's refusal, Gallenga's name was put forward by Michelangelo Castelli, the editor of *Il Risorgimento*, and on 28 September he left for Frankfurt, which he reached on 2 October, and where he was eventually joined by his wife.

In spite of the little faith he had in foreign diplomacy, Gallenga put all his efforts into the mission he was asked to perform. He was sent to Frankfurt to see whether better conditions for peace could be obtained from Austria, but the central government did not pay much attention to the change which had taken place in the Piedmontese legation, neither was it prepared to back Italy. By 12 October, Gallenga had still not been introduced to the *corps diplomatique*, as he complained to Lord Cowley.

I have been for some time expecting that Mr Schmerling as Minister of State for Foreign Affairs would officially introduce me to the *corps diplomatique*.

But, as I suppose in the press of business he has either forgotten or not deemed it necessary that such a presentation should take place, I would request your Lordship to grant me the honour of an interview.[2]

He was not surprised at the indifference with which his appointment was received, for he had always doubted whether Italy

---

[1] Abercromby to Palmerston, P.R.O., F.O. 67/155, No. 256.
[2] Gallenga to Cowley, 12 Oct., 1848, P.R.O., F.O. 519/157.

would find in Germany an ally against Austria. As was to be expected, the champions of German nationality 'were as anxious for the welfare of Italy as for their own' but for them, too:

at Trent, at Trieste, and the shores of the Adriatic, Austrian interests were also German interests, and the *natural* frontier of Germany must be drawn at the Mincio, or, at the utmost, at the Adige.[1]

Soon Gallenga realized that he had not been wrong in his judgement of German feelings towards Italy. Pan-Germanism was already so widespread that any loss to Austria would be felt as a loss to the whole Teutonic world. The only advantage to be gained from the situation was to make use of German and Austrian internal divisions.

Not long after his arrival, Gallenga sent a note to Schmerling, the head of the Austrian legation, asking for a public declaration on the Italian problem. He never received an official answer, since no one wanted to commit himself. For a while he thought of publishing his note, thus urging the Assembly to make a pronouncement on the subject, but in this he was strongly discouraged by Lord Cowley, who blamed his lack of discretion.

Should publications of this nature become common, all confidential communications would be destroyed between Governments who might as well conduct their affairs thro' the agency of newspapers.[2]

Perrone, then the Piedmontese Minister for Foreign Affairs, also disagreed with his chargé d'affaires about publishing his note.

By the middle of October, Gallenga felt that his mission was completely useless. However, he did not give up hope. He still believed that something could be done for Italy, if the immediate situation could be exploited. He wrote a rather touching letter to Perrone, in which he asked the minister to consider him as *l'enfant perdu* of Italian diplomacy, and declared himself ready to bear responsibility for any personal undertaking. He felt that the post between Turin and Frankfurt was far too slow. Contradictory news kept pouring in concerning the Viennese situation. Gallenga found himself in a totally German world, and acted in

---

[1] *Epis.*, vol. ii, p. 213.
[2] Cowley to Palmerston, 16 Oct. 1848, P.R.O., F.O. 519/148.

accordance with the development of the situation there: when Bruck was appointed Minister of Commerce at Vienna, he saw a chance of gaining something for Italy.

Bruck was a North German who had been director of the Austrian branch of Lloyd's at Trieste and was well acquainted with the Italian situation. He was sent to Frankfurt as a member of the Assembly and was later appointed Austrian plenipotentiary. In November, after the abdication of the Emperor Ferdinand, he became Minister of Commerce in the new Austrian Cabinet. Gallenga met with him in Frankfurt and had a chance of discussing Austro-Italian matters. Bruck thought that the Lombardo-Venetian provinces were a burden and a weakness to Austria rather than a useful possession, and was in favour of granting them independence. On the ground of that understanding and on hearing of his new appointment in Vienna, Gallenga drew up a scheme for a peaceful settlement, the conditions of which were as follows:

(1) Indépendance du Royaume Lombardo-Vénitien sous un Prince Autrichien.
(2) Nationalisation entière du personnel de l'armée et du Gouvernement à l'exception de la personne du Chef de l'État.
(3) Parme et Plaisance à la Sardaigne, Modène et Reggio à Rome.
(4) Massa Carrara et tous les territoires Modénais au Sud des Apennins à la Toscane.
(5) Indemnisation en argent à l'Autriche et participation de la dette publique.
(6) Alliance offensive et défensive entre la Sardaigne et le nouveau Royaume et s'il est possible avec les autres états de la confédération Italienne.
(7) Relations de commerce entre la Sardaigne, le nouveau Royaume (et s'il est possible le reste de l'Italie) d'un côté et l'Autriche et l'Allemagne de l'autre, autant c'est à dire qu'il y aura union entre ces deux pays.[1]

He was fully aware that 'ces conditions ne sont pas si avantageuses à la Sardaigne que celles qui paraissent dans les bases des Puissances médiatrices', but he was equally sure that those 'ne réussiraient

[1] Gallenga to Perrone, 29 Nov. 1848, Museo del Risorgimento, Turin, Registri della Segreteria Estera, 'Lettere ai Ministri d'Allemagna'.

jamais à faire accepter leur bases à l'Autriche sans la force'—and
France and Great Britain were not prepared to use military force
against Austria. Gallenga got in touch with Bruck and the Arch-
duke John of Austria, and was making plans for an Austrian
envoy to have unofficial talks with the government in Turin,
when Perrone openly condemned his action and recalled him.
It is difficult to say whether Gallenga's initiative would have ever
achieved its end. It is true that the Austrian territories in Italy
were not particularly profitable possessions. As Lord Cowley
pointed out to Gallenga, the occupation of Lombardy was a
question of time, for after all that had occurred in Italy, Austria
could hold it only at a ruinous expense for her finances. The surrender of Lombardy was to take place ten years later. At this
time, however, considerations of prestige prevented the apparently
powerful state of Austria from granting anything to defeated
Piedmont. Another reason which made Perrone condemn Gallenga's action was that he himself was more of a Piedmontese
than an Italian, and the expansion of Piedmont was more important to him than the establishment of an Italian confederation.
In Gallenga's plan very little was to be gained by Turin. The
plan, which suited the Federalists, did not satisfy the Piedmontese.
At the same time it was bound to encounter the complete disap-
proval of those who aimed at national unity. In the middle of
December, when Gallenga was recalled to Turin, the Perrone
Cabinet had fallen and Gioberti was elected. He gave power to
the most radical elements who were hostile to any moderate
policy. They wanted war even at the risk of a complete defeat.
This was to happen at Novara the following March.

A few conclusions can be drawn from Gallenga's diplomatic
experience: he was a bad chargé d'affaires and could hardly be
called a diplomat because of his lack of discretion, as appears from
Lord Cowley's letters, written at the time of his negotiations with
Bruck. We learn from one of them that Cowley, suspecting that
Turin and Berlin had made a direct proposal of peace to Vienna,
asked Gallenga whether he was aware of the circumstances. The
Italian at first denied it, but in a way which convinced Cowley
that he knew more than he chose to say.

After taking leave of me, he returned again, and said that as I might suspect him of a want of veracity, he would tell me the truth.[1]

This Gallenga did, behaving in a childish way. The choice of our writer as a diplomat might at first appear odd: he had no previous experience in this field and had not shown any particular aptitude for diplomacy. Like many others, he found himself in a position of political power because of the existing situation. The new Piedmontese government was associated with the Italian liberals, and new men were appointed in place of the old reactionary school. The policy pursued at this time was to be fully exploited by Cavour, who later looked for support from men from all parts of Italy. The Subalpine Parliament of the fifties acquired an Italian colour which had been lacking before.

Gallenga had a powerful intuition where political developments were concerned—this made him a remarkably good foreign correspondent in later years. His activity in Frankfurt is a good example of what Cavour was to achieve so successfully, namely to bring the Italian problem within the field of European diplomacy. Gallenga was convinced that little was to be gained from foreign help as such, but much could be done by tactful handling of the situation. Perrone himself seemed to have encouraged such an opinion, when on 5 November he wrote to his chargé d'affaires:

Dans un discours qu'il a prononcé avant hier à la Chambre des Députés M. le chevalier Pinelli a dit que jamais on n'admettrait dans la médiation d'autres Puissances que la France et l'Angleterre. Je dois vous dire que c'est l'opinion particulière de M. Pinelli, et non point celle du Ministère, qui agira d'après les circonstances et les intérêts du pays.[2]

The loyalty which Perrone later professed to France and Great Britain, when he proposed direct negotiations with Austria, meant little to Gallenga who after the Italian defeat wrote that, perhaps with the best of intentions, 'the two countries had

---

[1] Cowley to Palmerston, 10 Dec. 1848, P.R.O., F.O., 519/149, No. 323.
[2] Perrone to Gallenga, 5 Nov. 1848, Registri Segreteria Estera, no. 1, Turin.

murdered Italy. Without them, Piedmont and her allies would
have realized that it was impossible for them to hold the ground.'[1]

The failure of his diplomatic mission did not affect his position
in Turin. He continued to write for *Il Risorgimento* and published
a short pamphlet, *A che ne siamo?*, a summary of his previous
articles including his latest view on the situation.

Apart from Austria we have no enemies, if we show the world a
united front and show ourselves ready to fight for our sacred rights to
independence and internal order. Now then, where have we got to?

We have two democratic states in the centre, which are unfit for
any action either good or bad. In the north there is a mock democracy
and a mock tyranny in the south. And with them we must either declare war on Austria or make peace with her. . . . Now let us establish
two constitutional monarchies in the north and in the south. Let us get
control over the two central democracies and make them adjourn
their constituent assemblies, and open their enrolment lists. . . . Let's
learn how to govern and we shall win. . . . Let us show ourselves
strong, and treaties will be less ruinous.[2]

Gallenga was here referring to the Roman and Tuscan republics,
proclaimed by the Mazzinians who took over after the Pope and
the Grand Duke had fled, and to the Kingdom of the Two
Sicilies in the south and an enlarged monarchy in the north.

At the end of February, Gallenga went back to Frankfurt,
where he had left his family. A few weeks later, the armistice
having expired, the Piedmontese army was defeated at Novara
and Charles Albert abdicated in favour of his son, Victor Emmanuel II, thus putting an end to the war. Deeply affected by the
Italian failure, Gallenga decided not to return to Turin, but to
make his way back to London, which he did after spending
several months touring Central Europe. His going back to
England was often considered a voluntary exile, but his return
was prompted by practical considerations, such as family ties and
financial matters. He was aware that the Italian cause was lost for
the time being, as in July he wrote to Michelangelo Castelli, 'He
who in the present circumstances . . . would advocate war is

---

[1] *A che ne siamo?*, Turin, 1849, p. 10.
[2] Ibid., p. 51 and *passim*.

a murderer.'[1] He drew two main conclusions from his stay in Italy and Germany: first, the need to have one leading state, which would co-ordinate all Italian efforts and provide at the same time the ideal social structure for the future Italy; secondly, the necessity to relate the Italian question to the general European situation. Only a well-planned programme could achieve positive results in the future, but, at the time, peace was the best solution. By peace he meant not only the absence of an official state of war between the Italian states and Austria, but also the suppression of any violent uprising. Although short, Gallenga's stay in Italy had a decisive influence on his political thought: when he had left England he was imbued with the spirit of moderate liberalism, ready to support any Italian prince. He returned a loyal subject of the dynasty of Savoy and a conservative. His fiercest attacks on Mazzini and the democrats date from 1849. Hence the rather sceptical and critical attitude he developed towards men and institutions. The monarchical system, for example, appeared to him to be pre-eminently suitable for governing a country where education was, as yet, the prerogative of the higher classes, but he was far from having any blind love for royalty. This can be seen in his opinion of Charles Albert, which changed greatly over the years. The tyrant of 1833—who made blood flow copiously—was still in 1847 'an amphibious, equivocal character, half Jesuit, half headsman, ambitious yet fainthearted, never liked, never trusted by Austria; never esteemed, never fully given up by the patriots.' By 1848 he was 'the weak and yet noble king', who lost the chance of winning a campaign rather than have the Po valley ransacked by irregular troops. In 1849 after the defeat at Novara he was an unfortunate man expiating 'the inconsiderate sins of his youth'. The enigmatic figure of Charles Albert appealed to Gallenga more from the human than the political point of view. Even the few words he wrote in praise of the King during the 1848 campaign were dictated by contingent political impulses and not inspired by real admiration. Gallenga always considered him unequal to his task—

[1] *Carteggio politico di Michelangelo Castelli*, ed. by L. Chiala, Turin, 1890, vol. i, p. 51.

as can be seen in one of his last descriptions of the King. Though many years had elapsed since he met Charles Albert, this remains an interesting portrait of the Piedmontese sovereign, in spite of the fact that some of the details might have been slightly altered as years went by. In writing it, Gallenga had in mind the description left by D'Azeglio in *I miei ricordi*, from which he drew inspiration. The scene took place in Turin, in the summer of 1848, when Gallenga and other refugees formed a deputation and went to the King to pledge their faith and honour 'to stand by him in the name of the Italian Confederation'.

Poor King! He had had noble aspirations at various periods of his life. He had wished for good, but evil had been again and again too strong for him. He was in earnest now, at this last stage in his career, but how could any man know it? . . . He stood before the open window, all clad in his blue uniform, with his plumed cocked hat resting on his arm; a tall man, stiff and erect, lean and gaunt, all yellow like boxwood in his face, old, worn, broken in mind and body. He listened with some embarassment, he thanked us rather coldly; but asked, 'How any one could doubt the earnestness and steadfastness of his devotion to the nation's cause?'

'Sire,' I replied, 'your Majesty must be aware that reports are current about town that peace with Austria has already been secretly signed.'

My words touched him to the quick. His eyes flashed fire, and he moved forward a step or two, as if unable to control his emotion. 'Peace signed!' he exclaimed. Then he burst out in a bitter laugh. 'Gentlemen,' he said, 'if you know that, you are better informed than I am, or ought to be. . . . Take the word of a King and a gentleman. . . . Tell my people and your people that I have staked my crown, my life and that of my sons on the issue of this contest, and that my sword shall never be sheathed till we obtain a peace with which Italy may have reason to be satisfied.'[1]

Whatever his personal opinion of the king, Gallenga openly defended his policy in Great Britain, where the unhappy ending of the war seemed to have affected English sympathy towards Italy.

The English, accustomed to constant success, were ashamed of our

---

[1] *Epis.*, vol. ii, pp. 204–6.

failure, and no wonder. The very men who had most consistently taken up our cause, felt now as if they had been swindled out of their sympathies. As to the Ultra-Tories, the men for whom Austria had always been 'England's natural ally', and Italy merely a 'geographical expression', they treated us to their sneers.[1]

As soon as he got back to England, he started lecturing and writing about the reasons for the Italian defeat. He publicly attacked Gioberti and Mazzini, both of whom he thought responsible for Italian confusion, and supported Piedmont in a long article, 'Eighteen Months' Political Life in Italy', which appeared in December in *Colburn's New Monthly Magazine*, and which was later amplified and published in a volume, *Italy in 1848*. The work, which according to its author should have given the English public a true account of the campaign, heaped on him the hate and mistrust of all Anglo-Italian Mazzinians. They accused him of libellously describing the Lombards as cowards and of having betrayed the national cause. However, his opposition to the Mazzinians and his conservatism won him some popularity in Piedmont. By 1852 his reputation was so well-established that when Cavour went to France and England in quest of support from the Italian exiles, he called at 13 Kensington Gardens, where the Gallengas were then living. The interest Cavour had in winning Gallenga's support is quite understandable, for he was still a citizen of Parma and could, therefore, represent the Duchy in Piedmont. At the same time he held the chair of Italian at University College, London, and moved in the best literary and journalistic circles of the English capital. Cavour felt certain that he could secure Gallenga a seat in the Subalpine Parliament during the next general elections and asked him to return to Turin. Gallenga declined his offer, as he felt that he could better contribute to the Italian cause from England, a country which was now his home and to which a variety of indissoluble ties bound him. Despite his refusal, his relations with Cavour were very friendly for a while, and the statesman provided him with letters of introduction to several people, when Gallenga went to Piedmont to collect historical material for some books he intended to write.

[1] Ibid., p. 226.

On his way to Italy in the summer of 1852, Gallenga broke his
journey in Paris, and accompanied Cavour, who was travelling
back to Turin, on a visit to Daniele Manin, the Venetian dictator,
who after the fall of Venice had sought refuge there.

We found Manin—on the third or fourth floor of a house near the
Boulevards—a modest-looking, deep-eyed, high-browed personage,
who, knowing more of Piedmontese politics than I did, received
Cavour, the rising man, with greater deference than I had shown, but
was no less firm and explicit in his refusal of the parliamentary honours
intended for him, on the score of his inability to live in Turin without
the income he made in Paris out of his business as a teacher of languages. . . . Cavour soon perceived that he was in presence of too lofty
a character to be tempted by any proposal likely to clash with the
man's proud spirit of independence. . . . 'I see that I have no luck
anywhere', he said. 'Our friend here', pointing to me, 'will not consent
to come to Turin, because he is too well-off in London; and you—
you refuse because you are afraid of finding in Turin a harder life
than you have here.'[1]

Although his interest in politics was still great, Gallenga did
not take any active part in political events for a while and the
years between 1850 and 1854 were devoted to study and works of
scholarship, with the occasional odd article on the Italian situation. While working in London he kept in close contact with his
friends in Italy and a few trips to the North acquainted him with
post-war developments. In 1854 he thought that the fate of Italy
lay in the hands of the Piedmontese politicians and that something
could be achieved in the very near future. This time he accepted
Cavour's offer to enter the political arena, and, after being granted
Sardinian citizenship, he was elected to one of the Piedmontese
constituencies for Cavour's party. Thus he became one of the
deputies of the Subalpine Parliament. After some months of
political life, he wrote to Mayer full of enthusiasm and excitement.

Everyone here is in great anxiety because the Eastern situation may
change the fate of Europe and affect the development of the Italian
cause. We must be the first to cast our dice. You can see that there are

[1] *Epis.*, vol. ii, pp. 235–6.

times when it matters to be in Piedmont and carry some weight in public life.[1]

This letter was written at the end of January 1855, while discussions were held in Parliament about Piedmontese intervention in the Crimean war. When Cavour proposed it, Gallenga was one of the first to support him. In one of the few parliamentary speeches he ever made, he defended the alliance with the Western powers, pointing out that he did not think this alliance was something new.

I believe it to be a corollary and an inevitable consequence of what we did in 1848. Then popular unrest all over Europe threatened a general war, now we have come to a European conflict.... As in 1848, Europe is divided into two fields. . . . The two are engaged in a fight which this time must at least lead us to a decisive and final conclusion— a conclusion which we failed to reach in 1848.[2]

According to him, the cause of nationalism itself was at stake, for a Russian victory would mean the triumph of imperialism over the right to independence of individual countries. On the other hand, there was a chance that the victory of the Western powers would establish the principle of non-intervention all over Europe. He was greatly disappointed when at the Paris conference of 1856, which put an end to the war, France and England failed to do so.

It is a very great pity indeed . . . that the great principle of non-intervention was not agreed upon and firmly stipulated among the parties interested in the late Paris conference, and made a virtual condition to the signature of the peace of the 30th of March. Extremely unfortunate it is that England and France, with all the *entente cordiale* that they pretend to have sprung up between them dare not proclaim that only just and truly political principle for the rest of Europe. . . . The safest way of providing for the quiet of Italy and Europe is to allow . . . Italians fair play, to screen them from the Austrian interference.[3]

---

[1] Unpublished letter to Enrico Mayer, 23 Jan. 1855, Mayer Archives.
[2] Rapporti Parlamentari, 1854–5, pp. 1668–9, 5 Feb. 1855, Archivio di Stato, Turin.
[3] 'Italy and Piedmont, letter V', *Daily News,* 14 July 1856.

As he himself admitted, and his political rivals often pointed out, Gallenga was not a born orator, and very rarely took part in parliamentary debates. In the years he spent in Turin his main activity was journalism and he wrote for several Piedmontese reviews, such as *Il Cimento* and *Il Parlamento*. In the winter of 1855 he became special correspondent for the *Daily News*, taking the place held till then by Giovanni Ruffini. After twenty years absence from his country, interrupted only by short visits, he showed little understanding of the difficulties encountered by the newly established Parliament. In a letter to Mayer, Gallenga deplored the democratic freedom granted by the Statute.

What worries and irritates me is the dissolution of social and moral ties; without doubt the Piedmontese, who up to 1848 were the best people in Italy, if not the best on the Continent, are becoming corrupted by abuse of freedom: here we have a government which is immoral because of its weakness, immoral because of its indifference.[1]

He often compared Piedmontese political life to the English parliamentary system, and the comparison was all, of course, in favour of the latter.

Who cannot see how the English almost by instinct have built a political structure capable of permanent order and continuous experiment founded on a sound basis which promotes everlasting progress; a government which secures the maximum universal development, while preserving the most boundless individual freedom.[2]

Not only the political aspects of English life, but also the moral principles of the Victorian age were described by him as superior to Latin morals. A new satirical tone can now be found in Gallenga's writings. It is no wonder that his colleagues jokingly called him *novello Baretti*. His style acquired something of vivacity and violence, while it lost that detached serene tone which had scored so much success in his first articles in *Il Risorgimento*. He returned to Italy not as a *conciliatore* but as a moral censor. In little less than two years his criticism of such public evils as gambling-houses, begging religious orders, privileges granted to

[1] Unpublished letter to Enrico Mayer, 18 Mar. 1855, Mayer Archives.
[2] 'Sul progresso europeo', *Il Cimento*, Turin, Jan. 1855, vol. v, p. 9.

deputies, made him extremely unpopular, not only among the opposition, but even among members of his own party. When in 1856 an unknown episode of his life came to light, Gallenga found himself almost completely isolated. He resigned his seat in Parliament under circumstances which drew attention to his relations with Mazzini, now one of his greatest political enemies, but formerly a close political associate and a personal friend.

V

GALLENGA AND MAZZINI

I was walking at random in Upper Gower Street, when behind a ground-floor window there flashed upon me a pair of black eyes under a fine round forehead, which struck me as not unfamiliar, and could only belong to an Italian. As I went down street to the New Road, I was overtaken by a little man wearing green spectacles, who introduced himself as Usiglio from Modena, and told me I had been recognised as I passed by Mazzini, who wished to see me.[1]

Thus Gallenga recorded his meeting Mazzini again in England in 1839, when he had just arrived from America. Usiglio led him to the Genoese's house, where the two men renewed their acquaintance. They had previously met in Geneva in 1833, when Gallenga had already spent two years in exile, after his banishment from Parma. Although his visit had then been very brief, it is not surprising that Mazzini should at once recognize him, for the matter discussed among themselves in that far away summer of six years before was something which could not easily be forgotten. Gallenga, then an affiliate of Young Italy, went to Mazzini for advice and protection for a deed which he was determined to perform. He wanted to murder Charles Albert of Savoy, the then King of Piedmont, whom he considered the living symbol of tyranny and despotism. The first impression Mazzini had of Antonio was favourable, and in spite of his reluctance to back a political crime, in the end he accepted his proposal and gave him help and assistance. To understand why both men could consider such a desperate gesture as a way of reawakening the national conscience, which seemed to be dormant in Italy, one must bear in mind that the situation in the country then looked grimmer than ever. In spite of the hopes of many a liberal, the national movement had not gained any ground after the 1831 uprisings. The

[1] *Epis.*, vol. ii, p. 24.

country was split into many states, all of which were under Austrian influence, with the exception of Piedmont. But Piedmontese political independence did not coincide with social emancipation of the country. The government was most illiberal, and no constitution had so far been granted. Patriots were persecuted there as well as anywhere else in the Peninsula. The Kingdom of Savoy, then also known under the name of Kingdom of Sardinia, included Savoy, Nice, Piedmont, Liguria, and the island of Sardinia. The Genoese-born Mazzini was therefore a Piedmontese subject. Some years earlier he had been imprisoned because of his ideas and his being a Carbonaro, and once released from jail he was forced to go into exile. In 1831, when Charles Felix of Savoy died, the hopes of many Italian patriots revived, for the heir to the throne, Charles Albert, Prince of Carignano, had in his youth shown some sympathy for the Carbonari and the liberal movement.

From Marseilles Mazzini wrote him an impassioned letter, urging him to be the champion of Italian independence, but, greatly to his disappointment, the King began his reign on a conservative note. He not only rejected Mazzini's appeal, but even ordered his government to make representations to the French authorities, who asked Mazzini to withdraw from Marseilles—which he did, eventually settling in Geneva. From there he tried to keep alive the flame of Italian liberty, welcoming all exiles and continuing his writings for the national and social emancipation of his country. Underground plotting also continued in Italy, but no recent enterprise had been successful. Early in 1833 a revolutionary movement was discovered in the Piedmontese army, and several young soldiers were executed. Mazzini, who had been conniving at it from afar, was sentenced to death *in absentia*. In the same year one of his dearest friends, Jacopo Ruffini, committed suicide while in jail in Genoa. His mother and brothers, all of whom were devoted followers of Mazzini, had taken refuge in Geneva. It was at this distressing time of his life, when he was still suffering under the blow of Jacopo's death and the failure of the Piedmontese conspiracy, that Gallenga went to him. Antonio thought that the time had come to do something to relieve the sufferings of Italy and to make his name immortal. In this elated frame of mind he asked Luigi Melegari, an exile from Parma who lived in France and at the time an ardent Mazzinian, for a letter of introduction to the Genoese. Not long before he had joined Young Italy, under the name of Procida, for the reading of Mazzini's writings had aroused his enthusiasm and like most Italians he regarded him as the prophet and the moral leader of his country. For a short time the two young men—Gallenga was then twenty-three and Mazzini only five years his senior—were under the delusion, soon dispelled, that a political crime could alter the Italian situation. The plot had to be kept absolutely secret, if there were to be any hope of success. The secret was so well kept for such a long time that the main evidence now available is what both of them wrote some twenty years later. Thus Mazzini recorded their meeting in Geneva:

Not long before our expedition in Savoy, after many of ours had been executed in Genoa, Alessandria and Chambery, one night towards the end of 1833, a young man unknown to me called at the *Hôtel de la Navigation*; Luigi Melegari, now professor and deputy in Turin, then one of ours, had given him a note in which he recommended me his friend, who was determined to perform 'a noble deed', and wanted to arrange matters with me. The young man was Antonio Gallenga. He came from Corsica and was a member of Young Italy.

He told me that ever since the proscriptions had started, he had decided to revenge his brothers' blood and once and for all to teach tyrants that guilt was always followed by expiation; that he felt himself called to murder Charles Albert, the traitor of 1821 and his brothers' executioner; that he had nourished this idea in solitude till it had grown and become stronger than he himself, and other things besides.

I objected, as I have always done in similar cases: I discussed, put forward all arguments which might deter him from his plan. I told him that I considered Charles Albert worthy of death, but his death would not save Italy, that to take on himself the office of emissary of expiation he must be pure of any sense of mean revenge, and of any other feeling which was not pure, and once his mission was accomplished, he must be ready to cross his hands on his chest and die as a victim . . . defamed by men, as a murderer, and so I went on for a long time.

He had an answer for everything, his eyes shone while he spoke. He did not care for life, once his mission was over he would not withdraw a single step, he would cry: *Long Live Italy*, and die![1]

Once he decided to back Gallenga, Mazzini immediately set about helping him, and put him in touch with members of Young Italy. Thus he wrote to one of them, Pietro Olivero, asking him for a forged passport which would allow Antonio to travel safely inside Piedmont:

One of our young men will come to you, who deserves our veneration, so good, so holy he is. At all cost, it is absolutely necessary to find him a passport, as he will tell you. Everything depends on that.[2]

Provided with a passport the young man reached Piedmont, and in September he was in Turin determined to bring about the death of the King and to die himself. From Geneva Mazzini followed the development of the situation. The anxiety with which he kept inquiring about his movements shows the great importance he attached to the plot. On September 18 he wrote to Melegari:

By God, Procida! . . . I tremble at this delay. His secret is known to everyone.

Two days after, in another letter to the same, he wrote

I shall be deeply disappointed if Procida fails in his mission

and a week later, more and more worried about Antonio's delay, added

He promised to act, and from then on I haven't heard from him and this is bad, too bad for our attempt.

When by the begining of October, he began to doubt that Gallenga would ever carry out the assassination, he said:

I fear that Procida has weakened and I fear the time he has wasted will cost him dearly—five people know his secret and this not through me but through him, of his own free will by a formal announcement. It is a petty vanity which should not dwell in noble hearts like his.[3]

[1] *S.E.N.*, vol. 57, p. 142 and *passim*, to F. Campanella, 6 Oct. 1856.
[2] Ibid., vol. 5, p. 442, Mazzini to P. Olivero, Aug. 1833.
[3] Ibid., vol. 9, Mazzini to L. A. Melegari, letters of 18, 20, 27 Sept., and 3 Oct. 1833.

In effect something happened or rather did not happen, so Gallenga lost the opportunity of carrying out his plan and later abandoned it. Nothing is known about the actual reasons which made Gallenga change his mind, whether he acted thus because of personal fear or because of the sudden realization of the uselessness of such an action, which had been planned as an individual gesture to provoke some sort of popular reaction, and not as part of a well-organized plot. Gallenga blamed his failure firstly on the impossibility of finding a suitable weapon in Turin, then on the inefficiency of the local members of Young Italy, and finally he justified himself by saying that the police had grown suspicious, as can be seen in his rendering of the episode, written in 1855.

Supplied with a passport, money, and letters by Mazzini, he proceeded to Turin, in August, 1833, under the false name of Louis Mariotti. Mazzini's partisans at Turin had however either fled, or lived in fear and concealment. There was no one to give the stranger advice or direction, no one to furnish the means to carry his intent into effect, no one to take advantage of its probable issues. For nearly two months he watched for an opportunity to strike a blow. The attention of the police was at last awakened, and he was spirited away by a few friends, who had partly guessed his secret. Charles Albert hardly ever had a distinct idea of the designs that were harboured against his life; but as another emissary of Mazzini was soon after arrested, the bearer of a dagger with a hilt curiously wrought with precious stones in mosaic, which was identified as the personal property of the arch-conspirator, a vague impression remained, both in the King's own mind and in that of his most loyal subjects, that Mazzini did not shrink from the use of the assassin's knife. '*Ne vuole alla vita del Re*' (He is aiming at the King's life)—such was the quaint expression used with respect to Mazzini, which might be heard from a hundred officers in the Piedmontese army, during the campaign of 1848.[1]

However scanty is the information available, there can be no doubt that the 1833 plot was badly organized. Not only did Gallenga meet with several difficulties in Turin, but he even

[1] *History of Piedmont*, vol. iii, pp. 338–9.

forgot to provide himself with a weapon. So a man was sent to Geneva and Mazzini gave him a dagger wrought with precious stones. This never reached Gallenga for the young man carrying it was arrested by the police before arriving at Turin. This extraordinary story would be hard to believe, had not both Gallenga and Mazzini supplied evidence for it, but the unpractical and unrealistic aspects of the whole affair, which account for its failure, show how the motives which made them plot together were basically emotional and irrational.

Mazzini was deeply disappointed at the plot's failure, while Gallenga not only renounced his plan, but also abandoned any revolutionary activity, and broke all contacts with Young Italy and its leader. Probably ashamed of himself, he started wandering across Italy, North Africa, and eventually moved to America, apparently only engrossed in his own private welfare and in search of a position and a career. The incapacity to commit a political crime made him withdraw from politics altogether.

The unhappy ending of the 1833 affair had hardly left any resentment in Mazzini's mind, once he got over the initial disappointment. In 1835 on hearing that Gallenga was in Africa, he wrote to Melegari that he was sorry Antonio was so far away:

> Even if unfit for the enterprise he undertook, that young man is apt for other tasks and I should like him to be in France, or even in Italy.[1]

By then Mazzini had become aware of the sheer folly of their plot, and the improbability of its succeeding even if carried out. Another revolutionary attempt made in Piedmont shortly afterwards had also miserably failed: the expedition of Savoy, which took place at the beginning of 1834, when a band of Mazzinians crossed the border hoping to raise a revolt, but were immediately dispersed. The times were not ripe for actions of this sort.

When the two men accidentally met again in London, they were eager to renew their friendship. Gallenga was in desperate need of practical help, having just arrived from America almost penniless; as for Mazzini, it was typical of his warm and kind

---

[1] S.E.N., vol. 10, p. 318, Mazzini to L. A. Melegari, 28 Jan. 1835.

character to welcome his compatriots as friends. Love for their country was a deep bond for all exiles in those days, when repression inside Italy was still so violent. Mazzini introduced him to his circle of Italian and English friends, and it was at his house that Gallenga met Thomas Carlyle, Enrico Mayer, Lady Byron, and John Stuart Mill, and where he found work to enable him to earn his living during the first hard months of his stay in London.

Not only did Gallenga, alias Mariotti, enter into friendly relations with the Mazzinian circle, but he was also ready to support any of Mazzini's undertakings, such as *Il Comitato degli Esuli*, of which he was a member, and the Grenville School at Hatton Garden, where he taught occasionally. As previously mentioned, he wrote a rather moving tale in a good Dickensian style, *Morello*, in which Mazzini's school is mentioned and praised for its work. In 1844 and the following year, Gallenga attended the ceremonies for the anniversary of the school and spoke on each occasion. The first articles he published in English magazines were praised by Mazzini, who in a letter to his mother wrote:

> There is a young Italian here by the name of Gallenga who writes articles on Italian subjects for English reviews with good intent and enough talent. Recently he wrote one on Italian women who are too often spoken ill of here, which is patriotic and beautifully written, proving in short that Italian women are better than English and all other women. At the moment I wouldn't dare to assert it, but one day it will certainly be true, because we shall be better in everything than anyone else.[1]

Here Mazzini was reproaching Gallenga's excessive enthusiasm for his country, and yet sharing it in his belief that all Italians would eventually be better than anybody else. In 1844, when Mazzini's letters were being opened by the British government, thus violating the code of postal practice, Gallenga was at once at his side and wrote impassioned letters to the papers. Some of his interventions were so violent that Mazzini had to ask him to moderate his tone.

You praise the moderate tone of my letter on Lord Aberdeen's

[1] *S.E.N.*, vol. 20, p. 348, Mazzini to his mother, 22 Oct. 1841.

explanations; but you violate moderation far more easily than I. From the articles in *The Times* and the one in the *Herald* you should have gathered that *le mot est donné pour la réaction*, but woe to us if by a rash word we awake English self-esteem and make people turn against us.[1]

How justified Mazzini was in asking Gallenga to use more tact and diplomacy in his letters can be seen from one which appeared in *The Times* in February 1845.

Sir,

Would you oblige an ignorant foreigner by a correct definition of the word hospitality? You say in your paper of today—'We give these political fugitives security against their enemies' but you are aware that the same security is equally awarded to every pickpocket that runs away from a continental goal. It suits England as a commercial nation to open her harbours to the wanderers of all countries, and to do away with the inefficient and vexatious regulations of passports. Why is this wise and useful measure turned into a boon and favour to the political exile? Why is he expected therefore to abjure those principles for which he has sacrificed his own home? . . .

Sir James Graham would not dream of preventing Mr Mazzini from publishing his *Apostolato Popolare*, a copy of which would cost the life of any of his countrymen at home. Sir James Graham would not dream to shut [*sic*] Mazzini's school for the Italian boys, where, however, organ-grinders and image-sellers are taught the rights of man and hatred to Austria [*sic*]. Why, then, if the exiles enjoy the liberty of the press, the privilege of public assembly, and other rights common to every man that ever sets his foot on British shores, in spite of the Pope and Austria—why should not their letters be as sacred as those of the Lord Mayor himself? Oh, you say, they conspired against the security of the allies of England and the peace of Europe. If they do so, and if it be a crime to do so, are they not amenable to the British law? The Government proceeded against them on presumption; opened their letters, and never pretended to prove how far they were guilty.[2]

If we have quoted at length from Gallenga's letter, it is because it is interesting to note his attitude at that particular time, when

[1] Ibid., Appendix 3, p. 19, Mazzini to Mariotti, Mar. 1845.
[2] Letter to the Editor, *The Times*, p. 6, 24 Feb. 1845. I am indebted to W. J. Carlton for tracing this letter.

he was already well known in London literary circles and had made a reputation for himself. His backing of Mazzini was something more than the mere admiration of a disciple. In those years he gave his full and unconditional support to all Mazzini's activities, in spite of the fact that his political views were not always consistent with Young Italy and its doctrine. Gallenga's behaviour can be better understood when one bears in mind what he wrote to Piroli about Mazzini during the first war of independence.

I always thought and still think that he is the loftiest mind, the noblest heart of all who now live in Italy. I acknowledge in him that greatness of genius which without contention carries with itself minor minds. I realized that he alone watched for years in exile, while the whole of Italy was asleep, he alone fed the flame of Italian nationalism which was about to die out; and for a long time I was joined to him, with an inner conviction that I could not do anything better for the welfare of my country.[1]

It is because of the feelings here expressed that in 1846 we find Gallenga's signature as a secretary of Young Italy on a manifesto to the Swiss Government, and in 1847 we find his name, together with those of Mazzini, Giglioli, and Linton, on the *Proclama dell'Associazione Nazionale*. Up to then he was still Mazzini's follower, but he was already entertaining grave doubts about the value of Young Italy theories. Such doubts were quite well-known, so that as early as 1839, shortly after his return from America, Mazzini could say of Gallenga

his mind has developed intellectually, especially in the literary field, but he has waned politically. He doesn't speak of association or of anything else, but discusses the possibility that an Italian prince would free us, and similar utopias of positive men.[2]

As is also evident in 'Memoirs of an Italian Exile', a series of articles published in the *Metropolitan Magazine* between 1840 and 1842, Gallenga had begun to consider popular uprising as something childish and by no means the best way of uniting a country. In revolutions such as Italy had seen so far, too much was left to

[1] Gallenga to G. Piroli, May 1848, Raccolta Bertarelli, Museo del Risorgimento, Milan.

[2] *S.E.N.*, vol. 18, p. 125, letter to L. A. Melegari, 21 July 1839.

chance, and often warm-hearted patriots, who were ready to die in the heat of the moment, lacked the constancy to carry out a well-organized plan which, once they had got rid of foreign rule, would lead to a national government.

Gallenga also had little faith in the value of educating the masses as a means of bringing about a democratic government. The idea of a leader or of a leading state was gradually developing in his mind, though he was far from supporting Charles Albert.

My opinion is, that, as their universal hatred of Austria, and their fondness for the name of their country, are sufficient to unite the Italians under one common standard, it is the duty of everyone of us to follow that standard, by whatever man or party, and on behalf of whatever political principle, we may be called to join in.[1]

There is no doubt that he was already drifting away from Mazzini politically, and that what is considered his betrayal in 1848 was in fact an obvious consequence of such an idea. His support for some of Mazzini's undertakings sprang from the same source and not from a personal belief in his doctrine. He had, however, grown up in the atmosphere of Young Italy and owed most of his cultural background to it. Up to 1848 he was still under a strong Mazzinian influence where literary judgements and morals were concerned: one could almost say that in some of his critical evaluations of works of art he never departed from it, as can be seen in *Italy, Past and Present*.

In 1848, when the first war of independence broke out, Gallenga had been a rather weak Mazzinian for some years. When he was asked to review *Italy*, Mazzini asked for the freedom

de réfuter quelques erreurs qui son livre contient selon moi — si je pouvais dire sans crainte de mutilation ce que je pense être la vérité sur mon pays.[2]

Likewise, in 1847, when urged by Gallenga to lend his support to an uprising which had broken out in Messina, Mazzini felt the need to make sure of his friend's political belief, and asked him whether, if anything could be done, he was prepared to swear upon his honour that

[1] *Italy 1841*, vol. i, p. 378.
[2] *S.E.N.*, Appendix 2, p. 229, Mazzini to J. M. Kemble, Oct. 1841.

you will fight for our republican symbol and proclaim it, when necessary.[1]

His doubts about the adherence of Gallenga to the theories of Young Italy soon proved justified. In a short story which appeared in 1847, and which was later included in *Scenes from Italian Life*, Gallenga launched his first attack: the tale, entitled *Jacopo Ruffini*, relates in a highly dramatic tone the last moments of the young patriot who committed suicide for fear of betraying his friends. The death of Jacopo Ruffini was one of the bitterest sorrows of Mazzini's life. Years after the event had occurred, he is said to have called out his name in anguish, as if he was responsible for his friend's death. In Gallenga's story, the young enthusiastic Jacopo, confronted with imprisonment and death, goes through the awful ordeal of realizing that he is suffering for nothing. His sacrifice is useless, as his friends (Young Italy's friends) have abandoned him and betrayed the cause. He becomes aware of the pointlessness of underground plots and ends by killing himself in a moment of despair.

Jacopo Ruffini preserves much of the spirit of a romantic hero, a kind of Byronic figure reminiscent of *Jacopo Ortis*. The gravity of the attack on Mazzini is more moral than political. His name is not mentioned: the pessimistic conclusions Jacopo comes to about Young Italy are determined by what a police official tells him: only people fully acquainted with the Italian situation could be aware of the implications of Gallenga's story. Mazzini, of course, knew about it, for he wrote to Agostino Ruffini, Jacopo's brother,

Mariotti is the author of that piece on Jacopo you mentioned: it is a desecration.[2]

In the final edition of *Italy, Past and Present*, published in the following year, a whole chapter of the second volume is devoted to Mazzini and the National Association. Here the breach between the two men comes fully to light. Gallenga speaks of Mazzini as a man who combined 'the utmost stubbornness of the conviction and the fiercest intolerance of contradiction'. In the forties

---

[1] *S.E.N.*, Appendix 3, p. 343, Mazzini to Gallenga, Sept. 1847.
[2] Ibid., vol. 33, p. 320, Mazzini to A. Ruffini, London, Feb. 1848.

the principles of liberty and equality, unity and independence, on which the National Association was originally based, were no longer deemed realistic.

Although in the abstract, and in a general point of view, the emancipation of their country from foreign power is and ever was the object of all patriotic endeavours, though everyone felt that independence could only be secured by a bond of immediate, absolute unity, that a democratic form of government would be natural, and, as it were, indigenous in Italy . . . yet [they the Italians] did not all equally admit of the possibility of establishing a new republican state immediately on the basis of the present social edifice.[1]

The cold detachment with which he describes the unsuccessful revolts of Young Italy shows that he regarded them not only as risky but as a danger to the national cause. Only the blood of martyrs redeemed them. At this time he saw a far more concrete way of accelerating the process of unification in the various attempts made by the moderate parties which were forming in Italy. He was fully aware that war against Austria was inevitable, but underrated the importance of social problems which formed an essential part of Mazzini's doctrine. To Gallenga innovations in the political and economic fields could be introduced after the expulsion of foreign forces from Italian soil. The prominence of political factors over social considerations is a characteristic feature of the Risorgimento and of many similar revolutions. Men like Mazzini saw the great danger of supporting an established form of government which did not offer any guarantee of democracy and progress, for none of the Italian states provided an enlightened and satisfactory social structure. To put one of them at the head of the new nation was only changing from one form of oppression to another, and Mazzini remained faithful to the end to his ideal of *Dio e Popolo*.

When war broke out, Mazzini, Gallenga, and many other Italian exiles crossed the Channel on 28 March 1848. The time for action had come, and they were together again in spite of all their differences of opinion. They met other exiles in Paris, where the news had just come that Piedmont had joined the war and

[1] *Italy, P. and P.*, vol. ii, p. 24.

Charles Albert was leading the army. A new problem now faced Mazzini and his friends. They had left London on hearing that the Milanese had rebelled and were going to join the Lombards in the fight against the Austrians. Now the intervention of Piedmont brought a regular army into the war. Moreover, it was the only Italian state free from foreign interference and was bound to take the lead in the national movement. But could Charles Albert be trusted? Could the republican exiles accept a monarchy? Mazzini did not think so, but Gallenga disagreed. Now that war had been declared, he was no longer a politician, but a soldier, and his duty was to support the Italian army, no matter where it came from.

So they parted in Paris and never met again as friends, but only as political opponents. All through the war they put forward entirely different solutions to the Italian problem, their antagonism being clearly reflected in all their actions. Gallenga, who had in turn supported the *fusione* of the northern states with Piedmont and then Gioberti's idea of an Italian confederation, felt bitter towards Mazzini at the end of the war. In the leader of Young Italy he saw one of the main causes of the failure of the 1848-9 campaign. Mazzini was still extremely popular in Italy and his words carried great weight: the lack of unity among Italians, who were divided into royalists, federalists, and republicans—and the little support given to Charles Albert—could easily be imputed to him. Had he used his influence in favour of the Savoy dynasty, the defeat might not have been so complete: it might even have been avoided. In this vein Gallenga wrote 'Eighteen Months' Political Life in Italy', a long article in which Mazzini was spoken of with great respect as a man, but harshly criticized for his politics. His two attempts to establish a republican government in Florence and Rome were described as a proof of the failure of the democratic system. People who had never taken any part in public life, such as the Italians, could not suddenly become responsible citizens. Universal suffrage was useless, if not meaningless; the idea of an efficient people's government mere Utopian day-dreaming. What saved republicanism from shame and disgrace was the heroism with which the

Italians fought—the defence of Rome 'closed with brilliancy a revolution which would otherwise have left nothing behind but bitter remembrances'.[1] Mazzini saved himself from any further criticism only because he was faithful to his ideas and tried to put them into practice when the time came.

Gallenga now devoted himself completely to his new ideas, and tried to give the English public what he thought to be an impartial view of Italian problems. He was not indeed an unbiased judge, but there is no doubt that he did his best to revive English interest in Italian politics by pointing out actual difficulties. In *Italy in 1848* he made his views clear. He was by now a strong conservative and considered that the best form of government was an enlightened oligarchy. He felt deeply the necessity for an upper class to lead the state and provide stable guidance for the country. He had in mind something like the House of Lords and the British monarchy. He was aware that no such tradition existed in Italy, but for him history was there to prove that the lack of a monarchy had been the main reason for the wretched condition of Italy and her servitude to foreign power. He also tried to arouse general sympathy towards Piedmont, which was the only independent Italian state offering an ancient aristocratic rule. There was very little room, if any, for Mazzini's republic in his wide and thorough examination of the Italian situation after the defeat of Novara.

By the year 1850, Gallenga had earned the epithet of *tristo*[2] as appears from letters from Mazzini's supporters and critics, so that Gallenga had for a long time been considered as a kind of renegade and traitor. But a closer study of his writings proves that his change in attitude reflected a genuine development of his thought. His attacks on Mazzini were not of a personal kind, but the result of a disagreement with his doctrine. Though Gallenga did not possess the moral stature of Mazzini and was far more down-to-earth in his political beliefs, he was not an opportunist, and was prepared to face the consequences of his change of ideas, as can be seen at the time of the 1856 scandal, the best known episode in his life.

---

[1] 'Eighteen Months' Political Life in Italy', *New Month. Mag.*, vol. lxxxvii, no. 348, Dec. 1849, p. 408.　　　　　　　　　　　　　　[2] Wicked.

In his fervent campaign in support of Piedmont, which for him represented the sole hope of Italian emancipation, Gallenga decided to produce a work which would acquaint the English public with this small Italian state. With this object in mind, he wrote a *History of Piedmont*, which was first published in 1855 and translated into Italian the following year. It is a very extensive work covering the whole period of Piedmontese history from the beginning to Gallenga's own days. Contemporary events, including the 1848–9 war, and, in the Italian edition, the peace of Paris in March 1856, which marked the end of the Crimean war, are described in the last chapters of the book. Young Italy and Mazzini are, of course, mentioned. Among other criticisms, Gallenga condemns the recklessness of some of the activities of the National Association. To prove his point he quotes an episode from his own life, how in 1833 a young Italian, Luigi Mariotti, plotted with Mazzini against the life of Charles Albert. The episode is mentioned in both the English and the Italian versions, and although the author does not openly say that Mariotti and himself were the same person, the fact was well known. He always used the name of Mariotti until his marriage in 1847, and even afterwards he continued to use it as his *nom de plume*. When the book appeared in England, nobody seemed to pay any special attention to the episode, although Gallenga had been easily identified, as can be seen in a review of the book in the *Colburn's New Monthly Magazine* of December 1855, where the anonymous writer satirizes Gallenga's anti-Mazzinian feelings: 'But who was then the young fanatic Louis Mariotti?' But a fierce argument broke out as soon as the Italian edition was published in Turin. The attack which Gallenga launched against Mazzini's *matte congiure* brought blame and hostility on both of them. Gallenga's language itself had been sufficiently violent to rouse violent reactions, as we can see from the opening lines of his account of the plot against the king.

A young fanatic, weary of an exile's life, and nurtured in the classical ideas of Alfieri's patriotism, was with the chief of Young Italy, when Ruffini's mother, after the bloody catastrophe at Genoa, together with her family, sought refuge in Switzerland. Affected by that exhibition of acute sorrow, the would-be Brutus and Timoleon offered to avenge the desolate mother by taking the tyrant's life.[1]

L'Armonia, the organ of the catholic party in Piedmont, was one of the first papers to draw attention to the intended assassination. Don Margotti, the editor, seized the opportunity to prove not only how dangerous and extreme were the views held by the left-wing opposition, but also what kind of men belonged to the party in power, that is Cavour's. At the same time, on hearing of this new accusation, Mazzini, who was then in London, wrote an open letter to Federico Campanella who published it in *Italia e Popolo*, adding some harsh remarks on Gallenga's behaviour. In this letter Mazzini accused Gallenga of distorting the facts and concealing Mariotti's real identity, and he gave his own version of the episode. One of the main accusations that had been often levelled against Mazzini was of fostering murder and violence, and the abortive regicide of 1833 seemed to support it. However, the statute of Young Italy does not mention murder as a way of getting rid of tyranny, nor did Mazzini's theories encourage it. The idea of *God and People* is not basically individualistic, but collective, almost communist. Only the mysticism inherent in his belief could make Mazzini say

> He ended by convincing me that he was one of those creatures whose decisions lie between conscience and God, and whom Providence sends on earth from time to time to teach tyrants that the end of their power is in the hands of one sole man. And I asked him what he wanted from me.[2]

Moreover, anger and exasperation at Italy's conditions made them both hope that a badly-planned political murder might change the situation. Mazzini's letter was published in *Italia e Popolo* of 24 October 1856. In his answer to it, a few days later in *Il Risorgimento*, Gallenga stated that what Mazzini had written about the plot was true and that he himself was mainly responsible for it. A series of articles and letters then appeared in the Piedmontese newspapers condemning both Gallenga and Mazzini

---

[1] *History of Piedmont*, vol. iii, p. 338.
[2] *S.E.N.*, vol. 57, p. 143-4, to F. Campanella, 1856.

as promoters of political crime. Gallenga was accused of political vacillation, the regicide was dealt with as if it had actually taken place and soon the scandal developed to such proportions that on November 1 Gallenga had to resign his post in the Italian Parliament. The reaction against him was so violent that, just before retiring, he asked King Victor Emmanuel for a pardon, which was immediately granted, as is proved in a letter that Cavour wrote to him:

The King has received the letter which you sent him some days ago. His Majesty has asked me to inform you that, approving your feelings of repentance and devotion to the cause of our constitutional monarchy, which you expressed in it, and interpreting his noble father King Charles Albert's intentions, he forgets and forgives the events which force you to resign your seat in Parliament. In sending you this communication, I cannot help expressing my hope and desire that the future will offer you the opportunity of showing how sincere your repentance is, and how great is your love for the noble cause which the generous House of Savoy represents in Italy and Europe.[1]

It is quite obvious why the King forgave him so promptly: Charles Albert had not been blameless where political integrity and constancy were concerned. But if Victor Emmanuel was ready to take a sensible view of the matter, Cavour's party was not going to stand by Gallenga. They preferred to sacrifice him to public opinion rather than face a new struggle against their political opponents. Gallenga resigned under pressure from his own party. He was so worried about the unexpected development of the situation that he wrote to Panizzi asking him to defend him in England, when news of the scandal reached there. There was some reaction against him, but on the whole the scandal did not seriously injure his position. Instead the controversy lent support to Anglo-Italian opposition to Mazzini, which was spreading rapidly in the fifties.

If one looks closely at Gallenga's account of the 1833 plot and Mazzini's own account, one must admit that they both said the same things. They differed only about the reasons why the

[1] *Lettere edite ed inedite di Camillo Cavour*, ed. by L. Chiala, Turin, 1887, vol. vi, p. 46.

murder was not committed: Gallenga accused the members of
Young Italy in Turin of letting him down, while Mazzini imputed
the failure of their plot to him. Trying to clear himself of the
accusation of fomenting political crime, Mazzini stated that he
considered Charles Albert worthy of death, but that his death
would not save Italy, and went on to say that he pointed out all
the difficulties of the enterprise to Mariotti. But it is not easy to
understand why Gallenga should be accounted more guilty than
Mazzini, when the latter ended up not only by providing him
with a passport, but also by sending him a weapon. One must, of
course, bear in mind that they decided to kill Charles Albert after
one of the most unpopular episodes in the reign of the *esecrato
Carignano*.[1] Even now the 1833 trials remain one of the darkest
events in Piedmontese history. However, more than twenty
years later, because of changed political conditions, no one would
profit by publicly stressing the illiberal behaviour of the former
king. As a result all the blame was put on the two potential
murderers. The dispute with Gallenga is a further proof of the
increasing difficulties Mazzini was meeting and of his diminishing
popularity.

Gallenga was harshly criticized both by friends and opponents
for tactlessly revealing an almost unknown episode, or, as he
more poetically expressed it, for his *inconcussa fedeltà al vero*. Even
if the reasons for disclosing such a story were the result of his
antagonism to Mazzini rather than his 'devotion to truth', he
was right in bitterly stating that 'Newly born to a life of freedom,
we can easily soothe our conscience as long as we hope to cover
our actions in darkness'.[2] Many Italian politicians would have had
to admit a change in their political ideas, if they were to accept
publicly that from a potential regicide Gallenga could become
a strong and faithful supporter of monarchy. So many of the
men who formed the Cabinet and the Subalpine Parliament
had gone through a similar kind of experience, for they had
started their political career as militant Mazzinians and abandoned
Young Italy when facts proved that there was a quicker and

---

[1] Damned. Charles Albert was Prince of Carignano before becoming King
of Piedmont.   [2] Letter to the Editor, *Il Risorgimento*, 2 Nov. 1856.

easier way of uniting Italy by supporting Piedmont. Luigi Melegari, who sent Gallenga to Mazzini, provides a fair example. He
admitted knowing both Mazzini and Gallenga and having given
a letter of introduction to the latter, but strongly denied that he
had known anything about the plot. There can be no doubt that
he was aware of it: Mazzini's letters to him in 1833 are quite
clear on this point. When they were found in later years there
was evidence of erasures of whole passages, including the ones
mentioning Procida, alias Mariotti. The original text was restored
by means of a photographic process. Melegari went as far as
accusing *L'Armonia*—the organ of the catholic party—of libel and
won the case against the paper, because Gallenga and Mazzini did
not turn up to testify. As Gallenga sorrowfully stated, the time
for truth in Italian public life lay a long way ahead.

After 1856 the break between the two men was complete.
Gallenga continued to appear as a renegade and a traitor in the
writings of Mazzini and his supporters. He was also accused of
supporting an anti-Italian campaign when he was writing for
The Times in 1859, but in fact he was attacking Mazzini's politics
just as he had done earlier. The struggle between them was not of
a personal nature, in spite of the vehemence and violence which
informed some of their writings, for it reflected the battle of
ideas that had been going on since the French revolution all
over Europe, namely the development of conservatism and
liberalism, of right and left.

Shortly before his death, years after Mazzini himself had died,
Gallenga wrote:

I have always honoured that great man. I have found that he as an
Italian and Kossuth as a Hungarian were two great men enslaved by
an idea. For they were republicans and adverse to monarchy, they did
not believe it possible for the whole nation to be anything else, but
Mazzinian or Kossuthian.[1]

Now that the bitterness of their political differences was buried
in the past, he could look upon Mazzini as one of the greatest of
the Italians.

[1] P. Orsi, 'Antonio Gallenga', *Nuova Antologia*, vol. ccclx, p. 30, 1 Mar.
1932.

VI

LONDON 1849–1859

WHEN Gallenga made his way back to England in 1849, he hoped to be appointed *consigliere onorario di legazione* in London for the Piedmontese government, an honorary title which would have allowed him to maintain official links with Turin.

> I would need it as soon as I get back to London, so that I could get rid of my chair and my literary commitments and live only for politics and Italy.[1]

So he wrote to Michelangelo Castelli from Geneva in the summer, for he thought that such a title would give him a status enabling him to play an active role in favour of the Italian cause in England. The appointment did not come, and till 1854, when he was elected to the Subalpine Parliament, Gallenga continued his activities as a teacher and scholar, a career to which he returned after the 1856 scandal. His Chair of Italian at University College and his publications gave him a position of importance among the exiles, and it was this position rather than a recognition of his achievements during the 1848–9 campaign which brought him a visit from Cavour in 1852.

On his return to London, Gallenga found himself rejected by progressive groups in the capital with whom he had been associated in the forties because of his new political position, and only a few of his old friends remained faithful to him, Carlo Pepoli and Lady Morgan among them.

> Those English Liberals, whose love of Italy resolved itself into mere blind idolatry of Mazzini, put no limits to their abuse of what they called the 'Savoyard' or 'Royalist party'; and I have never forgotten the little scented note with which a gushing fashionable lady in Wilton Crescent intimated that 'She would never again be at home to any of

---

[1] L. Chiala, *Carteggio politico di Michelangelo Castelli*, Turin, 1890, vol. 1, p. 52, Gallenga to Castelli, 28 July 1849.

those apostates who had forsaken Mazzini'—little imagining that the reverse was the truth; that it was Mazzini who had deserted us.[1]

In the circumstances Gallenga drew closer to more conservative circles and his admission to the Athenaeum Club in 1853 can be looked upon as the official recognition of his new political leanings. His friendship with Vittorio Emanuele D'Azeglio, Massimo D'Azeglio's nephew and a Cavourian, then minister of Piedmont in London, who was his best man at his second marriage in 1858, dates from the early fifties. D'Azeglio's name also appears in the ballot held at the Athenaeum among those who voted in favour of Gallenga's admission. They also included Henry Crabb Robinson, the English journalist and diarist, who was a close friend of Gallenga's parents-in-law, the Schuncks, and for a while proved a good friend to him too. He was one of his referees when Gallenga applied for the Chair of Italian at University College, London, and it is in one of Henry's letters to his brother Thomas that we find a record of his hopes in 1848.

My old friend Prandi returns to Italy full of confidence that the Italian cause will triumph in spite of the counter-revolution in Naples. ... Gallenga, alias Mariotti, is returned, and he will stay in England, but he has also confidence—He is a convert to the party of Carl Albert the King of Sardinia who will probably be the King of Northern Italy— uniting Piedmont to the Lombard-Venetian State, Modena and Parma, —This will be a fine kingdom.[2]

It was mostly to Crabb Robinson that Gallenga owed his membership of the Athenaeum. In an autobiographical note at the foot of one of Gallenga's letters Crabb Robinson wrote in 1864:

I succeeded in getting Gallenga into the Athenaeum Club by great exertion and was made ashamed of my success afterwards by the development of his character. And yet he played an important part in the drama of his country. He was a man of great ability.[3]

[1] *Epis.*, vol. ii, pp. 226–7. The lady mentioned here is Arethusa Milner-Gibson who lived in Wilton Crescent.

[2] H. Crabb Robinson to Thomas, 2 June 1848, H.C.R. Correspondence, Dr. Williams' Library, London. Gallenga was then back in London because of his wife's illness.

[3] Ibid., Gallenga to Crabb Robinson, 4 Feb. 1850, footnote handwritten by Crabb Robinson, Aug. 1864.

No one can blame him for his judgement of the Italian writer, even less so when one reads Gallenga's letter to him on the subject of his assumed name Luigi Mariotti, the question of his real name having arisen at the time of his election to the Club.

My name—but I do not know which of my names. By the advice of Capt. Smyth, my seconder, I have requested the Committee to allow my real name to be substituted instead of the *nom de guerre* of Mariotti, which was first written down by mistake. . . . The real reasons of my first assumption of the name of Mariotti are simply these: in 1833 Mazzini wanted a messenger who would risk his neck by entering Piedmont to announce his forthcoming attack on Savoy: I offered for the tolerably venturous job, and as the name of Gallenga was already in the black list, I borrowed the passport of a good Swiss of the Canton Ticino, by name Luigi Mariotti.[1]

Crabb Robinson, a moderate in politics who viewed with sympathy the establishment of an Italian monarchy, was not likely to show much favour towards Mazzini, but even less towards one who had contemplated regicide. Nevertheless, there is no justification for Gallenga's lack of sincerity towards one of his referees who was also a close friend of the family: the long and untrue explanation given in this letter was proved false only three years later when his *History of Piedmont* appeared. Once he gained admission to the Club, Gallenga did not make himself very popular with it as can be deduced not only from Crabb Robinson's words, but also from his own account of it.

I cannot say I much valued the mere honour of belonging to a learned society; nor did I, at that time a quiet domestic character, frequently look in at the club. As members have to wait at least a score of years before they are balloted for, by far the greatest number consisted of twaddling and cackling fogies, whose bald pates, toothless gums, and rickety limbs sent a chill through my veins, and acted as an unpleasant reminder that I also had left the mid-career of life behind me. I met but few old friends, and made fewer new ones.[2]

[1] Ibid., Gallenga to Robinson, 11 Nov. 1852. This letter is wrongly dated 1853, for we know from the Athenaeum records that the ballot took place in February 1853.

[2] *Epis.*, vol. ii, p. 249.

Crabb Robinson was for a while one of the few friends whom Gallenga used to meet at the Club, but their relationship came to an end on the death of Juliet Schunck in 1855. Crabb Robinson's poor opinion of the Italian is not the only one on record. He was prepared to recognize in him a man of great ability sincerely committed to the cause of his country, but not equally reliable and sincere where his private life was concerned. The judgement passed on Gallenga by political opponents more than confirms his unpopularity: in 1858 Cavour wrote to Vittorio Emanuele D'Azeglio, who had been pestered by Antonio for an introduction to the English Court, just when rumours of the 1856 scandal reached London:

> Ne vous laissez pas attendrir par cet original. Il a été d'une incroyable indiscrétion.[1]

During the second war of Italian independence, when Gallenga was writing for *The Times*, Panizzi bitterly complained to Delane, then editor of the newspaper, about his violent criticism of Italy and the Italians. Although Delane defended him on this occasion and placed much confidence in him, and was indeed always his good friend, he was nevertheless aware of his eccentricities and difficult temperament. When in 1870 plans were made to send him to Paris on a mission as foreign correspondent for the London paper, Delane remarked that Gallenga would manage to quarrel with everybody in less than a month. He knew his man well: disillusion and disappointment in mankind and in himself had made Gallenga more and more difficult to deal with. From the early fifties dates that process of increasing isolation which in later years made him the lonely survivor of a lost age.

While trying to consolidate his social position, Gallenga was adding to his reputation as a writer. An article on Tasso which was a long review of Milman's *Life of Tasso*, a biography of the poet which had recently appeared, was the last thing he wrote on a literary subject, although his interest in literature remained till the end of his life. He also helped his friend Mayer to collect

---

[1] *Cavour e l'Inghilterra*, Bologna 1933, vol. ii, p. 196.

Foscolian manuscripts for Orlandini's edition of the poet. Rather amusing, to say the least, after all his fierce attacks on Young Italy and its leader, is what he wrote to his friend who had asked for assistance from both him and Mazzini.

> I am ready to help you. Send me all information you think useful and I shall set to work with all my zeal. Unluckily, and I don't know why, Mazzini does not want to see me and does not answer, when I write to him. Therefore I don't know what he's doing, whether he is engaged in some work, and we cannot work together. I don't know what evil spirit has so ill-disposed him towards me.[1]

Gallenga did his best to help Mayer: he employed a certain Cesare Agostini, an exile, as translator of some of Foscolo's English articles, printed an advertisement in *The Athenaeum*, contacted people who had known the poet, and succeeded in tracing letters by Foscolo. In 1851 in connection with his teaching at University College, Gallenga published his most popular and financially successful book, *A Grammar of the Italian Language,* which in a few years ran into several editions. It was followed by *A First Italian Reader* in 1852, and eventually a *Key to Mariotti's Grammar.* There is no doubt that Gallenga's literary activity declined after 1848, for his article on Tasso is nothing more than a biographical report, and one could hardly call his Italian text-books or his searching for Foscolo's papers literary works. His scholarship now developed in a different direction and his two major books which appeared in these years were of an historical character: *Fra Dolcino* and *History of Piedmont,* published respectively in 1853 and 1855.

An Historical Memoir of Fra Dolcino and His Times was the last book published by Gallenga under the name of Luigi Mariotti. It is the story of the heretical movement of the order of the Apostles, a dissenting Franciscan sect of the thirteenth century, led by Fra Dolcino. After a period of tolerance, the Pope launched a crusade against them: the heretics took refuge in the Alps above Vercelli, where they fought for two years against the papal army and managed to survive by ransacking nearby villages. The

---

[1] A. Linaker, *La vita e i tempi di Enrico Mayer*, Florence, 1898, vol. ii, p. 121.

movement, which had started as a peaceful reform, resorted to
violence till at last they were defeated, and most of the survivors
put to death with atrocious tortures, in 1307. The episode is
quoted by Dante in Canto XXVIII of the *Inferno*, and is one of
the many instances of rebellion against the rule and corruption of
the Church of Rome in the Middle Ages. Gallenga treated the
subject fully, firstly introducing a brief survey of heresy within
the Catholic Church from its earliest days, then dealing in greater
detail with those heretical movements which immediately preceded that of Fra Dolcino, such as the *Patarini*. After an ample and
exhaustive introduction, Gallenga portrays Dolcino and his followers from the early days of peaceful propaganda, moving from
place to place, throughout Northern Italy, until they attracted
the attention of the militant Church, and were forced to change
from men of peace into warriors. The book closes dramatically
with the defeat of the Apostles, and the tragic death of Dolcino
and his beloved Margaret of Trent, the woman who followed
him and his preaching and shared his fate. In dealing with a subject of this kind Gallenga leaves little to the imagination: he is
faithful to the historical evidence then available, and does not
turn the story of Dolcino and Margaret into a romance. *Fra
Dolcino* presents a unity of conception and a clarity of expression
which contrasts with many of his books. It is an historical work,
portraying not only facts, but also men and their drama. The story
of the beautiful Margaret and Dolcino had all the attraction of a
romance, and yet it never departs from historical truth. At the
same time information is never so arid or so abundant as to
impede the development of the narrative. Any inaccuracy or
occasional mistakes result from a lack of historical documents and
should not be imputed to Gallenga. The subject appealed to him
for several reasons: it belonged to the time of Dante, the period
of Italian history which he considered the greatest epoch of
Italian liberty. Heresy against the Church of Rome was for him
a sign of free thought and independence of mind. Moreover,
it was an early manifestation of a dissenting and protestant spirit
in Italy, a subject which had been dear to Gallenga from the days
of his article on Catholicism written while in America. In addi-

tion, the story of Dolcino and Margaret possessed an inherent interest and charm. In writing it Gallenga attempted, not unsuccessfully, to achieve 'the poetical beauty to which history is entitled to aspire' and which 'must be derived from intrinsic, not from adventitious sources'; which 'must have all the chasteness, the accuracy, and high finish of sculpture, in order to possess all its majesty and sublimity—its endless durability'.[1]

Gallenga's dramatic talent is seen in the following passage, where the hero, musing silently, after a victory over the papist army, is well aware that, in spite of his apparent success, the end is near, for his refuge in the Upper Valsesia could be nothing but a trap for him and his followers.

Dolcino, thus victorious on the summit of Mount Zibello, and on six other mountain-tops equally bristling with its citadels, lorded it over a desert. His present camp was vast, but hopelessly barren and waste. All round, south and east, the Bishop guarded every outlet, and interrupted all communication: on the west were mountains, ridge behind ridge, inhabited by all the terrors of a severe winter, and infinitely more formidable at that period than the high spirit and perseverance of modern curiosity has rendered them since. On the north, again, mountains, and beyond them the district of Varallo, such as it had been left after the unsparing devastations of the previous year. Further on again mountains and on the other side other valleys —those of Ossola on the north, and of Gressoney and Aosta on the west, where, had there been the slightest possibility of cutting one's way to them, the Apostles would have found the peasantry all in arms, fanaticised by their priests, sworn to their destruction.

Fra Dolcino, like a lion in the pit the hunter has dug for him, paced up and down that desolate valley of Trivero.[2]

The book also gains dramatic impact from frequent allusions to contemporary events, which make it more moving.

Heresy, at any rate, stands on no better foundations than sorcery: it was at the same stake that a multitude of crazy old women were consumed by slow fire, convicted 'upon their own confession' of flying through the air on a broom-stick. . . . Nor was it merely the terrible ordeal of bodily tortures that wrenched such avowals. Even in

---

[1] *Italy, P. and P.*, vol. ii, p. 123.   [2] *Fra Dolcino*, pp. 265–6.

more enlightened ages, in countries boasting of the abolition of the
rack, what fabric of guilt is it not in the power of the State-Inquisitor
to build up? At Venice or Milan, even at the present day, the ruler
has only to say 'Let there be a plot', and the mere moral torture of
harass and worry will hatch one for him on the shortest notice.[1]

Thus Gallenga wrote making a clear allusion to the martyrs of
the Spielberg, and to Austrian rule in the Lombard-Venetian
state. He was committed to the romantic view of the Middle
Ages, which saw in their freedom of thought and action a forerunner of nineteenth-century patriotism and liberty. Such an
interpretation adds to rather than detracts from the book, where
some aspects of the heretical movements of the thirteenth and
fourteenth centuries are acutely portrayed. The affinities between
the Franciscan orders and the Apostles—the anti-papal movement,
which inevitably took on a political hue identifying itself with
the Ghibelline party—the wait for the coming of a Saviour who
would rescue Italy from its present miseries, are all thrown into
relief. In his prophecies Fra Dolcino identified the Saviour with
Frederick II of Sicily, while Dante spoke of the *Veltro* and the
DVX.

Gallenga had put a lot of study and work into the writing of
Fra Dolcino, so that when it was published he felt utterly dissatisfied with the little success it obtained.

I relied on the interests of a Protestant community for its success;
but the book fell flat nevertheless. The press had hardly anything to
say in its praise or blame. The publishers dropped it at once as if it had
burnt their hands; and up to this day it is the most neglected and
utterly forgotten of all my poor productions.[2]

In spite of its unpopularity, *Fra Dolcino* did not go unmentioned
among people of culture. Charles Kingsley quoted it in *Two
Years Ago*, when the hero of the novel, reading it, felt inspired to
write a poem about

that sad and fantastic tragedy of Fra Dolcino and Margaret, which
signor Mariotti has lately given to the English public, in a book which,
both for its matter and its manner, should be better known than it is.[3]

[1] *Fra Dolcino*, p. 112.   [2] *Epis.*, vol. ii, p. 229.
[3] C. Kingsley, *Two Years Ago*, Cambridge, 1857, vol. i, p. 257.

It was also mentioned by Gerard Manley Hopkins who, in a note to his *Journal* of 2 May 1866, wrote that he thought all day of the terrible tragedy of Fra Dolcino.[1] Kingsley and Hopkins were both moved by the dramatic impact of the story, while justice to its historical qualities has been done recently by an Italian historian Anagnine, who in his study of the heretical movements of the fourteenth century, describes Gallenga's book as a 'noble, serene, and unbiased work'.[2]

The unity of conception and clarity of exposition which makes *Fra Dolcino* an artistically valid creation, is lacking in Gallenga's next history, the *History of Piedmont,* which caused him such great distress. The aim of the work was to study

the causes which led to the formation of the State of Piedmont and gave it stability; to bring the whole Past to bear on the whole Present; to inquire how far the long-continued success and advancement of that country has been owing to the mere advantages of geographical position, and to what extent it may also be ascribed to the peculiar genius of its Princes and the rare temper of its People.[3]

Ideally, therefore, the *History of Piedmont* is governed by the same principles of progress and development which governed *Italy, Past and Present.* Moreover, the book, which had been accused by the Mazzinians of being a eulogy of the House of Savoy, is in fact a eulogy of Piedmont and the Piedmontese.

The Princes of Savoy had, for the last three centuries, drilled a whole people into an army. The events of 1848 suddenly dignified that army into a people. The strictness and firmness of previous organization enabled the Piedmontese to be safely trusted with the two-edged tools of self-government. A constitution has been awarded to them, an ill-digested, ill-fitting patchwork of outlandish charters, but which, nevertheless, sanctions personal security and unbounded freedom of inquiry—the very substance of liberty all the world over.[4]

The book had two slightly differing editions: the English one

[1] *The Journals and Papers of Gerard Manley Hopkins,* ed. by H. House and G. Storey, London, 1959, p. 133. I am indebted to Mr. Storey for tracing this reference.

[2] E. Anagnine, *Dolcino e il movimento ereticale all'inizio del Trecento,* Florence, 1964, p. 1.

[3] *History of Piedmont,* vol. i, p. v.   [4] Ibid., vol. i, p. vi.

which was written before the Crimean war, and the Italian
edition which appeared in Turin in 1856 and covers events up to
the peace of Paris signed on 30 March 1856. The English edition
is divided into three volumes: the first, from pre-Roman times
till the year 1000; the second, from the year 1000 to the year 1559,
the date of the peace of Cateau-Cambrésis; the third from 1559
till the present day. The first two volumes are rich in information:
the descriptions of the dynastic successions in the House of Savoy,
and its relations with other reigning families of Europe are far too
detailed, and the material offered resembles the compilation of
a chronicle, and not that of a history. Gallenga himself was aware
of the major fault of his work and in the Italian version he tried
to obviate such mistakes: he condensed his material, and up to a
point succeeded in making the book more coherent. This edition
is slightly shorter than its English counterpart, in spite of the fact
that it covers a longer period. It is in two volumes, the first
covering the period from the origins to the middle of the fifteenth
century, while the second goes as far as Gallenga's own days. But
these alterations are more apparent than real, and the structure
remained the same. The attempt to present as one the history of
a region and of a dynasty, the destinies of which coincided only
after 1559, fails to produce an organic piece of work. Gallenga
knew that the history of Piedmont proper started only in the
sixteenth century, but was unable to reconstruct the events which
came before in a perspective that could satisfactorily portray the
history of a region which was not yet a national unity. For
reasons which were extrinsic to the book itself, the *History of Piedmont* enjoyed a great renown for a short time. Its real merits have
been assessed recently by an Italian historian, Aldo Garosci, who
remarked that this is the only history of Piedmont ever written,
for Gallenga was the first to consider the problem of the formation of the state. He studied how it was created, and how it grew
through the centuries, preserving its national characteristics, in
spite of foreign influences which affected the whole of Italy.
Gallenga compared Piedmont to other Italian States and explored
its relationships with the rest of Europe. In short, he went beyond
the boundaries of provincial history, and this places him above

other Piedmontese scholars, such as Cibrario and Provana, who remained prisoners of their parochial borders. This conception of history transcending national barriers—which was a basic idea in *Italy, Past and Present*—deserves no small merit and makes the reader wish that the author had made a better selection of the material available and had achieved a greater clarity of exposition, for his best passages are those giving an overall view of the period in all its complexity, whereas when going into detail he loses himself in trivialities. For instance, his advocating the continuity of one independent state south of the Alps at a time when all the other states in Italy had fallen under foreign rule is well expounded and at the same time convincingly presents the case for Piedmont as a state.

Republican times had done not a little in Italy towards producing that dead level upon which absolutism can best build its edifice. The Piedmontese were, of all people in Italy, the one amongst whom intensity of public life was most rapidly abating; on which, therefore, a new social order might be most easily established. It was neither the first nor the second generation of tyrants that could sit easy on the throne of Milan, Florence, or Parma; nor could the throne itself have been reared, in many instances, without the overwhelming interference of a foreign force. Everywhere in Italy there was long chafing and struggling. Every untoward event—the death of a prince, the march of a hostile army—was hailed as the signal of revolt. Even when rebellion was quenched, conspiracy would still be at work. Reft of his sword, the Italian had still his dagger,—a desperate, but by no means contemptible weapon, as Visconti and Sforza, Medici and Farnese, could attest. The Italian protested to the last,—he is still protesting. . . . But in the West, how striking the difference! Piedmont acquiesced in her new destinies, at once and for ever.

She accepted the Princes of Savoy as her native, legitimate rulers.

She was passively obedient to them in ordinary times,—heroically loyal in days of adversity.[1]

Gallenga was aware that such fidelity was not always a sign of the enlightened rule of the House of Savoy. Besides, the princes of Savoy never really felt Italian, not at least till the nineteenth

[1] *History of Piedmont*, vol. ii, pp. 244–5.

century, and even then only with the coming of Victor Emmanuel II in 1849. Only recently, therefore, Piedmont itself began to feel Italian, but now things were moving rapidly.

There are great facts, slowly and silently ripening in the womb of fate, with utter unconsciousness of the men that are mainly instrumental in their consummation. The race of Humbert only aimed at the increment of the State of Savoy; the result was the formation of the people of Piedmont. That people has, for the last seven years, been redeeming the Italian character, giving the lie to the ungenerous men who cried down a whole nation as hopelessly sunk and degenerate.

Piedmont is rehabilitating Italy, achieving a moral conquest a thousand times more glorious than any armed subjugation. Friends and foes will be equally convinced that either all Italy is to be raised to the level of Piedmont, or men must despair of God's justice upon earth.

In his bold, confident youth, an Italian patriot may have rejoiced in the firm belief that his age was destined to witness the rearing up of the whole edifice of Italian nationality. He must now be thankful to Heaven, if, dying, he can carry with him the conviction that the first stone—the corner-stone—is at least laid.

Italy may yet be a dream—but Piedmont is a reality.[1]

The turning of Piedmont into the 'corner-stone' of Italy implied the end of its existence as an independent state. In writing its history, Gallenga was conscious that these were the last days of Piedmont. His final pages, which cover the years between the creation of Young Italy and the establishment in Turin of a Parliament that was essentially Italian, and no longer regional, deal with political events which belong to Italian and not solely to Piedmontese life. Here Gallenga is no longer the historian, but the party man. The final chapters of the book are heavily biased, but they remain the liveliest of the whole work since in them we find echoed Gallenga's political passions: his love–hatred relationship with Mazzini, his now hostile judgement of Pius IX, and his lukewarm admiration for Cavour and the new King.

When the book was first published in England, it attracted

---

[1] *History of Piedmont*, vol. iii, pp. 451–2.

some interest. As the *Daily News* reviewer pointed out, it appeared at a propitious time, that is to say at the end of the war in the Crimea and on the eve of Victor Emmanuel's state visit to London in 1855. Another anonymous reviewer wrote:

King Victor Emmanuel II is daily expected on a visit to this country. An enthusiastic greeting is due to the prince, who, circumstanced as he has been, has not only defied Austrian insolence on the one hand, and Mazzini and his conspirators on the other, but has thrown down the gauntlet to the Pope; and while establishing constitutional liberty in his country, has at the same time rid it of the pious vermin with which it has been so long infested, and swept away the lazy herd of monks and friars.[1]

English interest in Italy had then been renewed by recent events. It was, however, mainly confined to contemporary Italy, which thus explains why both reviewers concentrated on the modern section of the history.

A year before *History of Piedmont* made its appearance, Gallenga published his memoirs of the 1831 uprising in Parma. They had already formed the subject of a series of articles in 1840, but he had not been satisfied with the initial rendering of the story and greatly elaborated it. *Castellamonte* is an autobiography of his early life and experiences, and together with the second volume of *Italy, Past and Present*, and some chapters from the *History of Piedmont*, it completes his picture of Italian life before 1848. Written in the first person, it opens with a recollection of school and University life in Parma, under Marie Louise: the episode of Melloni, the imprisonment at Compiano of Gallenga and his fellow-students, their subsequent liberation, the abduction of the bishop of Guastalla, the skirmish at Fiorenzuola, and the fall of Parma and Gallenga's flight from his native town. In short, it deals with all the events which preceded his banishment from Parma.

Castellamonte is a romanticized autobiography, and names of people and some facts have been altered, so that it is difficult at

[1] 'Review of *History of Piedmont*', *New Month. Mag.*, Dec. 1855, vol. cv, no. 420, p. 488. See also the *Daily News*, 6 Dec. 1855, p. 2.

times to distinguish between invention and reality: the book stands midway between history and fiction. Uberto di Castellamonte is the name chosen for the hero, a young man in his early twenties, still a student at Parma University. He is imbued with romantic ideas, ready to love and hate, impetuous and rash in his decisions. He is, of course, a replica of young Gallenga himself, or at least of what Gallenga thought he was in his youth. Events related are those which befell him, but whereas in real life he played a secondary role in the uprising, in his fictional transformation all events now naturally move around Castellamonte, who becomes the national hero of Parma. Castellamonte is the man who brings back to Parma the news of the defeat of Fiorenzuola, and he also incites the citizens of Parma to fight against Austria. There is an aura of grandeur and heroism about him, rendered by Gallenga's highly rhetorical style which gives impact to the situation, as for instance in the passage relating Castellamonte's haranguing of the Parmesans after the defeat.

There was an appalling silence, as I was hurried upstairs, and almost thrust upon that stage of popular oratory. Wide as the market-place is, its mighty area was all swarming with human heads. I looked down: more than ten thousands faces were turned upwards. I gazed far and wide upon that ocean of heads. . . .

'Countrymen', I began.

'Speak louder! speak out!' cried the sovereign populace.

'By God!', I muttered, 'I am not going to strain my lungs for your sake.'

'Countrymen', I repeated. . . . 'The Austrians have violated the non-intervention'.

A universal cry of astonishment.

'They have fallen upon us by night, like craven wolves; they have killed several of us, and taken the rest'.

A general shout of horror and indignation.

'A few of us have carved out our way by the might of the sword'.

'Hurrah!'

'Others have fought like men to the last. All is lost but our honour'.

'*Viva l'Italia!*'

'Countrymen! The Austrians are coming down upon us. Be men; be worthy of your name. If you are Italians, to arms! Avenge your brothers or share their fate. He dies well who dies for his country. To arms! Italians, to arms!'

As I said this, a genuine fit of enthusiasm raised me to my loftiest level. I grasped the hilt of my heavy sword, and unsheathing it, I waved it, like a maniac above the dazzled multitude.[1]

But after the defence is organized, and the night-watch begins, doubts arise in our hero's mind: when he discovers that the civic guards are asleep at the moment the Austrians are approaching Parma, he gives up all hope of defence and throws the key of the city to one of the populace. The town gates open to its invaders, and Parma surrenders without a fight. While the defence of the city is being organized in a crescendo of anxiety and uncertainty, portrayed in an elated style, the anti-climax of his decision to let the Austrians march into the city has a strongly satirical flavour. This mock irony pervades the whole of the book: from the exalted descriptions of noble deeds, from the high praise of patriotism, rebellion, and self-sacrifice one is suddenly brought face to face with everyday reality, which will not, of course, allow a practically unarmed city to fight against a regular army. However unreal the figure of Castellamonte is, Gallenga uses it quite subtly to portray a generation politically immature which was slowly awakening to a patriotic conscience. Castellamonte, alias young Gallenga, the scion of a middle-class milieu, saw the poetry of war in a horse and a sword, but did not realize its tragic reality. The spirit which pervades *Castellamonte* is a gently ironical reconsideration of youthful enterprises remembered twenty years later. Gallenga has a double attitude towards his hero, since he still admires Castellamonte's enthusiasm and easy heroism; at the same time he cannot help condemning the thoughtlessness of many of his actions. As he pointed out, it was as natural for him to be a hero at nineteen, as it was for him at forty to laugh at his own heroics. This double attitude towards the protagonist of the book is also reflected in the writer's evaluation of the early Risorgimento. For him the uprisings of 1820 and 1831 were heroic but ill-founded actions: the men who took part in them were great in their aspirations, noble in their intentions, but lacked

[1] *Castellamonte*, vol. ii, pp. 102–4.

an adequate social and civic conscience. Gallenga cannot help admiring them and yet laughing at them. This can be seen in the portrayal he left of some of the members of the provisional government and of the military characters who led the army of the little Duchy. Captain Melli is a good example: a Carbonaro at heart, but serving in Marie Louise's army, and in charge of the arrest of Castellamonte, after the students' rebellion against the removal of Professor Melloni from Parma University.

As I walked upstairs to find myself in the presence of Captain Melli . . . human heart could not have been readier for a death-struggle than mine was.

'Suffer me to ask you, Captain Melli', I commenced, in a tone of awful solemnity, raising myself to my full height, and disdainfully throwing my head backwards, 'to ask what offence I am charged with, or on what ground I have been violently summoned from my father's roof and brought before you?'

Captain Melli had a handsome, benevolent, dignified countenance. The military fierceness of his youth, if he ever had any, had in maturer years melted into the tenderness of domestic affections. There was a serene cheerfulness, a cordial affability in his manners, which strangely unfitted him for the stern duties of his office—an office to which he clung merely in consideration of his numerous family.

He had risen from his chair as I entered, and listened to my heroic *tirade*, merely waving his open hand downwards, as if endeavouring to allay the billows of a stormy ocean.

'I am a gendarme, and not a magistrate' he said at last, 'Your arrest has been effected in obedience to orders from on high'. He was quiet for a minute, and then added, slyly, 'and it was no fault of ours if you insisted on being *at home* to unwelcome visitors'.

I was little prepared for such words, and less for the fine significant smile that accompanied them; a smile that was afterwards clearly explained.

'We fully intended and expected', he continued, 'to find the nest cold and the bird flown . . .'

It was even so. Captain Melli was in the secret of the Carbonari and the warning which had reached me from various quarters, came originally from him.

I dare say I looked supremely silly; yet I made an effort and fell back on my former high-tragedy tone.

'Had I guessed' I said, very loftily, 'that you wished me to escape, that was an additional reason for me to stay'.

'I cannot say that I wish you joy of your intrepidity', the captain replied. 'In this country, and in such a case, you will find discretion invariably the best part of valour.'[1]

Marie Louise's paternalistic rule was not looking for victims who might become martyrs in the eyes of the people, and so tolerated men like Melli in her service. As can be seen from the previous scene, the tragic-comic elements of the situation are rendered in a highly satirical tone and, after giving the young man such wise advice, the captain and his prisoner sat down together for about two hours drinking coffee and talking about politics. To create such an atmosphere Gallenga makes ample use of rhetoric, interrupted by flippant and at times gruesome remarks. The result is often genuinely comic, as, for instance, in this description of one of the few and unsuccessful skirmishes of the Parmesans with the Austrian soldiers.

I bit my nether lip and set my teeth hard; and brandishing my sword with frantic rage, till the weapon quivered in my grasp, I aimed at the Croatian a blow. . . . My ponderous *Oderisi* fell with all its weight upon something that rang under the stroke. What, however, the result of the stroke was, I never had the means to ascertain; for, dragged by my valiant comrade, in much less than two seconds I found myself clear of the astonished enemy, and fairly out of the *mêlée*.

The Austrians, thus flurried of a sudden, were not, however, slow in recovering from their panic. They rallied; they closed their ranks after us; they drove back with their bayonets our less fortunate companions; and some of them turning abruptly, sent volley after volley in our direction, which had the effect of adding wings to our flight.

On we rode for our lives, without ever looking back, till we were fairly out of reach of their shot. The moment we halted, my poor charger gave one more desperate plunge and fell, head foremost, never to rise—the Croatian had buried his bayonet in his breast.

'My poor grey!', cried I, as I jumped to my feet, with the assistance of my friends. But I added with sorry pride: 'I hope my hand has avenged his fate!'

So saying, I lifted up my sabre.

[1] *Castellamonte*, vol. i, pp. 136–8.

Oh! the portentous thickness of an Austrian's skull. The brave ancient blade on which I had put such implicit reliance—which I had selected as the best in a hundred,—had snapped in twain.[1]

The main theme, of the book is, of course, the revolution at Parma. But there is also a second theme, Castellamonte's love for Sibilla, the beautiful, married, and much older Sibilla Sormani, too virtuous to yield to his passion. Following the fashion of the day, Gallenga deemed it necessary to introduce a love theme into the story, but he never was a good creator of fiction and the hero's love affair remains artificial and unreal. He had already tried his hand at fiction in two collections of short stories, *The Blackgown Papers* and *Scenes from Italian Life*, the only interest of which lies in the occasional remarks which supply evidence of Gallenga's own life or of Italian life in his day. Much later he was to produce two more novels, *Jenny Jennet, a Tale without a Murder*, published in 1886, and *Thecla's Vow*, which appeared posthumously in 1898. Both of them give evidence of his absolute lack of any talent as a novelist. *Jenny Jennet*, however, deserves to be remembered because of its famous reviewer, Oscar Wilde, who wittily remarked:

Mr. Gallenga has written, as he says, 'a tale without a murder,' but having put a pistol ball through his hero's chest and left him alive and hearty notwithstanding, he cannot be said to have produced a tale without a miracle.[2]

As soon as Gallenga departs from real experience he fails to achieve any result whatsoever. The following short extract from what should be a love scene between Castellamonte and Sibilla well proves the point.

'If I were to lay at your feet the sword of the successful champion of Italy—or if my name were not ingloriously in the list of the pro-scription—speak, what should I then be in the eyes of Sibilla Sormani?'
'In my eyes', she said hastily, rather answering looks than words. 'You, in my eyes?—Uberto di Castellamonte, once more beware of

[1] *Castellamonte*, vol. ii, p. 56–7.
[2] H. Pearson, *The Life of Oscar Wilde*, London, 1946, p. 123.

self. What? you are dealing in virtues, and claiming rewards? You tread in the path of honour, and would stoop to gather flowers? Oh! That I were indeed something to you! That I had it in my power to influence your course, and impress you with a sense of duty!'

The rebuke was not lost upon me. It scared my fancy out of some luxurious images on which it dwelt too dangerously; it sobered me at once. I cast down my eyes as if with a consciousness of guilt; and when I once more looked upon to address her, I felt that she was again for me the sacred unapproachable idol.

'You are a stern mentor, lady', I said.[1]

Here are all the ingredients of the cheap novelette, mitigated by a *stern* moralism which turns the heroine into a *mentor*. This could be interpreted as a satire on romance, in the same way as Gallenga was satirizing himself and the people of Parma, but the sections dealing with his love affair are lengthy and deprived of any ironical remarks, which so frequently occur in other parts of the book. Gallenga's own experiences provide the best parts of the novel. He also has a spontaneous feeling for the beauty of nature, and his descriptions of Parmesan countryside are usually neat, orderly, and serene, and provide a lovely and peaceful background to the action of the book. Even today *Castellamonte* preserves a freshness of feeling and a sprightliness of expression which make it readable and interesting to a modern reader. What mars the work—apart from points already mentioned— is the occasional clumsiness of Gallenga's English style.

When it was first published it met with devastatingly severe criticism in English reviews. '*Castellamonte* is one of the most discreditable specimens of book-making which has ever come under our notice' wrote an anonymous critic in the *Edinburgh Review*, while reviewing Ruffini's *Lorenzo Benoni* and Gallenga's work.

Though [the writer] had little to say—and that little was not worth saying, and it is not particularly well said—he has contrived, by trivial personalities, by tedious verbiage, by irrelevant episodes, by tawdry declamation, to spin it out into two worthless, wearisome, and dis- appointing volumes. How much of pure fiction, and how much of

---

[1] *Castellamonte*, vol. i, pp. 22–3.

romantic exaggeration he has allowed himself to mingle with the sub-stratum of facts, we have no means of detecting. . . . The only thing of moment—and this is conveyed faithfully enough—is the picture of mingled frivolity, imbecility, and cowardice,—of victory by accident, of resistance without purpose, of surrender without a struggle—which has been displayed time after time by nearly all the political movements in that unfortunate country.[1]

The critic failed to capture the satirical element contained in *Castellamonte*, an element which Gallenga introduced and de-veloped intentionally. In his memoirs he caught the ludicrous, almost comic aspect of an exaggeratedly romantic interpretation of life. *Jacopo Ortis* could not seriously be written again in the middle of the century. The refusal of the English and the Italian public to accept *Castellamonte* was based on moral grounds, that is to say on the difficulty of accepting satire as an alternative to the dramatic and emotional character in Pellico's and Mazzini's writings. There was an accepted way of writing about the Risor-gimento, which included D'Azeglio's witty complaisance, or Abba's earnestness, but which hardly allowed any room for comedy. There were, of course, some exceptions to this: for instance, Bini's *Manoscritto di un prigioniero*, written earlier by an ardent Mazzinian, or later some pages from *Il buco nel muro* by Guerrazzi. Bini, Gallenga, and Guerrazzi were not in any way making fun of the principle behind the Risorgimento. They satirized people and circumstances, but did not undermine the sanctity of the national cause. Patriotism and nationalism were very close to them, for they all played an active part in the Risorgimento. Satire was a way of pointing towards a more realistic approach to the situation, mitigating the inevitable excesses of an exalted enthusiasm. Even the *Edinburgh Review*, so fierce against Gallenga, recognized that the author was faithful to reality—or at least to some reality—in portraying the Parma society of 1831, but considered this faithfulness of little moment when compared to the grave, manly tone of *Lorenzo Benoni*, and to its 'elegance and idiomatic accuracy of style'. While there is

[1] '*Lorenzo Benoni* and *Castellamonte*', *Edinburgh Review*, Apr. 1854, vol. xcix, no. 202, p. 557.

no doubt that Ruffini's style was more polished and elegant than Gallenga's, one wonders how far apart the two writers really were, portraying as they did two facets of the same phenomenon and prompted by the same intense love of country felt in an entirely different way. The adverse criticism of Gallenga in the *Edinburgh Review* indicates one of the reasons why his writings fell into almost complete oblivion at the turn of the century, oblivion which may cause surprise if one compares it to the longer popularity enjoyed by the mediocre novels by Ruffini. Gallenga's interpretation and portrayal of the Risorgimento was not often pleasing to current standards of public opinion. If the reviewer of *Castellamonte* is representative of English public opinion, the writers of articles on Gallenga in the years which followed his death are representatives of that of Italy. They present a real travesty of the truth as regards Gallenga's life and activities, exercising a kind of censorship—not officially sponsored—in an attempt to make of Gallenga a figure in keeping with their easy myth of the Risorgimento, often over-simplified in its implications. This is evident in what Faldella wrote in 1897, two years after Gallenga's death, in an article where he used a letter written by Cavour to Cibrario in 1852, long before Antonio joined the Cavourian party, as proof of Cavour's high opinion of him.

All his life Gallenga was tortured by the remorse of his attempted regicide, as he confessed to me shortly before dying. But he will go in front of the throne of the Eternal God with the best diploma to which an Italian patriot could aspire. Not only has he the honourable pardon of the *Re Galantuomo*, interpreter of his noble father's soul, but also the following testimonial by Cavour, that is to say by the greatest artificer of national unity and constitutional freedom in Italy. 'I have the pleasure of highly recommending you Mr Gallenga . . . a very good Italian who, chased from his country, has worked to make her famous with his books rather than insulting her and afflicting her with secret plotting.'[1]

After resigning his seat in the Italian Parliament in 1856, Gallenga lingered in Italy for some months and returned to

[1] G. Faldella, 'Il pentimento di Antonio Gallenga', *Nuova Antologia*, 16 Oct. 1897, vol. lxxi, p. 661.

London in the spring of 1857. For a while he was, as he himself said, 'at a loose end'.

The spring and summer of that year—1857—may be considered the idlest period I ever remember spending in my life. I tarried in London all that season, little as I shared in its gaieties, haunting picture galleries, looking in at the rival opera houses, to which I could often have a free entrance, and brushing up such acquaintances as I had within a square mile or two of Hyde Park Corner.[1]

These months were not as carefree as Gallenga would like his reader to believe. In a letter to Panizzi, he asked him to defend him at University College, for he feared that Arrivabene, the man who acted as his deputy there during his long periods abroad, was plotting against him, and he seriously thought that he might lose the Chair of Italian, from which he eventually resigned in 1858. His fears were more imaginary than real: Count Arrivabene, an Italian exile who had settled in London, was always loyal to him, and there is no evidence that Gallenga was forced to resign from his professorship. He had, however, been experiencing some difficulties, and by the beginning of 1858 he grew so preoccupied with the rumours going round about his attempted regicide, that he returned to Turin and asked Cavour for a letter which would officially document the royal pardon.

Gallenga was longing for a full rehabilitation which would enable him to resume his political career in Piedmont. In October 1857 he wrote to some Italian friends—Domenico Carutti, the Piedmontese politician and journalist among them—asking for their support during the forthcoming elections, since he wanted to present himself as candidate in one of the colleges. Needless to say, this attempt never came to anything, and he returned to Italy only for occasional visits. After seeing Cavour in January, and obtaining the letter he wanted, Gallenga spent the winter in Italy, and in the following spring he was back again in London. For over a year he went to and fro between England and Italy, a thoroughly dissatisfied man, whose career, whether as journalist or politician, seemed to have come to an end. His only publication

[1] *Epis.*, vol. ii, p. 281.

of some importance which appeared at this time was a little book, *Country Life in Piedmont*, given to the press in the spring of 1858. It was the interest shown by the British public for the Kingdom of Sardinia which made him collect in a volume some of his Piedmontese correspondence to the *Daily News*, written two years before. The book met with some success, if we are to believe its author, who said in his memoirs that *Country Life* made up for some of the heavy losses suffered with the publication of *History of Piedmont*. Its attraction lies in the fact that it presented the English reader with life and tradition in small towns and villages outside Turin, that is to say in a part of the Italian peninsula which was still *terra incognita* for most English travellers, who were accustomed to making their way to Florence and Rome.

After the publication of *Country Life in Piedmont*, Gallenga was for a while involved in his own private concerns and thought that perhaps the time had come for retirement.

I was then in my forty-eighth year—a sober man, disenchanted of all illusions, as I thought, and cured of all ambition; with little regret for the past, and still less hope of the future.[1]

Nothing was further from what actually happened. At this time, he married again: his second wife, Ann Robinson, was a widow, ten years younger than himself, and she bore him two children. (By his first wife he already had a son, Romeo, who eventually returned to live in Italy and settled in Perugia, where the name of Gallenga has become famous. Romeo Gallenga Stuart, Romeo's son and Antonio's grandson, who was a politician at the time of Mussolini and an art critic, gave his family palace, *Palazzo Gallenga*, to the state and this is now the seat of the first Italian University for Foreigners, an institution well known all over the world.) Little is known about our author's private life: from the scanty information available his second marriage appears to have been happy; Ann was devoted to him and often accompanied him during his long journeys abroad. Their life, however, was troubled by sorrows caused by their children Mary Ann and Guy Hardwin. Mary Ann, an enterprising young girl, was among

[1] Ibid., vol. ii, p. 283.

the first women to go up to Cambridge, and she read mathematics at Girton in the eighties. To her parents' great distress she died in a road accident, when she was only twenty-four, not far from their home in Wales, where the Gallengas had retired. Guy Hardwin seems to have been an eccentric, conceited, and rather ignorant young man, and his relationship with his father deteriorated early, and so much, that, although Antonio died rich, he left his son only a small legacy of a hundred pounds. In 1915 Guy published a book, *The Last Soldier of Napoleon*, which was meant to be a diary left by Celso, Antonio's father. These memoirs, most of which are probably spurious, relate many amusing incidents, among them the episode in which Celso— or rather Guy since he was the editor of the book—attributed to Antonio Gallenga the authorship of Manzoni's *Il 5 maggio*. When Napoleon died, Celso, who had served him loyally for many years, went to his family

and talked much with them of my lost leader. My eldest son, a bright, if headstrong boy of nearly eleven must have been much impressed by what I said, for at a later date he wrote the following verses, much embodying what I had then said:

The Fifth of May[1]

There follows the translation of Manzoni's ode. Gallenga had, in effect, translated the poem into English years after Celso's death, and Guy attributed it to him: he would have turned in his grave at the thought that his son did not know his Manzoni.

Antonio and Ann were married in June 1858 at the Sardinian Chapel in London, and they immediately left for the continent, where they spent their honeymoon. On their return, Gallenga was offered a job as interpreter in a legal suit which was being held in Rome: Borghese versus the heirs of Lord Shrewsbury. No sooner was the offer made than the Gallengas set out again for Italy, and passing through Turin in October made their way to Rome. Here they remained for six months—during the first three Gallenga was occupied with the trial, the remainder of the time was spent in waiting for the birth of their first child.

---

[1] C. Gallenga, *The Last Soldier of Napoleon*, London, 1915, p. 132.

When at last they were ready to make their way back to England, Italy was up in arms. War had been declared by Piedmont and France on Austria on April 26; *de facto* most of Italy was involved in it.

We had hardly left Rome before we became aware that the whole youth of the country was stirring. Massimo D'Azeglio in Rome, and Boncompagni in Florence, sent out as extra-official Piedmontese agents, had suggested to the Pope's and the Grand Duke's Government the expediency of ridding themselves of revolutionary elements in their respective States, by raising golden bridges to the young volunteers on their way to the battlefields of Lombardy. The whole ablebodied population was soon on the tramp. We had them singing, shouting all along our route. Through Umbria and Tuscany, and from Florence to Pisa, and Spezia, and Genoa, the roads were swarming; the cities were wild with enthusiasm.[1]

The journey was long and interrupted by the movements of Italian and French troops, but eventually Gallenga succeeded, by means of coach and railways, in taking his family back to London. But

what home could there be for me in England while the destinies of Italy were being weighed in the scale?[2]

It was in this frame of mind that Gallenga left his family, and once again started hunting for a position which would allow him to return to Italy. He found an answer to his immediate problem in taking up journalism professionally, a career at which he had already tried his hand from time to time. Although nearly fifty, Gallenga now became foreign correspondent for *The Times*.

---

[1] *Epis.*, vol. ii, pp. 287-8.   [2] Ibid., p. 290.

VII

THE TIMES

As soon as he was back in London, Gallenga tried to re-establish his connection with the *Daily News*, hoping that they would send him to Italy as war correspondent. But the vacancy had already been filled. One of Gallenga's closest friends, Sir Francis Mowatt, then suggested *The Times* and gave him an introduction to the London paper.

On May 11—nearly three weeks after the French disembarkation and a fortnight after the Grand Duke of Tuscany and the Grand Duchess of Parma had fled from their capitals—no news having arrived from the Sardinian army, Morris resolved to bring in another man. Antonio Gallenga was an Italian rolling stone, now aged nearly fifty.[1]

Thus we read in *The History of 'The Times'*, but Gallenga has left us a far more vivid description of his first meeting with Mowbray Morris, *The Times*'s manager.

At one in the afternoon I called upon Mr Mowbray Morris, the manager of *The Times*. A West Indian by birth, still young, slender, dusky in the face with fine features and refined manners.

'How good of you to go out for us', he began, when we were seated, 'How good!'

'But I say, how kind of you to send me! You know nothing about me!'

'Perhaps you were not so utterly unknown as you imagined', he said, pointing to a book-shelf, where a copy of my *Italy, Past and Present* stared me in the face. 'That book has been on that shelf as a favourite ever since it came out—but now—about this war, Hardman, our own Turin correspondent writes that no 'press-gang' will be allowed at the front'.

'Let that be no hindrance', I said hastily. 'That rule will only apply to civilians and aliens. But I can don a uniform and go as a combatant.

---

[1] *The History of 'The Times'*, London, 1939, vol. ii, p. 284.

Cavour is my friend. I was till lately a deputy. Surely exception will be made in favour of me—an old patriot'.[1]

Gallenga's enthusiasm was easily aroused and he promptly forgot that his friendship with Cavour and other eminent politicians was, by now, more imaginary than real. Morris, however, was favourably impressed by him, and he wrote to Hardman, the paper's correspondent in Turin:

> You know him by reputation, and I think you will agree with me that no one can have a better chance of remaining with the army. He will leave London tomorrow evening and arrive I hope in Genoa on the 17th. His plan is to abstain from all communication with the authorities and to trust entirely to his own resources, and his well-established character as an Italian patriot.[2]

The Times had two other men in Italy, Wreford in Rome, and Eber, who had been sent as principal correspondent with the Sardinian army. Journalists, however, were experiencing difficulties with the Piedmontese and French authorities. The reason why Gallenga was brought in was that he should try and succeed where the others had failed, but by the time he reached Turin, Cavour and Napoleon III had relaxed their rules and the foreign press was able to join the army. The Italian campaign was great news in England and Morris did not recall Gallenga, but advised him to move elsewhere.

> There is no difficulty in the choice of the field. It is obviously Tuscany and the revolutionised states at present, and possibly the Kingdom of the Two Sicilies hereafter. It is generally supposed that Prince Jerome's army is intended to act in conjunction with the national Italian levies upon the extreme Austrian left, or in the event of action being inexpedient, to form the centre of the revolutionary party throughout Italy, collecting and protecting the native levies. To this army you should if possible attach yourself.[3]

Gallenga immediately went to Tuscany, where he joined Prince Napoleon Jerome's troops. Greatly to his disappointment, they were delayed and kept far from the battlefields of Lombardy

---

[1] *Epis.*, vol. ii, p. 293.   [2] *The History of 'The Times'*, vol. ii, p. 285.
[3] P.H.S., Morris to Gallenga in Genoa, 20 May 1859, MM. 9/383.

where the second war of independence was being fought and won. He found himself attached to the army of one of the least popular figures of the day, Prince Napoleon Joseph Charles Paul Jerome, cousin of the Emperor and heir presumptive to the throne of France. He had joined the Italian cause after his marriage with Princess Clotilde of Savoy, Victor Emmanuel's daughter, and he had been put in charge of the French troops in Tuscany. This ill-assorted marriage celebrated early in 1859, caused Gallenga to write:

There had been the sacrifice of the New Iphigenia, the Princess Clotilde, the pure-minded daughter of an old heroic line, wedded to that obese Plon-Plon, whose heroism no one would take for granted.[1]

In Florence, Gallenga met the prince, and he has left us an amusing portrait of that unpopular and grotesque figure, to whom he took a strong dislike.

I had solicited the Prince's gracious permission to travel with his staff, and obtained it at the close of a half-hour's interview. . . . I was not, I confess, greatly prepossessed with his presence. He had on a French Marshal's uniform, with a dainty red and golden kepi, and the smallness of the head-gear strangely contrasted with the full, broad, whiskerless face. Persons who had known him all their life and had seen him lately, had some difficulty in recognizing his fine features disguised as they were under the deep layers of the flabby fat with which, it seemed, the brief happiness of married life had compassed him round. The face was beaming with intelligence, no doubt, and the lineaments were certainly those of the great founder of his dynasty; but there was an oiliness about the skin, a twinkle about the eye, which had nothing in common either with the Napoleon of Arcole or with him of St. Helena: the expression was one of habitual simulation; and I felt all the time that I stood rather in the presence of a greasy monk or quibbling lawyer than of a soldier.[2]

Their meeting probably took place at the end of May, since on 10 June Morris wrote to Gallenga congratulating him on his success, for Prince Napoleon gave him permission to accompany him and circulate freely among his army. Gallenga followed the

[1] *Epis.*, vol. ii, p. 286.   [2] *Italy Revis.*, vol. ii, pp. 337–8.

slow and unsatisfactory movements of the troops as they crossed
Tuscany and eventually reached Lombardy. While Tuscany
accorded a warm welcome to the Prince, the soldiers under his
command felt dissatisfied. It seemed to Gallenga that Prince
Jerome's campaign was above all a diplomatic one. He accepted
the theory that it was Napoleon III's intention to have his cousin
made ruler of Tuscany instead of the Grand Duke. Rumours
were also going round among the soldiers which cast doubts
on the Prince's personal courage. There were political and
diplomatic reasons influencing the conduct of the Tuscan campaign and causing these delays which suited the policy of Napoleon III, for, in spite of his alliance with Piedmont, he was not
prepared to give his support to the creation of a larger Italian
state. Plon-Plon's troops reached Goito on 4 July on the eve of
the signing of the armistice at Villafranca. All that Gallenga and
the officers of the Tuscan divisions saw of that short but decisive
campaign was what was left of it at Solferino some days after the
battle which had given victory to the Franco-Italian forces.

The ground was still, fifteen days after the fight, thickly strewn
with soldiers' casques, cartridge-boxes and a variety of warlike wreck.
. . . The corpses seemed to have been buried with the utmost careless-
ness and indecent haste. Graves had not been dug, but the dead had
been laid in heaps in the furrows of the field where they fell, and a few
spadefuls of loose mould were thrown upon them. Beasts of prey of all
kinds, but especially cats—downright domestic cats; anywhere out of
Italy I might have thought them jackalls—were feasting on the remains;
half-fleshless bones had been dragged out of the heaving mounds here
and there, and the air was not free from that taint by which the
unhonoured dead can inflict their vengeance on the irreverent living.
The country lay still and calm; the pale young moon strove to out-
shine the faint last streaks of waning sunset. There lay the plain, the
fought-for hill, the solitary tower in its summit. We might have passed
by, and never dreamt that on that very spot, so few days before, 400,000
men had met in deadly struggle. . . . Had it not been for those desecrated
bodies, the scene would have been one of ineffable rural repose.[1]

It was with this sad picture in his mind and with bitter thoughts

[1] *Italy Revis.*, vol. ii, pp. 351–2.

about Villafranca—which he shared with the majority of Italians —that Gallenga returned to England as soon as the armistice was signed. From London he went straight to his country home in Llandogo, in Wales, and there he immediately received the following letter from Morris, surprised and annoyed at his sudden return.

I am very sorry you are returned so suddenly. . . . Our wish was that you should visit the Duchies and Florence and afterwards Rome or any other place where events claimed a record. Relying upon you I have recalled two of our correspondents from Italy who seemed less fit than yourself to be the historian of the movement now imminent. One of these is already returned and the other is daily expected. Thus you see, I am in a dilemma, and as you are the chief cause, you will I am sure do your best to help me out of it. The only way is for you to return to Italy without delay, prepared to move from place to place and go wherever the chief interest may call you. I can offer you the same terms as before—that is £80 per month; but it is not in my power to make a permanent engagement.[1]

Gallenga accepted this proposal and returned to Italy forthwith and spent most of his time of the following four years there. His connection with the London newspaper, which had started on a temporary basis and was still so in July 1859, was eventually made permanent and lasted till 1884. Most of the time he acted as foreign correspondent, and became one of the major figures among the journalists of the day, as is evident in this report of him, in *The History of 'The Times'*:

Antonio Gallenga was one of those rare journalists who achieved success both as a foreign correspondent and as a writer of leading articles. Delane placed much confidence in his articles upon foreign subjects, although they always required 'translating'. Between 1866 and 1872 Gallenga wrote a large proportion of the foreign articles, but his work was repeatedly interrupted by service as a correspondent, for his best talents were in that direction.[2]

Professional secrecy, strictly kept then as now at Printing House Square, and anonymity make it difficult to trace all Gallenga's

---

[1] P.H.S., Morris to Gallenga in Llandogo, 26 July 1859, MM. 9/476.
[2] *The History of 'The Times'*, vol, ii, pp. 451–2.

contributions to the newspaper. But he helps us himself: for he collected together his *Times* articles and published them in book form, just as he had done earlier with his writings for the *Daily News*. Volumes such as *Two Years of the Eastern Question* or *A Summer Tour in Russia*, are collections of former articles slightly adapted and arranged in chronological order. Such works had great political interest, since they stated the official opinion of *The Times*. *The Invasion of Denmark*, for instance, written at the time of the Prussian-Danish war in 1864, was immediately translated into Danish. His articles on Italy were collected and condensed into two works, *Italy Revisited*, which appeared in 1875, and *The Pope and the King*, published in 1878. It is from these that we shall draw when illustrating his Italian experiences as a British journalist.

Gallenga spent most of the latter part of 1859 in Florence. Early in January 1860, Morris asked him to go to Rome. But he was denied permission to stay by the Papal authorities. Their resentment was not of a personal kind. Recent events had made the Pope fear for the loss of his states, or at least of a part of them, and the openly pro-Italian policy of *The Times* was looked upon with suspicion. Much angered by the treatment received by his correspondent, Morris wrote:

I have received your letter describing the manner of your expulsion from Rome, and informing me that you would arrive in Florence on the 2nd of this month. As you had prepared me for this disastrous termination of your Roman mission, I am not surprised: but my indignation is not the less on that account. I shall look forward with all the greater eagerness to the speedy overthrow of these imbecile tyrants. The important question, however, for the moment is—how you can best be employed for your own advantage and ours.[1]

Gallenga wasted no time and spent the following months travelling throughout Northern Italy. In March he was in Turin for the opening of the new session of Parliament, and at this time he had a chance to see how influential *The Times* was, a fact he had been aware of for some time.

It was not long before I felt that *The Times* was a power—a power

[1] P.H.S., Morris to Gallenga, 6 Feb. 1860, MM. 9/650.

greater than any of the most colossal European Empires; and I found out that of that power I was the mouthpiece, and—so to say, the accredited Ambassador. However insignificant a pigmy a correspondent might be, he became taller and more conspicuous than any giant the moment he stood on one of the pinnacles of that wonderful edifice of Printing-House Square.[1]

He was in fact re-elected to Parliament by the district of Castellamonte. Cavour supported him as is known from a letter to Vittorio Emanuele D'Azeglio, in which he wrote:

Je l'ai laissé nommé député. Cela lui donnera une plus grande autorité auprès du *Times*. Il faut espérer qu'il en fera bon usage.[2]

Thus the position which he had to resign in 1856 was now granted him, a proof of the authority and prestige enjoyed by the London paper.

So far his experiences in Italy had been interesting but of no great moment, but in the following August the situation changed, for, quite by chance, Gallenga became an eye witness of one of the most stirring and fateful events of Italian history. This was the Expedition of the Thousand, which led to the annexation of the Kingdom of the Two Sicilies, and which inspired some of his most brilliant articles. Among the Italian dynasties the Bourbons had always distinguished themselves for their illiberality. Not even the death of Ferdinand II, *Re Bomba*, which occurred in May 1859, improved the situation, as his successor, the weak and inefficient Francis, continued in his footsteps, regardless of the changed political conditions inside the Peninsula. The misrule of the Neapolitan court had been publicly denounced to the world's public opinion by Gladstone in 1851, at the time of his visit there. After the second war of independence, restlessness in the kingdom was growing very fast. In the spring of 1860 news reached Piedmont of an unsuccessful revolt which had broken out in Sicily. Garibaldi immediately decided to gather together some of his Red Shirts and formed an expeditionary force which early in May

---

[1] *Epis.*, vol. ii, p. 313.
[2] *Cavour e l'Inghilterra*, Bologna, 1933, vol. ii, p. 93, Cavour to D'Azeglio, 7 July 1860.

5 *King Victor Emanuel II welcomed by the London Corporations during his state visit, December 1855*
The Illustrated London News, 29 Dec. 1855

6 *Garibaldi enters Naples, September 1860*

Oil by Antonino Licata

sailed from Quarto near Genoa, heading for Sicily. Garibaldi and the Thousand—so were his followers called on this occasion—received a warm welcome in the island, and by August they had defeated the royal troops and freed the region from Bourbon rule. The expedition was great news in England. Originally *The Times* had appointed Eber as a special correspondent in Naples and Sicily, but, carried away by his own enthusiasm for the Italian cause, the journalist had joined the Garibaldians, and his reporting for the paper was greatly handicapped by his military enterprises. In August Morris decided to send Gallenga, who set off at once and landed at Palermo on the 10th. Garibaldi was then making preparations to move from Sicily to Calabria, for he intended to reach Naples from the south. Gallenga joined him and his troops and sailed with them on board the English vessel *Amazon*, which took them to Messina. From there they crossed the straits and landed in Calabria. Gallenga had therefore a chance to report for *The Times* on that part of the expedition which took the Thousand from Reggio Calabria to Naples. The situation was extremely chaotic, and there was no organized defence against the Red Shirts. Thus Gallenga wrote commenting on the desolate conditions of the Bourbon troops:

It was, I believe, the first instance in history in which a conquering and a vanquished army were seen marching side by side, and almost promiscuously, without any hostile feelings, without any wish to harm, but also without any power to help each other. The sufferings of the dispersed Neapolitans were dreadful to behold, and at every step, as the numbers increased, rose in intensity. We must have passed at least as many as 25,000 in our progress. As they laid down their muskets, every man of them cut a stick out of the hedge, and began tramping. Footsore, and many of them shoeless, almost naked some of them—for they sold all available garments—they crept along, parched, burnt, starved.[1]

In this conquered and tattered army, the supreme witness to the decadence of Bourbon rule, were sown the seeds of that brigandage which later was to produce grave disorders and almost insoluble problems for the new nation.

[1] *Italy Revis.*, vol. ii, p. 378.

Gallenga was close to Garibaldi's headquarters most of the time. During the latter part of the expedition he travelled with Colonel Peard, Garibaldi's Englishman, C. S. Forbes, a British naval officer, and Colonel Fabrizi. According to Trevelyan[1] they had been asked by the General to precede his troops and report on the Neapolitan forces. While Garibaldi advanced along the coast, moving at a slower pace, they travelled inland from Cosenza to Eboli. On 4 September, they reached Auletta where an amusing episode took place, which gave them the opportunity of accelerating the fall of the Bourbons.

We had for some time been amused by the stir Colonel Peard's appearance created among the astonished natives. His long beard and Calabrian hat caused him to be mistaken for Garibaldi, and the reception he met with everywhere was perfectly overwhelming. It was to no purpose that we honestly tried to undeceive the frantic multitude. They professed that 'they would respect the General's *incognito*, but they could not be deceived as to his likeness, having seen so many thousands of his photographs.' . . . The people's obstinacy at first embarrassed us, and annoyed the Colonel; but in time we perceived that this premature announcement of Garibaldi's arrival could not fail to add to the enthusiasm of the bands hastening in arms from the neighbouring country, and to strike dismay and confusion among the royal troops.[2]

In the end, Peard and his friends decided to exploit the situation to Garibaldi's advantage. They sent despatches which spread false and alarming news about Garibaldi's movements in reply to inquiries made via telegraph by the Neapolitan authorities and addressed to the local gendarmerie. Moreover, Gallenga telegraphed some of his friends in Naples—General Ulloa among them—confirming that Garibaldi had already reached Eboli and Auletta, and that the Caldarelli brigade had joined the Red Shirts. As a result, Salerno was evacuated by the Bourbon troops, and the King decided to retreat and abandon Naples. The initiative taken by Peard and Gallenga well illustrated the chaos in which the kingdom lay. The conquest of the mainland by the Red Shirts

[1] G. M. Trevelyan, *Garibaldi and the Making of Italy*, London, 1911, p. 338 and *passim*.

[2] *Italy Revis.*, vol. ii, p. 393.

presents some tragi-comic incidents which greatly contrast with the heroic and fierce battles fought elsewhere by Garibaldi and his troops. The Bourbons of Naples ended their rule in a comic opera atmosphere. On 7 September Garibaldi entered the capital; by the 10th of this month, the campaign having come to an end, Eber resumed his journalistic activities and Gallenga returned to Turin. As already mentioned, he was on the same steamer which took Garibaldi to Messina, and thus he had a chance to observe him closely.

The General moved among the various groups upon deck with a kind and an apt word for each of them—evincing that readiness of recognition, that perfect accuracy of recollection, that memory of men and things and circumstances, however trifling, which have ranked among the innate privileges of royal or heroic greatness. He had on his usual Dictatorial suit, the unfailing red flannel shirt, with a silk bandanna kerchief thrown loosely and widely round the neck, by way of a scarf, light gray trousers, and the modern wide-awake hat with a turn-up brim. The prodigious breadth of the General's shoulders, his colossal chest, and the natural dignity and lion-like majesty of his countenance again and again inclined the beholder to overrate his real stature, which was certainly not above the middle size. . . . The hair on a near inspection was dark-brown—darker by far than the beard, which was tawny or reddish. The beard was worn full and long. The cheek-bones were high, and the nose came down between them in a perfectly straight long line, even with the slightly slanting forehead. The complexion of that part of the face which was not hid by the beard, was not merely bronzed or sunburnt, but had a peculiar sanguine hue, and was thickly studded with endless freckles. This remarkable tint, the features, the colour of the beard, together with the calm but deep expression of the eye, had contributed to give his countenance that unmatched character which won him the appellation of the 'Lion-face'.[1]

Gallenga may have lingered too long on the physical appearance of Garibaldi, but there was something so commanding in his looks that one could not but be attracted by him. In 1860 the General was at the climax of his career, at a particularly happy

[1] Ibid., vol. ii, pp. 363-4.

moment when his military success coincided with his political achievement. In 1875 Gallenga wrote:

Such was the man fifteen years ago, and such was at that time the adoration of men for him. People had not then heard of Aspromonte or Mentana, or of the disastrous repulse in the Tyrol of 1866, or of the absurd crusade on behalf of Gambetta's Republic in 1870. Nor had the hero's speech at the Peace Congress at Geneva, that 'there could be no question whether or not St. Peter had been in Rome, since he, Garibaldi, could give them his word of honour that no such man as St. Peter had ever existed', as yet been reported in the newspapers. It was only too easy in later times to under-rate Garibaldi's political or social abilities, as it had been to over-estimate his military capacity. Garibaldi was neither infallible in council nor, as it turned out, invincible in the field. But it was too hard to say that 'the ass's head was associated in him with the lion's heart'. As a brave and good man—the most well-meaning and self-denying of men—Garibaldi stands alone in our age, and full justice will be done to his character when all that has been or may be imputed to him on the score of want of judgement and discretion shall be utterly given to oblivion.[1]

Not only was Garibaldi extremely popular with his soldiers, but he was also met with a warm welcome in his march through Calabria. The march of the Thousand from Reggio to Naples is described by Gallenga with vivid details, adding another page to the illustrious records of those days.

Garibaldi had not taken a large force with him from Sicily, and with the exception of a few chosen bands, such as the Chasseurs des Alpes and his veteran company of Genoese sharpshooters, it was as inefficient as it was numerically inadequate to the enterprise. Such as it was however little was ever or anywhere seen of it. It was usual with Garibaldi to issue marching orders and then set off, himself first with such of his staff as chose to follow, taking for granted the army would come next, but seldom being at the trouble [sic] to ascertain whether it did or not. A general staff, a commissariat, an ambulance, all the appurtenances of a well-appointed military establishment, were supposed to exist; but everything must have been left at a great distance behind, as within several miles of the Commander-in-chief I seldom saw more than about forty or fifty, some of them not very soldier-like, and others

[1] *Italy Revis.*, vol. ii, pp. 369–70.

very sorrily mounted, horsemen. Nothing could be more comical
than the blank look of surprise with which the mayors and other
notables of the Calabrian towns we rode into, after all due humble
obeisance and greeting to the Liberators, looked over the General's
shoulders, and seeing nobody behind him but that motley staff, asked,
'Le truppe dove le avite?'[1]

After leaving Naples, Gallenga returned to Turin where he kept
his headquarters till the summer of 1863. While in Piedmont, he
regularly attended Parliament. His participation in parliamentary
life was not very active or in any way remarkable, but as a deputy
he had a chance to witness some of the most momentous events
in the history of the new nation. In February 1861 Victor Emmanuel was proclaimed King of Italy, and Turin became the
capital of the country, which now included most of the Peninsula
with the exception of Rome, the Venetian Provinces, Trieste, and
the Alto Adige. In the following June Camillo Cavour, the greatest *artifice* of Italian unity, died. He was succeeded first by the Tuscan Bettino Ricasoli, then by the Piedmontese lawyer Urbano
Rattazzi. Neither of them was equal to him. Rattazzi especially
gained for himself the reputation of being an intriguing politician
and a poor statesman, and he lacked the capacity to face up to the
complex political situation confronting him. While on one hand
the followers of Mazzini and Garibaldi were urging for a further
aggrandizement of the nation, the French were now protecting
the Pope and opposing any manœuvre aimed at making Rome
the capital of Italy. Rattazzi's fame is unhappily linked to the
episode of Aspromonte, in which Garibaldi, marching with some
volunteers towards Rome in the hope of renewing the easy
success of the expedition of the Thousand, was stopped in Calabria
by regular Italian troops and wounded. This happened in 1862:
Rattazzi had at first secretly encouraged Garibaldi's action, ready
to act as Cavour had done over the Kingdom of the Two Sicilies,
that is to accept the *fait accompli*. But fears of French reactions
made him change his mind and use force against Garibaldi. This
was a most unpopular gesture, and Gallenga reacted violently to

[1] Ibid., vol. ii, pp. 372–3.

it by trying to promote a vote of no confidence against his cabinet but he was unsuccessful.

As in his previous parliamentary experiences, Gallenga was most interested in the problem of public morality, and his name is linked with two episodes: Persano's promotion to the rank of admiral, and the Bensa affair. It was while Rattazzi was Prime Minister that the first of these episodes took place.

> Somehow my bold onset on Rattazzi at the beginning of his administration, however politically questionable, had been morally honourable, and it won me a certain amount of popularity which urged me on to take a more active part in Parliamentary proceedings than my position as a foreign journalist seemed to warrant. I was always ready to take up questions of public morality. On the eve of the downfall of the Rattazzi Ministry, Vice-Admiral Persano, who had held the portfolio of Marine in that Cabinet, had been cool enough to raise himself to the rank of Admiral.[1]

Gallenga attacked Persano but failed, for Rattazzi and most members of the Parliament backed the newly appointed Admiral. Carlo Pellion di Persano has gone down in history as the man who led the Italian fleet at the battle of Lissa in 1866 and lost. But if he allowed himself to be defeated then at a crucial point in the third war of Italian independence, now, in 1862, with the help of Rattazzi, Persano bravely withstood the attack Gallenga launched on him, and did not resign from his new appointment. This incident, however, gave Gallenga the reputation of an *enfant terrible*, and it was to him that the Italian colony in Tunis addressed themselves when complaining against the newly appointed Italian consul, Enrico Bensa. Little is known about this man, who, according to Gallenga, styled himself the 'King's Private Secretary'.

> [Bensa] had been one of those minions whom the *Re Galantuomo*— whose private tastes were not as irreproachable as his public conduct —employed for services from which men with clean hands would have shrunk.[2]

As is well known, King Victor Emmanuel II had a great weakness for female company, and kept several mistresses. Although we

---

[1] *Epis.*, vol. ii, pp. 329–30.   [2] Ibid., vol. ii, p. 331.

do not know what the King's Private Secretary's duties were, one can easily surmise that they had something to do with his amorous life. Knowing far too much about his master's private life, Bensa tried to take advantage of the situation and blackmailed him. A way of getting rid of him, when he became a nuisance to Victor Emmanuel, was found by Rattazzi who had him appointed Consul-General at Tunis. Bensa's behaviour was as bad there as it had been in Turin. According to the complaints which reached Gallenga,

kept in his pay a band of bravoes with whom he enforced his pleasure by threats and deeds of violence, terrorising the whole colony.[1]

On 28 March 1863, Gallenga put down a question in Parliament about him. In three weeks' time, before his question had been fully answered by the Minister of Foreign Affairs, Bensa had resigned and the case was considered closed. The incident would have been of little consequence, had not the name of Bensa been connected with that of the Royal family.

The King, seeing that the Ministers were acting upon my unrelenting pressure, looked on my conduct as the result of a deliberate hostility against his person; and as he, very naturally, thought I was ill-requiting his noble interference in my behalf, in that crisis of 1856 in which he had come forward as my only Italian open friend—he now conceived against me a deep resentment, the symptoms of which became perceptible at no distant period.[2]

Once again, as in 1856, Gallenga proved unpopular with the people of his own party, the *destra storica*. As Arrighi wrote, Gallenga always searched in Parliament for those thorny questions which so much irritated 'our peaceful and happy deputies'.[3] For the time being no sign of displeasure from the King was shown to Gallenga, and when the session broke up he returned undisturbed to London, where his articles for The Times had met with the approval of the right wing, but with great hostility from the Mazzinians.

By the summer of 1863 the Italian situation seemed to have

---

[1] Ibid., pp. 332–3. [2] Ibid., vol. ii, p. 334.
[3] C. Arrighi, *I 450 ovvero i deputati del presente e i deputati dell'avvenire*, Milan, 1865, p. 221.

come to a standstill as far as revolutions and expansion of the kingdom were concerned. Subsequently, foreign interest in Italy greatly decreased, while new and more exciting events were happening on the international scene, and Gallenga was sent elsewhere. As Mowbray Morris told him, the interest of the English public had been for the last twelve months exclusively absorbed by the outbreak of the Civil War in America. It was to the United States that Gallenga was immediately sent. Only in September 1864, when plans were made to move the capital from Turin to Florence, Italy attracted English interest once more, since the question of the capital was closely connected with that of Rome and the temporal power. Apparently the decision to make Florence capital of Italy, which became effective in 1865, was taken in order to reassure Napoleon III and the Pope that no further attempt would be made against Rome. In effect it was a first step towards conquering the city, for as soon as the Pope was deprived of French protection in 1870 because of the Franco-Prussian war, the Italians seized the opportunity and freed the city, leaving to the Church the possession of the small Vatican city. In autumn 1864 *The Times* decided to send Gallenga to Turin again, so that he could closely follow the development of the situation. But now the consequences of the Bensa affair made themselves felt, and prevented him from carrying out his task. Gallenga arrived just after the people of Turin had revolted because of the decision to remove the capital to Florence, when the Italian government put down the rebellion with unnecessary severity and not without bloodshed. But Gallenga could not concentrate on public matters since Bensa was back in Turin, anxious to challenge him to a duel. Gallenga refused to fight and left the city. Eventually, however, pressed by friends, he decided to return to Turin and face Bensa, but the latter disappeared and was never heard of again. This incident prevented Gallenga from working for *The Times* in Italy, since he was informed that it was the King's opinion that 'in the present, unsettled state of men's minds in the city, a private quarrel, with which his Royal name would naturally be mixed up, might furnish a further pretext for new popular disturbances'.

The Times then sent him as correspondent elsewhere. Earlier in 1864 he had resigned his seat in Parliament owing to his inability to attend the sessions. The years between 1864 and 1873 saw him moving from place to place. In 1866 he was in Spain, and later the same year, during the third war of Italian independence, he was in London writing leading articles on foreign affairs; between September 1868 and July 1869 he went to Spain at the time of the dethronement of Queen Isabella; in 1870 he was war correspondent for the Franco-Prussian war; in 1873 he was in Cuba. Apart from a fleeting visit to Italy in September 1871 for the opening of the Mont Cenis tunnel, most of his time was spent far from his native country, so that when he was posted to Rome in 1873, he could speak of his ten years' absence.

My task was assigned to me in Italy, where I was desired to give my impression of the progress that country had made. . . . I crossed the Alps through the new tunnel, and proceeded, *via*, Turin, Bologna, and Florence, to Rome, where I arrived in May of the third year after the transformation of the Papal city into the capital of United Italy.

My stay in Rome lasted a little above two years, though I wandered from place to place almost incessantly, especially during the malaria season, visiting all the cities, describing all the provinces, and examining all political, social and other questions.[1]

After the fall of Rome, Italy had come to the end of her territorial claims. The Italians and the Austrians had accepted the position made for them by the 1859 and 1866 wars, and 'as Italy has really no designs on Trieste, and none on Trent, unless it might be had by peaceful means, it is felt that no subject of direct collision between the two States can arise'.[2] As Gallenga said, a long period of peaceful coexistence lay ahead for the two countries, a period which should have been conducive to the accomplishment of national integration and amalgamation of the peninsula, a process started by political unification.

Gallenga's first impression of the new country was inevitably disappointing. Like the majority of his contemporaries who had fought and suffered for the independence of their land, he felt that the new Italy was an *Italietta*, petty and bourgeois, which now

[1] *Epis.*, vol. ii, pp. 359–60.   [2] *Italy Revis.*, vol. i, p. 228.

under one flag, combined not only the virtues but also, and above all, the vices of the several badly governed Italian states. Gallenga's views at this time are clearly seen in a conversation which he reported as having taken place among Italian deputies, while travelling from Bologna to Rome.

My fellow travellers fell almost unwittingly on that universal topic—public affairs, and then their manner was at once sobered, and a vein of sadness broke in upon their lively discourse. It was impossible, they thought, that Italy could ever regret having bravely asserted her right to self-government, but it would be vain to deny that she has not yet governed herself quite as wisely as might have been expected.

Their countrymen, they said, had been adroit politicians, but indifferent legislators and helpless administrators. The race of Cavours was extinct, and the country had no statesman at its head. . . .

They could see nothing but shortcomings in the home administration; they complained of the frequent miscarriage of justice, of the inefficiency of the police, of unsafe prisons; the perpetual cropping up of brigandage, murder stalking about in broad daylight; the law nowhere revered or obeyed; the re-organization of the Army and Navy slow and costly; public education an egregious failure. . . . To hear them, it would seem that not one of the fond dreams they had cherished in their youth, when they conspired as patriots of the Young Italy school, had proved true.[1]

Even before unification was finally achieved, many patriots had been aware of the difficulties facing the country, Gallenga among them, for as early as 1855 he wrote:

That Italy is sick, and grievously sick, no man will be bold enough to gainsay; nor will any man dare to assert, that the only evils she is suffering from are the Austrians and the Pope, although they may be the original causes of all her malady.[2]

Yet most of the men who fought against the Austrians had often neglected social and economic problems for political and nationalist claims. Few were those who in the early Risorgimento felt the emancipation of their country as a regeneration of habits and customs. Gallenga's own experience is significant as indicative of a general Italian trend. Mazzini, who was the forerunner of

---

[1] *Italy Revis.*, vol. i, pp. 12–13.　　　[2] *Country Life*, pp. 130–1.

those who did not close their eyes to social problems, belonged to a minority. Most of his followers sooner or later abandoned his views and put social questions aside. Once the country was united, all these problems could no longer be ignored. *Italy Revisited* is an excellent document giving evidence of the general conditions of Italy at a time when some of its age-old problems had come to the fore, some of which are still unsolved today, such as the difference between North and South, the *mafia*, the Alto Adige question, and corruption in bureaucracy and in public life.

The real strength of the country lies in the superior intelligence and culture, in the industry and energy, and in the higher moral character of those twelve or fourteen millions of northern people, who speak dialects hardly Italian, yet who have most powerfully contributed to work out the destinies of the nation.[1]

Thus Gallenga wrote, lamenting that with the transfer of the capital to Rome, the Italians who did not want to be 'Piedmontized' were being rapidly 'Neapolitanized'. Brigandage in the peninsula and *mafia* in Sicily were among the greatest evils of the southern regions. But brigandage was a problem not only in the former Kingdom of the Two Sicilies, for Gallenga also records, with the *camorra* in Naples, the *accoltellatori* in a northern district, Romagna. He showed himself more optimistic towards the solution of this problem than events later justified. As for the Alto Adige question there is something strikingly modern in his remark:

Nothing sounds more pathetic than the complaint of German travellers, who declare that the sight of so many old German strongholds in the Tyrolese valleys being now *Verwalsched*, or Italianized, by the advancing tide of Southern immigration, gives them a feeling of homesickness.[2]

These words were written at a time when Trent and its region were still under Austrian rule. The Italianization of that area had started a long time before it actually became part of the Italian kingdom. But these are only marginal observations on Italian life: what seemed above all to be wanting, according to Gallenga, was a civic conscience. Moreover, the lack of properly organized

---

[1] *Italy Revis.*, vol. i, p. 18.   [2] Ibid., vol. ii, pp. 224–5.

industry in the South caused many people to flock into state-paid jobs.

The corruption and disorder which had sunk so deeply into every department of the public service in the southern districts under Bourbon rule is rapidly tainting the whole administration of the Italian kingdom, while any reform tending to introduce order and economy is obstructed by the preponderance of those very southern provinces where reform is more sorely needed.[1]

Not every aspect of Italian life, however, appeared unfavourable to him. There were symptoms of national revival, which might have been the forerunners of a true and general modernization of the country. History has shown that progress and emancipation came much more slowly than Gallenga expected. What to him appeared to be vital signs of progress were the spread of education, the building of new roads and new railways throughout the country, the interest and study put into agriculture and industry in some areas of the Peninsula, for example, in Romagna and throughout most of the Po valley.

Look all around about this little town of Parma. Its population has not dwindled, its territory has not lost its fertility. It is on the contrary better cultivated and more productive than at any former period. It is no longer cramped with jealously-guarded borders. It enjoys the amplest freedom of commerce; its fruits are carried all over Lombardy; its splendid cattle finds its way across France to the English butcher's stall.

It was instances of this kind which made him say that

we must be allowed to hope that this general discouragement and this sluggish and despondent decay, are merely transient.[2]

Progress came to those parts of the country which were potentially rich and modern and which had been previously handicapped by the existence of too many borders. Apart from the Po valley, signs of activity and new life were visible in Florence and throughout Tuscany, where Gallenga had a chance to admire the work which men like Ginori and Peruzzi were doing for industrial and

---

[1] *Italy Revis.*, vol. i, pp. 254–5.   [2] Ibid., vol. ii, p. 92.

agricultural development. Now, he was praising and admiring
the social work which had already been started by some of the
leading aristocrats in Tuscany in 1840, but to which he had then
refused to contribute. Gallenga also saw the sign of a reawakening
in the growing phenomenon of emigration, which caused so
many Italians to leave their country and seek their fortune overseas.

Something very new and hardly conceivable, it is said, must have
come upon Neapolitans and Sicilians to send them forth in quest of
such distant homes, and the causes, it is added, must be sought in the
general distress of the country, in the heavy taxation, and in the
severity of the new system of military duty. Those easy-going,
indolent Southerners have been roused from their habitual apathy by
what was meant as a tender of rights and liberties, but which has
actually turned out an infliction of burdens and responsibilities.[1]

Those new burdens were not entirely negative, since they made
people aware of their own wretchedness and made them search
for a better life. Bourbon rule was paternalistic, and corrupt; the
new Government was strict, but not so corrupt. What the southern
regions lacked, according to Gallenga—and in this he was right—
was an enlightened and active middle class which would promote
private enterprise.

Gallenga's writings on Italy in the seventies are not only a political and economic document. They also have a social character
in so far as they illustrate the new life and habits of the Italians,
when a new generation was rising, while so many of the older
men were rapidly disappearing. He attended many ceremonies
commemorating the deaths of many illustrious people of the
Risorgimento. In November 1873 he was present at the uncover-
ing of the Cavour monument in Turin.

A gathering of Cavour's friends round Cavour's monument, however imposing, could not fail to be a melancholy sight, for the man
summed up an epoch and a generation; and it is appalling to consider
the havoc which death had made, not only among the Balbos, the
Alfieris, the Revels, Perrones, Giobertis, D'Azeglios, and the hundreds
who opened the way for his success, but also among the Farinis,
Lafarinas, Cassinis, and other men whom he distinguished as his

[1] Ibid., vol. i, p. 288.

followers, and on whose co-operation his achievement mainly depended. The ranks both of Cavour's seniors and juniors have been thinned with equal ruthlessness; and, in her eager and almost morbid anxiety to honour the dead, Italy would seem to evince misgivings about her ability to replace them. In every instance in which the men now trusted with her destinies appear somewhat unequal to the task before them, the loss of Cavour occurs to men's mind.[1]

The day after Cavour's monument was unveiled, a similar ceremony was held for Massimo D'Azeglio, and this could not fail to suggest a comparison between them.

Unquestionably Cavour had by far the larger brain, letting alone the fact that he was more successful. Cavour was one of the world's greatest workers; D'Azeglio was simply an *amateur* in politics, as in all literary, artistic and even military pursuits. Both of them loved their country, but with Cavour patriotism was a task, with D'Azeglio, in a great measure, a sentiment. Cavour chose public life as a business; D'Azeglio entered it from a sense of duty, and as a matter of irksome necessity. Neither of them had the least faith in the possibility of a United Italy; for Cavour, after sounding Manin in Paris, in 1852, came back to Turin giving him up as 'an unpractical man who was still dreaming of Italian unity'—a dream which Cavour himself was soon destined to bring to a reality. And D'Azeglio, who died before the annexation of Venice and Rome, questioned whether, even if it was possible 'to make Italy' it would be found equally practicable 'to make the Italians'.[2]

Thus Gallenga wrote giving his final judgement on two men, both of whom he knew and admired, but only one of whom he truly loved and respected: D'Azeglio.

The funeral of Manzoni in Milan in 1873 gave Gallenga a chance to lament Italian decadence in the field of literature. But here, his point is not fully proved: he had far too long been estranged from the literary world, and his judgement is very superficial. Far more interesting is the portrayal he left us of Victor Emmanuel II and Pius IX who lived to see Rome become the capital of Italy and who had both played a prominent role in the history of their country. In describing them, Gallenga also portrayed the strained relationship between the state and the Church.

If the subject were not too serious and fraught with too much danger, it would be impossible not to laugh at the efforts which are being made to find room enough in Rome for the King and the Pope. . . . Most assuredly the position of the old Pontiff becomes daily more intolerable. From his windows in the Vatican he can see the King's banner waving from the roof of what once was his Palace on the Quirinal. In the stillness of his apartment he may hear the trumpets of the troops who stormed his capital, and the shouts of the populace which once were so enthusiastic for him, now greeting the constitutional sovereign on his way to open Parliament.[1]

In writing about the King and the Pope, Gallenga could not resist the temptation to launch into some of his anti-clerical attacks, which were also directed against the bigotry of the House of Savoy. It was his opinion that only reluctantly had Victor Emmanuel been talked into depriving the Pope of his temporal possessions.

Had the King had his own way the Pope would never have been robbed of one inch of his territory, there would never have been one monk the less in Italy, nor would the Church have lost one farthing of her revenue. . . . Victor Emmanuel is, in his own way, a believer. He has been trained in a school where veneration for the sacred character of the priesthood is the beginning and end of religion. He is not the man to sneer at excommunications, or to sleep quietly under the Pope's curses.[2]

Victor Emmanuel was a man whom Gallenga admired for his personal qualities, such as courage, and his fidelity to the Italian cause, but, as an individual, he appeared to have a good many faults.

When the present generation and the next have passed away, there will perhaps be a King of Italy resident in Rome. But that must be a sovereign of a different stamp from Victor Emmanuel II. . . . Rome is to many strangers a somewhat objectionable summer residence; but the King seems to find it an equally irksome sojourn in winter. He appears for one day to open Parliament; on the morrow he leaves for

---

[1] Ibid., vol. i, pp. 105, 112–13.   [2] Ibid., vol. i, p. 116.

a fortnight at Naples; he will be back by and by for another day, but go on to Florence for a month. . . . Victor Emmanuel is nowhere at home in a town, but least of all in the Pope's city. It is always in spite of himself that Victor Emmanuel plays a monarch's part, though, to do him justice, he can play it with sufficient dignity and grace. His instincts are those of a soldier and sportsman; it is only under a tent or in a gamekeeper's lodge that he seems to breathe freely.[1]

He did not consider Victor Emmanuel a great statesman. Like Garibaldi, the King was brave and courageous in war-time, but naïve and uncouth in politics. Both Garibaldi and the King lacked the diplomacy and refinement of political thought of men such as Cavour and D'Azeglio. Pius IX was, according to Gallenga, a better politician than Victor Emmanuel II, but his activities were undermined by a basic weakness, which, as in the case of Charles Albert, made him waver between liberalism and extreme conservatism. At the time of his election to the Holy See in 1848 Pius IX had roused the hopes of Italian patriots because of his liberal attitude: he was among the first Italian princes to grant a constitution, but he changed his attitude towards the national cause during the first war of independence, frightened as he was of the success of the most radical elements. Gallenga blamed the Pope's change of mind on external influences, and on political events, which, ever since the first war of independence, had threatened him with the loss of his states. Gallenga did not deny Pius IX Christian virtues: the Pope in fact proved generous enough to forgive the Italian King on the eve of his death, and did not deprive him of his benediction in *articulo mortis*. He was also a spiritual leader and took a keen interest in the moral unity of the Church: in 1869 he organized the Ecumenical Council—which was suspended because of the 1870 events and never re-summoned. The Pope's goodwill, however, should not be taken as a sign that the situation between Italy and the Holy See was in any way easing. While in Rome, Gallenga was a witness of the ever-growing difficulties of the coexistence of the two powers. As in the case of the Venetian republic, the Papal States continued to exist as a political entity for some time after they had ceased to

[1] *Italy Revis.*, vol. i, pp. 383-4.

be a prosperous and active nation. The manœuvres to keep the Papal possessions independent and prevent Italy from conquering Rome—manœuvres which Austria and France in turn performed —reflected European political issues rather than a belief of the Catholic Church in the divine right of temporal power. In spite of the fact that the Pope could not be brought to acquiesce in the loss of his states, Pius IX knew that his power as a Prince was at an end, and even given the chance he would have refused to take them back.

Gallenga's book on the Pope and the King ends with the accession to the throne of Humbert I and the election of Pope Leo XIII in 1878. The new King was in his early thirties when he ascended the throne. He had married Margherita Teresa Giovanna, a Princess of Savoy and his cousin, who was a strong-willed woman, well-educated, and cultured. They both tried to turn the Piedmontese monarchy into an Italian institution, and although Humbert was not as popular as his father, he tried to establish contacts with the whole country. His reign was apparently tranquil, no further general wars troubled it, but there was great social unrest throughout the country, and he fell a victim to it when in 1900 he was assassinated by an anarchist. Leo XIII was a much abler man than Pius IX and although he always defended the power of the Church, he was wise enough to avoid too much friction with his neighbouring nation. Notwithstanding the differences in personality and temperament between them and the two former leaders, the situation in Rome did not alter and, in spite of a few signs of improvement in the situation, nothing really changed. The Church still represented a powerful secular organization, and was still far from turning into a spiritual power only. For once Gallenga did not dare to forecast the future: a few months' reign was too short a time to judge either Humbert I or Leo XIII.

In April 1878 Gallenga was recalled from Rome and sent out to Greece and Constantinople. Although he was nearly seventy, he continued to act as correspondent, but his contributions to the paper became less frequent. The retirement of J. T. Delane, who left *The Times* in 1878 and died the following year, marked the beginning of the end of Gallenga's career. The new editor, T. Chenery, continued to employ him for some short missions, and for the writing of biographies, reviews of books, and headed-articles. Gallenga's last long missions were a ten months' journey to South America (October 1879–June 1880) and another to Russia the following year. Chenery was editor for a very short period, since he died in 1883, and his successor, G. Buckle, dispensed with Gallenga's services almost entirely. Nobody can blame the editor of *The Times* for considering the Italian too old for further missions abroad. Gallenga was the only one who did not think of himself as old. When in 1884 he asked to be sent to Morocco, the reply was as follows:

[Although there is] no doubt that in spite of the burden of years you would do your work as creditably as on former occasions, at seventy-four you surely cannot expect us to send you on such a mission or to be consenting parties to your going. *The Times* has to consider what is due to your age if thro' excess of zeal you fail to do so.[1]

In the same year Gallenga published an autobiography, *Episodes of My Second Life*, which covered his life to the time of writing; and this put an abrupt end to his connection with *The Times*.

Circumstances connected with a recent publication of yours rendered it absolutely necessary to terminate your engagement with this office; and I find myself obliged to be the medium for conveying to you the painful intimation. From the long standing connection with *The Times* you must have been fully aware that its leader writers are bound to secrecy; yet you have openly violated our confidence in this respect and done so in terms as regards three editors under whom you have served which I forbear to characterize. The Proprietors have been more considerate towards you than you have been of them. They have authorized me to send you the enclosed cheque for £300, the amount of a year's salary in advance. With this, however, your engagement on our staff must now absolutely and entirely cease.[2]

When reading Gallenga's memoirs today, one cannot help smiling at what *The Times* considered a severe breach of confidence, but, as was customary at Printing House Square, the most abso-

---

[1] P.H.S., 10 Oct. 1884, L.B., 20/240.
[2] Ibid., 6 Dec. 1884, L.B. 20/688.

lute professional secrecy was required from all its contributors. All he revealed concerned his relationship with the various editors under whom he worked. Moreover, he made some fleeting allusions to the role played by *The Times* in the political field; disclosed on which errands he was sent, and also made some irreverent remarks on the character of his employers. Far from being 'racy', as Frank Giles suggests,[1] his memoirs are tame by modern standards, and pleasant to read. Throughout the years Gallenga had never learnt to be discreet, and so retirement, which would shortly have come in any case because of age, was now forced upon him.

[1] F. Giles, *A Prince of Journalists: the Life and Times of De Blowitz*, London, 1962, p. 58.

VIII

THE LAST YEARS

THE book which caused such annoyance at Printing House Square is a diary, and, unlike *Castellamonte*, a true account of Gallenga's life. Moreover, together with *Italy, Past and Present* it constitutes his best work. Its value lies not only in the information it supplies about so many aspects and people of the nineteenth century, but also in the attractive way in which the story is told. Like many other famous memoir-writers he caught the spirit of his times and his name deserves a place beside those of D'Azeglio and Abba, as well as of Lady Morgan and Bulwer-Lytton and other illustrious Victorians who cultivated the art of writing about themselves.

Episodes of My Second Life begins where *Castellamonte* ends. It opens with a description of the crossing of the Atlantic in 1836, when Gallenga emigrated to the New World. It is in two volumes: *American Experiences* and *English Experiences*; the first dealing with his stay in the U.S. from 1836 till 1839, the second beginning in 1839 with his move to London. From that year he was always linked with Great Britain, either professionally or for family reasons, hence the title of his second section: *English Experiences*, in spite of the fact that a good deal of his time was spent away from England. His memoirs are *episodes*, for his intention was not to write an accurate and strictly chronological account of his life, but to recall the main events he had witnessed during his career. Personal events, such as family happenings, are dealt with briefly, while ample space is dedicated to Italian politics, the first crossing of the Atlantic, and his meeting with famous men. In his own words:

On the 15th August, 1836, I was born again. . . . I embarked at Gibraltar for New York. I was then five-and-twenty years old. Up to that date I had been an Italian; henceforth, without laying aside my national identity, I would have to take up as much of the garb and language, of the habits of thought and of the nature and temperament of an alien race, as I might deem desirable or find inevitable. It was the beginning of a new life.[1]

The first thing that strikes one in the *Episodes* is the different amount of space given to the two periods; the first, the American, covering three years only, occupies the whole of the first volume; while the second accounts for all the years from 1839 to 1884; and the nearer we come to the present day, the shorter the narrative, the more concise the description. This is due in part to the desire to interest a reading public more inclined to be attracted by events far away in the past; but it is also and chiefly due to the way in which Gallenga looked back on his life. No doubt he considered his American experiences important: greatly influencing his personality, they helped to bring him to full maturity; and they gave him his first introduction to the Anglo-Saxon world and culture. Moreover, the way of life in the New World in the 1830s was varied and adventurous, in a country where the sophisticated society of Boston coexisted with the roughness of the pioneers of Tennessee. To young Gallenga, America was still a colony.

The real business for a real man in a colony is to make money, and that can best be done by agricultural, manufacturing, mining, or trading industry, followed up into the highest branches of land speculation, banking and financing.[2]

Thus he wrote lamenting his failure to make his stay in the United States a financial success. Gallenga's experiences in Boston, his impression of men such as Longfellow, Prescott, and Everett have already been illustrated; he has equally interesting and informative views of the other facet of American life which he saw, that of the still wild country, the old *Far West* or the America of slaves and plantations, where men made great fortunes, but knew little about culture. In the summer of 1838, he travelled to Nashville in Tennessee hoping to find some sort of remunerative employment at the University there. He had been introduced to

[1] *Epis.*, vol. i, pp. 1–2.   [2] Ibid., vol. i, p. 370.

John Bell, a resident of Nashville and the Speaker of the House of Representatives, by his friend Edward Everett. His trip proved a failure, for he found no suitable job, and after spending the summer with the Bell family, he returned to New England in the autumn. As Garosci has pointed out, there are many inaccuracies in his description of University institutions in Nashville and of some of the people he met there. Gallenga himself admitted that

the Episodes of my life, which I am here attempting to recall, are so far back in the past, my remembrance of them is so hopelessly faded and blurred, that the *retentive* faculties must, almost unconsciously, fall back on the resources of the *inventive*; so that it becomes extremely difficult, even for myself, to determine where the *Vrai* ends and the *Vraisemblable* begins.[1]

But nevertheless his pages on the American *frontier* have a tone of reality and sincerity in the atmosphere he succeeds in creating.

It would be interesting to revisit these remote Alleghany districts and see the improvements the lapse of nearly two generations may have effected. But at the time of my journey, August, 1838, they still exhibited many of the features of pioneers' life. The land had been seized by immigrants from the Maritime States, where it was held of little account by the owners of tobacco, cotton, and other plantations relying for existence on negro labour. It was for a long time the refuge of the 'mean whites' of the South, and of the lawyers and parsons, pedlars, and land-sharks of the North. But it was marvellous to see the fertility of the virgin soil of those clearings. There had been no time to cut down the trees; their gigantic stems were still everywhere cumbering the ground, charred or bleached, as they had been hastily half-burnt or 'girdled', withering on their roots with all their bare branches sprawling in the air, and looking like a forest of portentous ghosts as we passed them in the twilight or moonlight; yet between those trunks, and amidst that wreck, broad patches of Indian corn were struggling into existence, growing to a height and luxuriance to which even the richest flats of my native North Italian region have nothing to compare. Flocks and herds, though ill-tended, were glorious. Lack of bread and meat was unknown here, and in the houses where hospitality was tendered, although in most instances mere log huts, there was an air of plenty, comfort and even neatness which the roughness of the

[1] *Epis.*, vol. i, pp. vi–vii.

road and the backward look of the country had fully prepared us to appreciate.[1]

The society which Gallenga found in Nashville was a far cry from the cultured circles of New England, and his time spent there was given more to exploring and watching local life than to any literary enterprise. His companions were the two young sons of Mr. Bell, who showed him life in the countryside and in the plantations where tobacco, maize, and rice were grown.

In so far as I could see of the condition of the plantations I visited, I felt then, as I did subsequently in the West Indies, in Brazil, and elsewhere, that the treatment of the blacks was as good as their owners, in consideration of their own interest, could make it, for the slaves had in their master's estimation the value of cattle, and were tended with as much care and tenderness as would be bestowed on useful dumb creatures. It was not the lash, but the dread of the lash, that kept them to their work. . . . The negro slave was certainly better fed, better lodged, merrier and happier, than the Irish or Lombard free labourer is at the present time. It was not as injurious to the physical condition of the blacks, who, as it turned out, would not have been better off if left to themselves—that slavery might be considered an unmitigated evil. It was rather in its effects on the character of the whites that it was really and fatally objectionable, for . . . it created among them a spirit of caste, a conceit of race, a superiority of colour, which, however, based on undeniable natural difference, could never be reduced to organised artificial distinction.[2]

As can be seen from this passage, the defender of the Italian nation and its right to independence did not take up the cause of civil rights for coloured people, for he judged them unfit for emancipation, and had no doubt as to the superiority of the white race.

In spite of his criticism of American life and his often biased judgement of people and situations, his pages on America have a liveliness which is sometimes lacking in the second part, dealing with England. The author himself cherished the memories of those early years with mixed feelings: nostalgia for his past youth and attraction and distaste for a country where he failed to settle permanently, but where he would have liked to belong. Although

[1] Ibid., vol. i, pp. 329-30. [2] Ibid., pp. 348-9.

he never openly admitted his interest in the New World, it is symptomatic that, in spite of his experience in Nashville, after only three years in Europe, he set off again across the Atlantic, hoping to make a permanent home in Nova Scotia.

Inaccuracies are also present in the second volume: it has been largely drawn upon for the preceding chapters, with confirmation of Gallenga's information from external evidence, whenever possible. This has proved that his inaccuracies have usually been involuntary and not significant. For instance, he transposes the date of publication of his article on Tasso from 1851 to 1858. But since he is trying to portray a world which was fast disappearing rather than supply the historian with a chronicle, the fault is in itself a very minor one and does not detract from the historical value of the book, taken as a document of society and a way of life. The major alteration in the work is Gallenga's own self-portrait. If it is quite human that he should try to make his behaviour appear better than it actually was, it is difficult to believe that he was as shy and self-restrained as he makes out himself to be.

Still the greatest hindrance to my success as a journalist lay in my invincible shyness, my unwillingness to push myself forward; my self-respect and sense of dignity and regard for other men's susceptibilities, which forbade my forcing my company on people who seemed to have no wish for it, which wearied me with long attendance in antechambers, made me scorn information obtained by backstairs influence—made me, in short, not sufficiently presuming and indiscreet, or not sufficiently *flunkeyish* for an 'Interviewer'.[1]

It is impossible to recognize here the Gallenga who pestered Henry Crabb Robinson unceasingly for admission to the Athenaeum Club, or who, after the 1856 scandal, dared to ask Vittorio Emanuele D'Azeglio for an introduction to the Court of St. James at the very moment when rumours of the scandal had reached the English capital. These are, however, the faults of the man and not of the writer. It must also be added that, although *Episodes* is written in the first person, the narrator himself does not play a great part in it. He happens to be the protagonist of the

---

[1] *Epis.*, vol. ii, pp. 365–6.

story, but he appears more as a witness of events than a major figure in them. Unlike the account of his early life in *Castellamonte*, here the world does not revolve around the author, other people and facts take the major role as time progresses. Witness the portraits he has left us of Longfellow, Carlyle, Charles Albert, and his pages on the meeting between Cavour and Manin in Paris. To all these should be added his description of Dickens, his former friend and pupil, just before he died.

It was only a few days before his decease that Dickens walked past the table at which I was writing at the Athenaeum—Dickens, gray-haired, careworn, and oh, *quantum mutatus!* so absent and absorbed in his thoughts that I deemed it indiscretion to address him. Was he the Dickens I used to see almost daily at his house in Devonshire Terrace, where, like a Napoleon, he kept his tame eagle—a bright-eyed, ready-witted, somewhat gushing, happy man, cheered by the world's applause, equally idolised by his wife, by his children, by every member of his family, while as yet not even the shadow of a cloud had risen to darken the light of his household? Was he the Dickens who dwelt with so much zest and humour on the horrors of our first voyage to Yankeeland, and who entertained me with good-natured banter about the oddities of some of my friends?[1]

The book reflects not only political events and episodes in the life of great men, but also scientific discoveries, such as the expansion of the railway system, the improvement of maritime transport, the discovery and introduction of the telegraph, which over a period of fifty years had changed the face of the world and brought countries nearer to each other. The tone itself in which it is written is far more controlled and down-to-earth than the style of any earlier work. Traits of realism and conciseness of style were already present in *Italy Revisited*; but while that book is a collection of journalistic writings, *Episodes* presents unity of conception and is an original creation. This more moderate and controlled style is indicative of the detachment of the writer: the book is mainly concerned with recalling the past and attempting to put on paper memories which would otherwise be lost. Gallenga himself notes that in his days there was

[1] Ibid., vol. ii, pp. 372–3.

no end of Memoirs, Confessions, Reminiscences, personal gossip of every description. And it is, perhaps, all this vast farrago of retrospective literature that warns us that our World is getting old and given to twaddle.[1]

He was seventy-four when this work was published and he had still about ten more years to live. After his dismissal from *The Times* he retired to Llandogo in Wales, where he had a country house, from where he sent the occasional article to English and Italian magazines. At the time of the publication of *Episodes*, his reputation was still very high, as reviews of it show. See, for instance, the review in the American magazine *The Nation* which compared Gallenga's dislike of American life to that of Trollope and Dickens; or the one in the *Fortnightly Review*, where we read

Mr Gallenga occupies a prominent place in that brilliant galaxy of special and war correspondents, the other particularly bright stars of which are W. H. Russell, Sala, Forbes, and Cameron of the *Standard*. He has also, as a political writer, especially on foreign affairs left behind him a reputation in Printing House Square which will never be forgotten.[2]

This last judgement, however, proved wrong. Gallenga's fame was declining fast, in spite of the fact that he continued to write.

Among the several articles of interest, published after his retirement, is 'Italian Social Life', which appeared in the *National Review*. His attitude to Italy has now become even more severe than in *Italy Revisited*, where a certain serenity of judgement is still preserved. His disappointment has become more bitter, and the article contains some stern criticisms of life in Italy.

The Italians do not work enough, or rather, those who do work are pressed upon too heavily by those who do not. The drones are killing the bees.

Hunger is not a sufficient inducement to rouse the energies of a whole nation; and ambition, emulation, all those generous instincts by which such energies are multiplied, are still dormant in Italian hearts. One could scarcely name another European nation so barren

---

[1] *Epis.*, vol. i, p. vi.
[2] T. H. S. Prescott, 'Men of Letters on Themselves', *Fortnightly Review*, vol. xxxvi, no. 216, p. 844, 1 Dec. 1884.

in every branch of high trade and industry, of science and literature, nay, even of art and music, as Italy is in her twenty-fifth year of emancipated existence. Are we told that all the faculties of the struggling people are absorbed by politics? But look at the political press! Are not the Italian papers too worthless to bear a comparison even with their Spanish contemporaries?

Politics in Italy are, unfortunately, the only lucrative calling. The living forces of the nation are exhausted, not to support, but to pamper the Government. The limbs are fagged and jaded to fill the torpid over-grown stomach.[1]

What was still lacking was, according to Gallenga, a satisfactory system of education, for 'the fact is, that the life of new Italy can hardly be said to have fairly begun', and 'to affect and modify Italian nature will take no end of time and patience'. If we have quoted from this article it is because it contains the themes and ideas which were to be more fully developed in Gallenga's last book on Italy, *Italy, Present and Future*, or rather *L'Italia presente e futura*, for it first appeared in Italy, then in England. Gallenga had been a stranger from Italian life for too long so that his picture is distorted and untrue. His last work on Italy falls into two sections, the first dealing with military forces, foreign and domestic policy, State and Church relationships, the second with education and the arts and sciences in Italy. The plan is ambitious, and the work was probably meant to be a continuation of *Italy, Past and Present*. But Gallenga's creative period, which had earlier shown signs of exhaustion, was over. *Italy, Present and Future* would have been put to better use had it been written as a series of political speeches from some extreme right-wing member of the Italian Parliament than as a book *da Italiano per gli Italiani*. His disappointment in his country now becomes tinged with bitter pessimism. Not all of his criticisms are unfounded, and there is little doubt that the generation that came to power after the re-unification of the country did not always prove enlightened or efficient in running it. Nevertheless, many of Gallenga's attacks on Italy and the Italians are weak and unjust, especially when from some general considerations he begins to analyse the present

[1] 'Italian Social Life', *National Review*, Oct. 1884, vol. iv, no. 20, p. 256.

situation. After many years of residence abroad the separation between the writer and his country was complete. Even granting that his political position was more conservative than before, some of his suggestions and proposed remedies are unrealistic and show the same lack of understanding of Italy, for which forty years before he had blamed the English. It is enough to quote what he has to say on private and state schools in Italy.

Clearly the care and education of the lower classes in Italy, and especially in the country, should not altogether fall on the government, but should also partly devolve on the upper social classes. It should rely on private rather than on public charity.[1]

This was written after he had harshly complained about the Italian upper classes and their lack of interest in the welfare of the country. Moreover, Gallenga who had always been anti-clerical, and blamed the Catholic clergy for many of the evils of the country, now had second thoughts about a government which introduced lay education on a large scale.

In a country going through a period of transition, where the law has undeniably lost not little of the curb it should put on men's worst propensities, the sudden and total removal of religious guidance in the training of youthful minds must undoubtedly be fraught with serious danger.[2]

No mention is made of the reasons which made a state school the most suitable and the quickest way of accelerating the process of national amalgamation, so often hoped for by Gallenga himself. In reading his pages on education one cannot help feeling that what he had in mind was something like the English system of education, regardless of the actual conditions of schooling in Italy. This attitude is certainly amazing, if one thinks of the interest he had taken in the problem in earlier days. Any further examination of the book only brings more evidence of this severance between the man and his country. As superficial as his remarks on education or on Italian politics are his observations on the literature of the day. When writing of Carducci, Rapisardi, or Guerrini, he sums up his views on contemporary poetry thus:

[1] *Italy, P. and F.*, vol. ii, .p 135.   [2] Ibid., p. 17.

[it has] made but little headway into foreign countries, and least of all into England; for it does not seem fit for translation, and it is not, fortunately, very intelligible to English readers in the original.[1]

Of some historical interest are his words in praise of De Amicis, because they bear witness to the popularity of this author in England, but on the whole, a deeper analysis of the text only goes to show that *Italy, Present and Future* is only a promise—never maintained—of a work parallel to *Italy, Past and Present*.

Already at the time of the publication of *Italy Revisited*, Gallenga had been considered too severe a judge of Italian life, as can be seen in *The Times* book review of 11 November 1875. When 'Italian Social Life' was written, Grazia Pierantoni Mancini, an Italian novelist, wrote to Gallenga, reproaching him for his strictness.

> How severe you are with your countrymen, Mr Gallenga! My heart bled for them when I read those telling words, which must have made the reader cry out: this Italian whips his people as no foreigner would ever dare to do. Shall I dare and disclose my thought to you? I think you overdo it and paint people in a conventional manner, as customary in foreign novels, where the Italian always plays the part of a spy, or of a stabber or a coward.[2]

Her words could also be applied to *Italy, Present and Future*, which found a warm welcome only with the *Dublin Review*, a Church magazine which disapproved of the taking of Rome from the Pope, and considered that most of the ills of contemporary Italy were due to the sacrilegious suppression of the temporal power.

If one looks at the poor quality of these late writings by Gallenga, one sees that he had outlived his times; and he could not adjust himself to the new classes which had come to power and the new ideas which governed them. There is something touching and pathetic in some of his letters to Italian friends in his last years. Thus he wrote in 1889, to Emilio Broglio, the former Minister of Education:

[1] Ibid., p. 59.
[2] Unpublished letter, Pierantoni to Gallenga, undated (probably 1884), Museo del Risorgimento, Rome.

Your letter to Bonghi which was printed in the *Fanfulla* of the 22nd, gave me a stab in the heart, hearing you talk of the last gulf of our life, and I four years your senior, and until yesterday strong and healthy sailing through the sea of life, but now tormented by a bronchitis which may very well take me to my haven even before this letter reaches you.

Now since you think we are both moving towards the same end, let's thank heaven for granting us time to say good-bye, and to recall the days when we worked together in Parliament; as for myself I do so with great affection and respect, at least as much as that shown to you by Bonghi. You speak of bad health, I recognize in your physical weariness, some sort of moral uneasiness and discomfort. Bonghi speaks of oblivion and ingratitude to you from your country and I, who have almost always lived far away, long time ago had guessed what Bonghi discovers now.

The letter continues with Gallenga sorrowfully applying to himself and his works what had happened to Broglio.

I wrote many books on Italy in English and they were not read. . . . I published one in Italian two years ago, and no one wanted to read it. . . . Let's resign ourselves to live in obscurity, and forgive our country for her ungratefulness and oblivion.[1]

Gallenga felt bitterly that neglect and oblivion were surrounding him. Most of his contemporaries had died, and his last years were troubled by private sorrows, such as the death of his only daughter and his long quarrels with his son Guy Hardwin; but he still found solace in writing. In 1890 he published a short book, *Lettere Inglesi*, a collection of articles on English life, and in 1895, on the eve of his death, at the venerable age of eighty-five, he contributed a series of articles for the Roman paper *Il Fanfulla*, under the title 'Ottantacinque anni di vita', which are an abridged Italian version of *Episodes*. These articles, the compilation of which was interrupted by his death on 16 December, do not add much to our knowledge of him and the information contained in them is often marred by inaccuracies of detail. His memory was fading fast, as is also evident in some of his letters to the historian Pietro

[1] Gallenga to Broglio, unpublished letter, 25 Feb. 1889, Museo del Risorgimento, Milan. Ruggero Bonghi was an Italian scholar and politician, who had been Minister of Education from 1874 to 1876.

Orsi, where well-known facts, such as his meetings with Mazzini, had been completely forgotten or altered.

When the news of his death became known, a few obituaries were published in English, American, and Italian magazines and newspapers. All of them concentrated their interest on the man and his political activities rather than on the writer. Although his works were mentioned, no special consideration was given to them, as is seen in his obituary in *The Times*. But the best *in memoriam* that he could have hoped for, giving the truest picture of his career, is to be found, not in any obituary, but in the words of one of his closest friends, G. A. H. Sala, the writer and journalist, writing only a year before his death.

Was there ever a more valiant and indefatigable journalist and *littérateur* than Antonio? In the interest of the great journal of Printing House Square, he had repeatedly travelled through Spain and Italy, through the Spanish Antilles and South America; and he had been in the United States when the great Republic was in the midst of war. He had been a deputy of the Italian Parliament; he had been, I fancy, mixed up with a good many political conspiracies; and in addition to all this, he had led two lives; for in his youth he had been a teacher of languages in England under the *nom de guerre* of Luigi Mariotti. I picked up the other day, at a second-hand bookstall, a copy of Mariotti's *Italian–English Grammar*—fifteenth or twentieth edition. Somebody must have made a mint of money out of that grammar. . . . I rejoice to say that, although in his old age he had suffered a bitter bereavement in the death, by a cruel accident, of his beloved and accomplished daughter, he still lives, a substantial country-squire at The Falls, near Monmouth. He has written a small library of books of travels, and of political essays. He served *The Times* for a quarter of a century, and must have composed thousands of leaders on foreign subjects, and columns of special correspondence from abroad. For many years he has been a member of the Athenaeum Club; and yet not very long since, when I was asked by the pert young editor of a weekly paper to give him a list of eminent journalists whose portraits he might engrave, and I mentioned the name of Antonio Gallenga as that of one of the most gifted and most distinguished members of my craft, the pert young editor stared at me and said he did not know who Antonio Gallenga was.[1]

¹ G. A. H. Sala, *Sala's Life and Adventures*, London, 1895, vol. ii, pp. 285–6.

After the long silence which has followed Gallenga's death, many reasons justify a revival of interest in him and in his work. The part he played in Anglo-Italian society was twofold; he was a politician and a writer; a man of action and a *letterato*. After closely examining his political activities, it must be conceded that their importance is limited, Gallenga being only one of many exiles in Great Britain who took part in the struggle during the Risorgimento. The 1833 episode, or his diplomatic mission to Frankfurt, or even his subsequent career as an Italian deputy did not to any remarkable extent affect the history of his country. His political career alone does not justify a full study of his life. Indeed, as long as his writings were neglected, the interest of historians was confined to the 1833 episode, so closely linked with Mazzini and the history of Young Italy. It is Gallenga's writings that bear testimony to his real contribution to the development and to the understanding of his times. Some of these were mere political pamphlets, the interest of which is short-lived, for they are soon superseded by subsequent events, as in the case of *Democracy across the Channel*. Others, such as *Latest News from Italy* or *Italy in 1848* are chronicles of the times, of importance only to the historian. Some of Gallenga's works, however, go beyond that. His *Italy, Past and Present* is one of the links in the transition from the literary histories of the Enlightenment to those of the romantic school; but this was not recognized, for even if famous men such as Longfellow or Prescott praised it highly, the book never gained the reputation it deserved. It was at a disadvantage from the fact that it was written in English and published in England, where it did not easily fit into any tradition: and by the time Gallenga became known in Italy as a writer, it was too late for the work to be of interest to Italian scholars. It was only in the eighties that Gallenga's connections with Italian publishers were fully established, and then his works appeared at the same time in English and Italian. His two histories which reveal his qualities as a scholar and a historian, *Fra Dolcino* and *History of Piedmont* also failed to gain the reputation they deserved for the reasons we have seen. Together with the critic and the historian, Gallenga is also to be remembered as a diarist, a writer who in his

7 *Italian emigrants leaving for America after the unification of the country*
Oil by Oddone Tomasi

8 *King Humbert I at the opening of Parliament in Rome*

two autobiographical works showed a penetrating and intelligent observation of English and Italian society. With his later books on Italy, that is to say with his writings for *The Times* on Italian subjects, he contributed to keeping alive in England the interest in Italy and in things Italian. In these works he merits special attention because of his portrayal of unknown aspects of Italian life to men and women who had a stereotyped idea of Italy. He often roused the anger of Italianists but we have already pointed out how, at least as late as 1875—the year of the publication of *Italy Revisited*—his picture of Italian society, though tinged with political passion, was altogether truthful. Detrimental to the quality of his writings was his being forced to use the English tongue. However good his knowledge of English—and on occasions he writes brilliantly, if, perhaps, a little too flamboyantly —he does make grammatical errors, his syntax can be awkward, and at times a somewhat monotonous repetition of certain constructions is apt to pall. But for a writer whose English is not his native tongue he has a wealth of vocabulary, his best passages produce a real English prose rhythm, and, whatever his faults of style, these never obscure his meaning, which is always abundantly clear. Gallenga is not the artist who creates from imagination, nor is he to be evaluated as a stylist; he is of interest as a critic and as a *raconteur*, as the chronicler of his age who knew how to tell his tale, and who often saw deeply into the scene he observed. Few Italian exiles, if any, who made England their home, have, with their knowledge of the language and familiarity of the English way of life, so imbibed an English way of thought. Gallenga, while never ceasing to be an Italian exile with a most fervent love of his country, yet comes to appreciate, and so makes his own, English habits and modes of thought, that he judges his Italy from the standpoint of the moralizing English Victorian. It is this unique mixture of the staid Victorian English gentleman and the ardent, impulsive Italian patriot which makes his works such interesting and fascinating reading. Journalist, critic, memorialist, historian; but he will also be remembered as a perfect example of a phenomenon of Victorian England: a true Anglo-Italian of a hundred years ago.

LIST OF ABBREVIATIONS

A.B.M.: Ann Brown Memorial Papers, Providence, Long Island.

B.M.: British Museum Library.

Castellamonte: A. Gallenga, *Castellamonte. An Autobiographical Sketch Illustrative of Italian Life during the Insurrection of 1831*, 2 vols, London, 1854.

Country Life: A. Gallenga, *Country Life in Piedmont*, London, 1858.

Democracy: A. Gallenga, *Democracy across the Channel*, London, 1883.

D.N.B.: Dictionary of National Biography.

Epis.: A. Gallenga, *Episodes of My Second Life*, 2 vols., London, 1884.

Fra Dolcino: L. Mariotti, *An Historical Memoir of Fra Dolcino and His Times*, London, 1853.

History of Piedmont: A. Gallenga, *History of Piedmont*, 3 vols. London, 1855.

Italy P. and F.: A. Gallenga, *Italy, Present and Future*, 2 vols., London, 1887.

Italy 1841: L. Mariotti, *Italy: General Views of Its History and Literature in Reference to Its Present State*, 2 vols., London, 1841.

Italy, P. and P.: L. Mariotti, *Italy, Past and Present*, 2 vols., London, 1848.

Italy Revis.: A. Gallenga, *Italy Revisited*, 2 vols., London, 1875.

Met. Mag.: *Metropolitan Magazine*.

New Month. Mag.: *Colburn's New Monthly Magazine*.

North Am. Review: *North American Review*.

Oltremonte: *Oltremonte ed Oltremare: Canti di un Pellegrino dati in luce da Luigi Mariotti*, London, 1844.

P.H.S.: *The Times* Archives, Printing House Square.

P.R.O.: Public Record Office.

S.E.N.: *Edizione nazionale degli Scritti editi ed inediti di Giuseppe Mazzini. Epistolario.* Imola, 1906–43.

BIBLIOGRAPHY OF
ANTONIO GALLENGA'S WRITINGS

BOOKS

The books are listed in chronological order. The date is that of the first edition; the place of publication, unless otherwise stated, is London. Reference is given when the books appeared anonymously or under the name of Luigi Mariotti. An asterisk marks the works which were published while writing for *The Times*.

1827   *Ode a Macedonio Melloni per l'elezione di lui alla Cattedra di Fisica nella D. Università di Parma* (anonymous), Parma.

1838   *Romanze* (anonymous), Cambridge, Massachusetts.

1841   (L. Mariotti) *Italy: General Views of Its History and Literature in Reference to Its Present State*, 2 vols.

1844   *Oltremonte ed Oltremare: Canti di un Pellegrino dati in luce da Luigi Mariotti.*

1845   (L. Mariotti) I. *The Age We Live In. A Mock Heroic Lecture;* II. *Bull and Nongtongpaw, or National Characteristics.*

1846   (L. Mariotti) *The Blackgown Papers*, 2 vols.
       (L. Mariotti) *Italien in seiner politischen und literarischen Entwickelung und in seiner gegenwärtigen Zustanden*, trans. by J. B. Seybt, Leipzig.

1847   (L. Mariotti) *Latest News from Italy.*

1848   (L. Mariotti) *Italy, Past and Present*, 2 vols.
       (L. Mariotti) *Present State and Prospects of Italy.* (This book is the second volume of *Italy, Past and Present*, published separately).

1849   *A che ne siamo? Pensieri d'un Italiano d'Oltremonti*, Turin.

1850   (L. Mariotti) *Scenes from Italian Life.*

1851   (L. Mariotti) *Italy in 1848.*
       (L. Mariotti) *A Practical Grammar of the Italian Language.*

1852   (L. Mariotti) *First Italian Reading Book.*

1853   (L. Mariotti) *An Historical Memoir of Fra Dolcino and His Times.*

1854   *Castellamonte. An Autobiographical Sketch Illustrative of Italian Life during the Insurrection of 1831*, 2 vols. (First published anonymously, reprinted in 1856 under the name of A. Gallenga).

1855   *History of Piedmont*, 3 vols.

1856 *Storia del Piemonte dai primi tempi alla pace di Parigi del 30 marzo 1856*, 2 vols., Turin.

1858 *Country Life in Piedmont.*

1861 *Manuale dell'elettore*, Siena.

1864 *The Invasion of Denmark in 1864*, 2 vols.
*Krigen i Slesvig 1864 (Oversat efter Mr Gallenga's Breve til *The Times*, med nogle Forkortelser og Forandringer), Copenhagen.

1870 *A Key to the Exercises in Mariotti's Italian Grammar.*

1873 *The Pearl of the Antilles.*

1874 *La Perla delle Antille*, Milan.

1875 *Italy Revisited*, 2 vols.

1877 *Two Years of the Eastern Question*, 2 vols.

1879 *The Pope and the King. The War between Church and State in Italy*, 2 vols.

1880 *South America.*

1882 *A Summer Tour in Russia.*

1883 *Un viaggio estivo in Russia*, Parma.
Democracy across the Channel.
Iberian Reminiscences, 2 vols.
La democrazia di là dello Stretto, Parma.

1884 *Episodes of My Second Life*, 2 vols.

1886 *Jenny Jennett: a Tale without a Murder*, 2 vols.
L'Italia presente e futura, translated by Sofia Portini Santarelli, Florence.

1887 *Italy, Present and Future*, 2 vols.

1890 *Vita Inglese: lettere agli Italiani*, Florence.

1898 *Thecla's Vow.*

ARTICLES

The articles are listed in chronological order; when introducing a series bearing the same title, full references are given for the first article, followed by the date and number of the next issues. When a series covers more than one year, the full title is repeated for the first issue of each year.

1838 'Last years of Maria Luisa', in *North Am. Review*, April, vol. xlvi, no. 99.

'Romantic Poetry in Italy', in *North Am. Review*, July, vol. xlvii, no. 100.

1839 'Catholicism in Italy', in *The Christian Examiner*, January, vol. xxv, no. 90.

'Historians of Italy', in *North Am. Review*, April, vol. xlviii, no. 103.

'Italy by an Exile', in *Met. Mag.*, Oct., vol. xxvi, no. 102; Nov., vol. xxvi, no. 103; Dec., vol. xxvi, no. 104.

1840 'Italy in the Middle Ages', in *North Am. Review*, Jan., vol. l, no. 106.
'Historical Publications in Italy', in *British and Foreign Review*, Jan., vol. xi, no. 22.
'Italy by an Exile' (cont.), in *Met. Mag.*, Jan., vol. xxvii, no. 105; March, vol. xxvii, no. 107; April, vol. xxvii, no. 108; June, vol. xxviii, no. 110; Sept., vol. xxix, no. 113; Nov., vol. xxix, no. 115.
'Memoirs of an Italian Exile edited by Eli Blackgown', in *Met. Mag.* Feb., vol. xxvii, no. 106; March, vol. xxvii, no. 107; May, vol. xxviii, no. 109; July, vol. xxviii, no. 111; Oct., vol. xxix, no. 114; Dec., vol xxix, no. 116.
'Caterina de' Medici', in *Foreign Quarterly Review*, Oct., vol. xxvi, no. 51.

1841 'Italy by an Exile' (cont.), in *Met. Mag.*, Jan., vol. xxx, no. 117.
'Copyright in Italy', in *Foreign Quarterly Review*, Jan., vol. xxvi, no. 52.
'Memoirs of an Italian Exile edited by Eli Blackgown', in *Met. Mag.*, Feb., vol. xxx, no. 118; March, vol. xxx, no. 119; May, vol. xxxi, no. 121; June, vol. xxxi, no. 122; July, vol. xxxi, no. 123; Aug., vol. xxxi, no. 124; Sept., vol. xxxii, no. 125; Oct., vol. xxxii, no. 126; Dec., vol. xxxii, no. 128.
'Italian Drama', in *Foreign Quarterly Review*, April, vol. xxvii, no. 53.
'Education in Italy', in *Foreign Quarterly Review*, July, vol. xxvii, no. 54.
'The Women of Italy', in *Foreign Quarterly Review*, Oct., vol. xxviii, no. 55.

1842 'The Aristocracy in Italy', in *Foreign Quarterly Review*, Jan., vol. xxviii, no. 56.
'Memoirs of an Italian Exile edited by Eli Blackgown', in *Met. Mag.*, Jan., vol. xxxiii, no. 129.

1843 'The Last of the Carbonari', in *New Month. Mag.*, Sept., vol. lxix, no. 273.
'Red-Coats and Black Gowns', in *New Month. Mag.*, Dec., vol. lxix, no. 276.

1844 'The Last of the Contrabbandieri', in *New Month. Mag.*, Oct., vol. lxxii, no. 286.

1845 'Town Life in Italy: The "Veglione"', in *New Month. Mag.*, Feb., vol. lxxiii, no. 290.
'Morello, or The Organ Boy's Progress', in *New Month. Mag.*, Oct., vol. lxxv, no. 298.

1847 'Present State and Prospects of Italy', in *New Month. Mag.*, Feb., vol. lxxix, no. 314.
'The Spirit of Dante', in *New Month. Mag.*, May, vol. lxxx, no. 317.
'The Casino', in *New Month. Mag.*, July, vol. lxxx, no. 319.
'Manzoni', in *New Month. Mag.*, Sept., vol. lxxxi, no. 321.

188   BIBLIOGRAPHY

1847 'The Italian Crisis', in *New Month. Mag.*, Oct., vol. lxxxi, no. 322.
      'The Last Hours of Jacopo Ruffini', in *The Keepsake*.
      'The Italian Programme', in *New Month. Mag.*, Nov., vol. lxxxi, no. 323.

1848 'Maria Luisa and Carlo Ludovico', in *New Month. Mag.*, Feb., vol. lxxxii, no. 326.
      Lettera a Giuseppe Piroli, May, Parma.
      'Agli Italiani di Piemonte e Lombardia: parole di un conciliatore', in *Il Risorgimento*, 18, 19, 24, 28, 29, 30 August; 1, 6, 9 September; ibid., 'La Confederazione Italiana', 9, 12, 19, 22, 23, 25 September.
      'The "Veglia": Country Life in Italy', in *New Month. Mag.*, Sept., vol. lxxxiv, no. 333.

1849 'Eighteen Months' Political Life in Italy', in *New Month. Mag.*, Dec., vol. lxxxvii, no. 348.

1850 'Christmas in Italy', in *New Month. Mag.*, Jan., vol. lxxxviii, no. 349.

1851 'Love and Madness of Tasso', in *New Month. Mag.*, Jan., vol. xci, no. 361; Feb., vol. xci, no. 362.

1852 'Piedmont', in *Edinburgh Review*, July, vol. xcvi, no. 195.
      'Fra Dolcino', in *New Quarterly Review*, vol. ii.

1855 *Daily News* file: correspondences from Piedmont.
      'Cenni etnografici sul progresso europeo', in *Il Cimento*, year III, vol. v, pp. 1–14; 'Paralleli etnografici: Celti e Teutoni', ibid., pp. 266–79; 'Contrasti di carattere nazionale: operosità italiana e straniera,' ibid., pp. 470–85; 'Studi etnografici: Lingua e nazione', ibid., pp. 781–95; 'Sviluppo di uno Stato morale in Piemonte', ibid., pp. 1069–88.

1856 *Daily News* file: correspondences from Piedmont.
      'La letteratura italiana all'estero', in *Il Cimento*, year IV, vol. vii.
      'L'Inghilterra e la pace', in *La Rivista Contemporanea*, March, year IV, vol. vi.
      'La Francia e la pace', in *La Rivista Contemporanea*, April, year IV, vol. vi.

1857 'La nostra prima carovana', in *La Rivista Contemporanea*. Dispense, nos. 1–2.

1859–84—for Gallenga's correspondences see *The Times* file and books marked with an asterisk.

1881 'Italy: Her Home and Foreign Policy', in *Fortnightly Review*, July, vol. xxx (New Series), no. 175.

1883 'L'Italia, il suo commercio e le sue colonie', in *Nuova Antologia*, 15 June, vol. lxix.

1884   'Italian Social Life', in *National Review*, Oct., vol. iv, no. 20.

1888   'Italy in England', in *National Review*, May, vol. xi, no. 63.
       'France and Italy', in *Contemporary Review*, Oct., vol. liv.

1889   'Mr Gladstone and Italy', in *National Review*, June, vol. xiii, no. 76.

1895   'Ottantacinque anni di vita', in *Il Fanfulla*, 9, 12, 15, 19, 26 August;
       5 September; 4 and 24 October.

SOURCES CONSULTED

UNPUBLISHED

Acts of Naturalization, P.R.O.

Ann Brown Memorial Papers, Providence, Long Island.

The Athenaeum Club Records.

Carteggio Giobertiano, Biblioteca Civica, Turin.

Foreign Office Papers 1848, P.R.O.

Lettere ai Ministri d'Allemagna 1848, Archivio di Stato, Turin.

MSS., Biblioteca Labronica, Leghorn.

MSS., Biblioteca Nazionale Centrale, Florence.

MSS., Museo del Risorgimento, Milan.

MSS., Museo del Risorgimento, Rome.

MSS., Museo del Risorgimento, Turin.

E. Mayer Papers, Mayer Archives.

Panizzi Papers, B.M.

Rapporti Parlamentari, Archivio di Stato, Turin.

Registri Segreteria Estera, Archivio di Stato, Turin.

H. C. Robinson's Correspondence, Dr. Williams' Library, London.

Somerset House Archives.

The Times Archives.

PUBLISHED

Sources are listed in alphabetical order

GENERAL

D. E. D. BEALES, *England and Italy, 1859–60*, London 1961.

C. P. BRAND, *Italy and the English Romantics*, Cambridge, 1957.

E. CASA, 'Commemorazione di Antonio Gallenga', in *Archivio Storico per le Province Parmensi*, vol. v, Parma, 1896.

C. CAVOUR, *Carteggio Cavour e l'Inghilterra*, Bologna, 1933.

A. COPPI, *Annali d'Italia dal 1750 al 1860*, Florence, 1860.

Dictionary of National Biography.

Dizionario del Risorgimento Nazionale, Milan, 1933.

'A. Gallenga', in *Men of the Time*, London, 1884.

A. GAROSCI, *Antonio Gallenga. Avventura, politica e storia nell'Ottocento italiano*, Turin, 1964.

Grande Dizionario Enciclopedico U.T.E.T.

BOLTON KING, *A History of Italian Unity*, London, 1889.

D. LEVI, 'Antonio Gallenga', in *Il Risorgimento Italiano*, edited by L. Carpi, Milan, 1884.

A. LOMBROSO, 'Antonio Gallenga', in *La Rivista di Roma*, 25 Nov., 10 Dec. 1907, anno XI, fasc. xxii.

Edizione nazionale degli Scritti editi ed inediti di Giuseppe Mazzini, Imola, 1906–43.

G. MAZZONI, *Storia letteraria d'Italia*, vol. ii, Milan, 1913.

P. ORSI, 'Antonio Gallenga', in *Nuova Antologia*, March 1932, vol. ccclx.

A. PARISET, *Dizionario biografico dei Parmigiani illustri*, Parma, 1905 .

H. W. RUDMAN, *Italian Nationalism and English Letters*, London, 1940.

A. SIGNORETTI, *Italia e Inghilterra durante il Risorgimento*, Milan, 1940.

C. TRABUCCO, *Questo verde Canavese. Paesi e personaggi*, Turin, 1957.

M. C. W. WICKS, *The Italian Exiles in London, 1816–1848*, Manchester, 1937.

CHAPTER I

E. CASA, *I moti rivoluzionari accaduti a Parma nel 1831*, Parma, 1895.

E. EVERETT, *Orations and Speeches on Various Occasions*, Boston, 1836.

P. P. FROTHINGHAM, *E. Everett, Orator and Statesman*, New York, 1925.

V. GABRIELI, 'W. H. Prescott e la storia come arte', in *Studi Americani*, no. 4, Rome, 1958.

C. GALLENGA, *The Last Soldier of Napoleon*, London, 1915.

A. LA PIANA, *La cultura americana e l'Italia*, Turin, 1938.

H. W. LONGFELLOW, *The Poets and Poetry of Europe*, Philadelphia, 1845.

F. O. MATTHIESSEN, *American Renaissance*, New York, 1941.

The Correspondence of W. H. Prescott, 1833–1847, ed. R. Wolcott, Boston, 1925.

W. H. PRESCOTT, 'Mariotti's Italy', in *North American Review*, April 1842, vol. liv, no. 115.

Regia Deputazione di Storia Patria, *I moti del 1831 nelle Province Parmensi*, Parma, 1931.

M. TABARRINI, *Gino Capponi, i suoi tempi, i suoi studi e i suoi amici*, Florence, 1879.

Life, Letters and Journals of G. Ticknor, ed. G. S. Hillard, Boston, 1909.

F. VIGLIONE, *La critica letteraria di H. W. Longfellow*, Florence, 1934.

VAN WYCK BROOKS, *The Flowering of New England, 1815–1865*, London, 1936.

CHAPTER II

G. ARTOM-TREVES, *Anglo-Fiorentini di cento anni fa*, Florence, 1953.

C. BIRCHENOUGH, *History of Elementary Education in England and Wales from 1800 to the Present Day*, London, 1938.

C. BROOKS, *Antonio Panizzi, Scholar and Patriot*, Manchester, 1931.

W. J. CARLTON, 'Dickens Studies Italian', in *The Dickensian*, May 1965, vol. lxi.

C. DICKENS, *American Notes*, Greenwich, Conn., 1961.
Letters of Charles Dickens, London, 1880–2.
Pictures from Italy, London, 1907.

C. H. FIRTH, *Modern Languages at Oxford, 1724–1929*, Oxford, 1929.

J. FORSTER, *The Life of Charles Dickens*, London, 1928.

E. G. GARDNER, *History of the Italian Department*, London University College, 1924.

W. K. HANCOCK, *Ricasoli and the Risorgimento in Tuscany*, London, 1926.

A. LAMBRUSCHINI (editor), *La Guida dell'Educatore*, 1836–45.

A. LINAKER, *La vita e i tempi di Enrico Mayer*, Florence, 1898.

G. MACPHERSON, *Memoirs of the Life of Ann Jameson*, London, 1878.

Mazzini's Letters to an English Family (1844–1872), ed. E. F. Richards, London, 1920–2.

Lettere di G. Mazzini ad Aurelio Saffi e alla famiglia Crawford (1850–1872) ed. G. Mazzatinti, Rome, 1905.

Oxford University Historical Register, 1200–1900, Oxford, 1900.

G. PIOLI, *Istituzioni e amici superstiti di G. Mazzini a Londra*, Florence, 1914.

The Correspondence of W. H. Prescott, 1833–1847, ed. R. Wolcott, Boston, 1925.

M. TABARRINI, *Gino Capponi, i suoi tempi, i suoi studi e i suoi amici*, Florence, 1879.

F. VIGLIONE, *Ugo Foscolo in Inghilterra*, Catania, 1910.

E. R. P. VINCENT, *Gabriele Rossetti in England*, Oxford, 1936.

T. WHITAKER SCALIA, *Sicily and England*, London, 1907.

CHAPTER III

W. BINNI, *Storia della critica*, Florence, 1960.

G. A. BORGESE, *Storia della critica romantica in Italia*, Milan, 1949.

M. CATAUDELLA, *Il romanzo storico italiano*, Naples, 1960.

B. CROCE, *Storia della storiografia italiana nel secolo XIX°*, Bari, 1921.

F. De Sanctis, *Storia della letteratura italiana*, Milan, 1917.
  Teoria e storia della letteratura, Bari, 1926.

C. Dionisotti, *Vita di Carlo Botta*, Turin, 1867.

P. Emiliani-Giudici, *Storia delle belle lettere in Italia*, Florence, 1844.

The English Catalogue of Books, 1835–1863, London, 1864.

U. Foscolo, *Opere edite e postume*, Florence, 1850–90.

A. Galimberti, *Dante nel pensiero inglese*, Florence, 1921.

E. Garin, *L'umanesimo italiano. Filosofia e vita civile nel Rinascimento*, Bari, 1952.

P. L. Ginguené, *Histoire littéraire d'Italie*, Paris, 1811–35.

W. Gladstone, 'Leopardi', in *Quarterly Review*, March 1850, vol. lxxxvi, no. 172.

H. Hallam, *View of the State of Europe during the Middle Ages*, London, 1818.

U. Limentani, *L'attività letteraria di G. Mazzini*, Turin, 1950.

G. Mazzini, *Scritti editi ed inediti*, Rome, 1881.

L. Settembrini, *Lezioni di Letteratura Italiana*, Florence, 1964.

J. C. L. De Sismondi, *De la littérature du midi de l'Europe*, Paris, 1813.
  Histoire des républiques italiennes du moyen âge, Paris, 1809–18.

G. Tiraboschi, *Storia della letteratura italiana*, Modena, 1772–95.

P. Toynbee, *Dante in English Literature from Chaucer to Cary, 1380–1844*, London, 1909.

R. Wellek, *A History of Modern Criticism: 1750–1950*. II: *The Romantic Age*, London, 1955.

CHAPTER IV

Carteggio politico di Michelangelo Castelli, ed. L. Chiala, Turin, 1890.

Lettere edite ed inedite di Camillo Cavour, ed. L. Chiala, Turin, 1883–7.

F. Curato, 'Il Parlamento di Francoforte e la prima guerra d'indipendenza', in *Archivio Storico Italiano*, 1952–3, nos. 399–401.

M. D'Azeglio, *I miei ricordi*, Milan, 1964.

G. Del Bono, *Cavour e Napoleone III*, Turin, 1941.

Epistolario di Luigi Farini, ed. L. Rava, Bologna, 1911–14.

L. Scarabelli, 'Correspondence from Parma' in *Il Risorgimento*, 17 May 1848.

A. J. P. Taylor, *The Italian Problem in European Diplomacy, 1847–49*, Manchester, 1934.

W. von Willisen, *La campagna d'Italia del 1848 esposta e giudicata dal maggiore prussiano W. von Willisen*, Turin, 1848.

'Proclama al Popolo Britannico', *Il Risorgimento*, 23 Sept. 1848.

CHAPTER V

G. BRIANO, *Rivelazioni importanti*, Turin, 1856.

H. N. GAY, 'Mazzini e Antonio Gallenga, apostoli dell'indipendenza italiana in Inghilterra', in *Nuova Antologia*, 16 July 1928, vol. cccxxxviii.

G. O. GRIFFITH, *Mazzini, Prophet of Modern Europe*, London, 1932.

S. MASTELLONE, *Mazzini e la Giovane Italia, 1831–1834*, Pisa, 1960.

G. MAZZINI, *Scritti editi ed inediti*, Rome, 1881.

E. MORELLI, *Mazzini in Inghilterra*, Florence, 1938.

—— *Giuseppe Mazzini. Saggi e ricerche*, Rome, 1950.

A. OMODEO, *Difesa del Risorgimento*, Turin, 1951.

F. PINELLI, *Storia militare del Piemonte*, Turin, 1855.

G. PIOLI, *Istituzioni e amici superstiti di Giuseppe Mazzini a Londra*, Florence, 1914.

I. RAULICH, 'Mazzini e la trama del Gallenga', in *Nuova Antologia*, 16 June 1920, vol. ccxc.

CHAPTER VI

E. ANAGNINE, *Dolcino e il movimento ereticale all'inizio del Trecento*, Florence, 1964.

C. BINI, *Manoscritto di un prigioniero*, Milan, 1961.

Carteggio politico di Michelangelo Castelli, ed. L. Chiala, Turin, 1890.

I. ELLIOT, *Index to the Henry Crabb Robinson Letters in Dr. Williams' Library*, London, 1960.

G. FALDELLA, 'Il pentimento di A. Gallenga', in *Nuova Antologia*, 16 Oct. 1897, vol. lxxi.

E. G. GARDNER, *History of the Italian Department*, London University College, 1924.

F. D. GUERRAZZI, *Il buco nel muro*, Lugano, 1862.

The History of 'The Times', vol. 11, London, 1939.

The Journals and Papers of Gerard Manley Hopkins, ed. H. House and G. Storey, London, 1959.

C. KINGSLEY, *Two Years Ago*, Cambridge, 1857.

A. LINAKER, *La vita e i tempi di Enrico Mayer*, Florence, 1898.

E. J. MORLEY, *Henry Crabb Robinson on Books and Their Writers*, London, 1938.

H. PEARSON, *The Life of Oscar Wilde*, London, 1946.

'*Lorenzo Benoni* and *Castellamonte*' in *Edinburgh Review*, April 1854, vol. xcix, no. 202.

'Review of *Fra Dolcino*', in *New Quarterly Review*, 1853, vol. ii.

'Review of *History of Piedmont*', in *New Month. Mag.*, Dec. 1855, vol. cv, no. 420.

'Review of *History of Piedmont*', in *Daily News*, 6 Dec. 1855.

'Review of *History of Piedmont*', in *British Quarterly Review*, Jan. 1856, vol. xxiii, no. 45.

'Review of *History of Piedmont*', in *Westminster and Foreign Review*, Jan. 1856, vol. ix, no. 17.

T. SADLER, *The Diary, Reminiscences and Correspondence of H. Crabb Robinson*, London, 1869.

CHAPTER VII

G. C. ABBA, *Da Quarto al Volturno. Notarelle di uno dei Mille*, Florence, 1925.

C. ARRIGHI, *I 450 ovvero i deputati del presente e i deputati dell'avvenire*, Milan, 1865.

Atti del Parlamento Italiano. Sessioni 1860–63, Rome, 1883.

G. BANDI, *I Mille*, Milan, 1960.

A. CALANI, *Il Parlamento del Regno d'Italia*, Milan, 1860.

G. DEL BONO, *Cavour e Napoleone III*, Turin, 1941.

F. GILES, *A Prince of Journalists: the Life and Times of De Blowitz*, London, 1962.

The History of 'The Times', vol. ii, London, 1939.

A. J. JEMOLO, *Chiesa e Stato in Italia negli ultimi cento anni*, Turin, 1955.

W. MATURI, *Questioni di Storia del Risorgimento e dell'Unità d'Italia*, Milan, 1951.

'Review of *Italy Revisited*', in *The Times*, 11 Nov. 1875.

Lettere e documenti del Barone Bettino Ricasoli, ed. M. Tabarrini and A. Gotti, Florence, 1892.

L. RIDOLFI, *Cosimo Ridolfi e gli Istituti del suo tempo*, Florence, 1901.

T. SARTI, *I rappresentanti del Piemonte e d'Italia nelle tredici legislature del Regno*, Rome, 1880.

G. M. TREVELYAN, *Garibaldi and the Making of Italy*, London, 1911.

Garibaldi and the Thousand, London, 1909.

M. B. URBAN, *British Opinion and Policy on the Unification of Italy, 1856–1861*, Scottdale, 1938.

CHAPTER VIII

'Antonio Gallenga: Obituary', in *The Athenaeum*, 21 Dec. 1895.

'Antonio Gallenga: Obituary', in *The Times*, 19 Dec. 1895.

G. ARANGIO RUIZ, *Storia costituzionale del Regno d'Italia*, Florence, 1898.

T. H. S. PRESCOTT, 'Men of Letters on Themselves', in *Fortnightly Review*, 1 Dec. 1884, vol. xxxvi, no. 216.

'Review of *Episodes of My Second Life*', in *The Athenaeum*, 14 Feb. 1885.

'Review of *Episodes of My Second Life*', in *The Nation*, New York, 26 Mar. 1885.

'Review of *Italy, Present and Future*', in *The Academy*, 1887, no. 31.

'Review of *Italy, Present and Future*', in *The Dublin Review*, April 1887, vol. xvii, no. 2.

G. A. H. SALA, *The Life and Adventures of G. A. H. Sala Written by Himself*, London, 1895.

INDEX